2009 SUPPLEMENT

to

CASES AND MATERIALS

on

NONPROFIT ORGANIZATIONS

THIRD EDITION

By

JAMES J. FISHMAN
Professor of Law,
Pace University School of Law

STEPHEN SCHWARZ
Professor of Law Emeritus,
University of California, Hastings College of the Law

FOUNDATION PRESS
2009

© 2008 THOMSON REUTERS/FOUNDATION PRESS

© 2009 By THOMSON REUTERS/FOUNDATION PRESS

      195 Broadway, 9th Floor

      New York, NY 10007

      Phone Toll Free 1–877–888–1330

      Fax (212) 367–6799

      foundation–press.com

Printed in the United States of America

ISBN 978–1–59941–663–2

PREFACE

This 2009 Supplement updates *Cases and Materials on Nonprofit Organizations* by summarizing the major developments that have occurred since publication of the Third Edition in July of 2006. It is organized to parallel the main text, with appropriate cross references to chapter headings and page numbers. This Supplement covers significant developments through July 1, 2009, including the many tax-related provisions of the Pension Protection Act of 2006 ("PPA 2006") affecting nonprofit organizations and their donors. References throughout the Supplement to the legislative history of PPA 2006 are to Joint Committee on Taxation, Technical Explanation of H.R. 4, the "Pension Protection Act of 2006," as Passed by the House on July 28, 2006, and as Considered by the Senate on August 3, 2006 (JCX-38-06), August 3, 2006 ("PPA 2006 Technical Explanation").

An Appendix to the Supplement includes the statutory text for the major PPA 2006 changes, with new or revised language in italics; the full text of the Uniform Prudent Management of Institutional Funds Act ("UPMIFA"); final Treasury Regulations on the relationship between the inurement and private benefit doctrines under I.R.C. § 501(c)(3) and the § 4958 intermediate sanctions penalty regime; new final and temporary regulations eliminating the public charity advance ruling process and changing the computation period for organizations seeking to be classified as public charities under §§ 170(b)(1)(A)(vi) and 509(a)(2); and the revised Form 990 annual information return.

JAMES J. FISHMAN
STEPHEN SCHWARZ

July 2009

TABLE OF CONTENTS

[This Table of Contents correlates the 2009 Supplement to the Table of Contents in the text, indicating the pages in the Supplement that contain material supplementing that covered under the listed original headings. Italics indicate new or substantially revised material.]

PART ONE

INTRODUCTION

CHAPTER 1

AN OVERVIEW OF THE NONPROFIT SECTOR

A. INTRODUCTION

Page 17:

At the end of the carryover paragraph, insert:

2006 Legislation. Just a few weeks after the Third Edition of the text was published in the summer of 2006, Congress enacted the most significant nonprofit tax legislation in several decades as part of the Pension Protection Act of 2006 (hereinafter "PPA 2006" or the "2006 Act"). This legislation was signed by President Bush on August 17, 2006, which is the "date of enactment" for purposes of its many effective dates. PPA 2006 includes carrots and sticks – a handful of charitable giving incentives along with various provisions to curtail abuses and improve accountability. The major changes affect donor-advised funds, supporting organizations, noncash contributions and, to a lesser extent, private foundations.

PPA 2006 is discussed throughout this Supplement in connection with the topics to which it relates. The statutory text of major provisions is reproduced in the Statutes and Regulations Appendix, *infra*, at page 89 et seq.

Further Rumblings On Hold. Since the enactment of PPA 2006, interest in pursuing nonprofit sector tax reforms has abated but not totally disappeared. Senate Finance Committee ranking member Charles Grassley, often with the cooperation of committee chair Max Baucus, continues to lead the charge for more accountability through periodic press releases, inquiries and reports. The Finance Committee's focus has been primarily on nonprofit hospitals, large university endowments, lucrative intercollegiate athletic programs, executive compensation, and media ministries.   Both the House and Senate taxwriting committees have expressed interest in the scope of charity and whether § 501(c)(3) organizations are providing a sufficient public benefit by conducting charitable programs commensurate in scope with their resources.

With the downturn in the economy and the arrival of a new President, priorities have shifted. Comprehensive tax reform now seems unlikely in the near term, but more targeted changes are still possible later in 2009 as part of the federal budget process or to help finance health care legislation.

C. CHARITY, PHILANTHROPY AND NONPROFIT ORGANIZATIONS: A HISTORICAL INTRODUCTION
Page 43:

After the carryover paragraph, insert:

NOTE: SOCIAL ENTERPRISE ORGANIZATIONS

Social enterprise organizations are for-profit firms committed to philanthropic activity. They have been characterized as "for-benefit corporations," falling between traditional businesses and charities, and are said to inhabit a "fourth sector" of society composed of organizations driven by social purposes and financial promise.[1] A recent catalyst for social enterprise investment was the announcement in 2006 that the Google Corporation would commit one percent of the company's stock worth $1 billion, and one percent of its annual profits over the next twenty years to invest in businesses with a social purpose.[2] Initially, Google established a traditional private foundation and contributed $90 million to it. The second philanthropic vehicle, Google.org to which most of the support is being given, is a for-profit corporation. Other businesses and entrepreneurs, such as private equity funds, have also formed large pools of capital for social purposes outside of charitable tax exempt structures.[3] What are the legal differences between traditional charities and social enterprise organizations?

The social enterprise movement is based upon the belief that market forces offer a more flexible, efficient and effective approach to promoting the public good than traditional charitable nonprofits, such as private foundations, which are subject to a restrictive regulatory regime.[4] Social enterprise corporations harken back to the cooperative movements in England and the United States in the nineteenth century. Social enterprise organizations are unconcerned with the tax issues that envelope traditional charitable activity. They are fully taxable, can issue shares of stock and return profits to investors. Their proponents argue that private sector interests will be encouraged to invest in social enterprises because they will derive a financial return while providing a public benefit.

---

[1]Stephanie Strom, Make Money, Save the World, Businesses and Nonprofits are Spawning Corporate Hybrids, N.Y. Times, May 6, 2007, § 3, at 1. The other three are the government, private and nonprofit sectors.

[2]Nicole Wallace, Blending Business and Charity, Chron. Philanthropy, Sept. 28, 2006, at 14; Katie Hafner, Philanthropy Google's Way: Not the Usual, N.Y. Times, Sept. 14, 2006, at A1.

[3]See Stephanie Strom, What's Wrong With Profit, N.Y. Times, Nov. 13, 2006, at F1; Jenny Anderson, A Hedge Fund With High Returns and High Reaching Goals, N.Y. Times, Nov. 13, 2006, at F14.

[4]See *infra* Chapter 7.

Vermont became the first state to enact legislation that recognizes a social enterprise firm as a separate legal form of organization. See 11 Vt. Stat. Ann. § 3001(23) (2008). The "low profit limited liability company," or "L3C" is organized for a business purpose but: (1) significantly furthers the accomplishment of one or more charitable or educational purposes within the meaning of § 170(c)(2)(B) of the Internal Revenue Code, (2) might not have been formed but for the L3C's relationship to the accomplishment of charitable or educational purposes, and (3) no significant purpose of which is the production of income or the appreciation of property. If a company later fails to satisfy any of these requirements, it ceases to be an L3C and exists as a regular limited liability company. Similar legislation has been enacted in Michigan, Wyoming, North Dakota, and Utah, and L3C bills are pending in several other states. For a discussion of these approaches, see Michael D. Gottesman, From Cobblestones to Pavement, The Legal Road Forward for the Creation of Hybrid Social Organizations, 26 Yale L. & Pol'y Rev. 345 (2007); Dana Brakman Reiser, For-profit Philanthropy, 77 Fordham L. Rev. 2437 (2009).

A major purpose of the L3C structure is to permit private foundations to become co-owners or lenders by making what are known as "program-related investments" ("PRIs"). PRIs count as qualified distributions for purposes of the five percent payout requirement imposed on private foundations and they are exempted from certain penalties on imprudent investments.

For-profit public benefit ventures raise several questions. Does the creation of such hybrid forms of organization serve to blur the line between for-profit and nonprofit entities? See *infra* Chapter 6, at page 593 of the text. Are they charities? Are they more efficient and effective than traditional charities?[5] Are social enterprises permanent entities or merely reflections of transitory stock market success or rising earnings? Should they receive tax benefits? If so, under what circumstances?[6]

---

[5]The advantages of social enterprise firms compared to traditional charities and the structuring options are discussed in Robert A. Wexler, Social Enterprise: A Legal Context, 54 Exempt Org. Tax Rev. 233 (2006) and Robert A. Wexler, Effective Social Enterprise – A Menu of Legal Structures, 63 Exempt Org. Tax Rev. 565 (2009). For a criticism of social enterprise for nonprofits, see Ben Casselman, Why "Social Enterprise" Rarely Works, Wall St. J., June 1, 2007, at W3.

[6]For an argument that for-profit entities should receive the same tax advantages as nonprofits, see Eric Posner & Anup Malani, The Case for For-Profit Charities (September 2006), University of Chicago Law & Economics, Olin Working Paper No. 304, available at SSRN: http://ssrn.com/abstract=928976 (there is no good argument for making those tax subsidies available only to charities that adopt the nonprofit form).

PART TWO

ORGANIZATION AND OPERATION OF NONPROFIT ORGANIZATIONS — THE STATE PERSPECTIVE

CHAPTER 2

FORMATION AND DISSOLUTION

C. PURPOSES AND POWERS OF NONPROFIT CORPORATIONS

2. COMMERCIAL PURPOSES

Page 83:

Delete the Note beginning on page 83 through the end of the third paragraph on page 85, and replace it with the following:

NOTE: COMMERCIAL PURPOSES AND PROPERTY TAX EXEMPTIONS

At one time, many states thought there was an impenetrable barrier between business and charitable activity. Thus, New York's Membership Corporation Law, the predecessor to its Not-for-Profit Corporation Law, did not permit organizations involved in business-type activities to incorporate as a charity. As the business-charity boundary became more ambiguous, such as with low income, nonprofit, non-governmental housing developments, the law changed. New York created a special category of nonprofit corporation that engaged in activities for business or quasi-business purposes.[1] Other states reached an expansive view of nonprofit activity by decision, and later in reaction to pressures on the tax base retreated.

A nonprofit organization's commercial activities may raise questions as to its qualification for state property tax exemptions. An illustrative case is State v. North Star Research and Development Institute, 294 Minn. 56, 200 N.W.2d 410 (1972), which involved a corporation established by the University of Minnesota and several for-profit corporations which contributed land, financial support, and granted low interest loans. North Star was formed to engage in research for

---

[1] N.Y. Not-for-Profit Corp. L. § 201 * * * "Type C– A not-for-profit corporation of this type may be formed for any lawful business purpose to achieve a lawful public or quasi-public objective.

scientific purposes in the public interest and for the benefit of the Twin Cities area. The basic idea behind the creation of North Star was to attract smaller companies to the Twin Cities to stimulate the local economy and to provide access to a research center for companies too small to support one on their own. The University also was concerned about the amount of applied research as distinguished from basic research conducted by university faculty and students. University officials believed that North Star's development would relax the pressure upon the university by fulfilling the needs of industry for applied research. North Star engaged in a broad variety of research projects for governmental clients and for private industry.

The issue was whether North Star was a business conducted for profit or a purely public charity. If the latter, its property would be exempt from property taxation. The Supreme Court of Minnesota, with two judges dissenting, held that the phrase "nonprofit corporation" meant a corporation formed for a purpose not involving pecuniary gain to its shareholders or members and paid no other dividends or other pecuniary remuneration. The test was not whether the corporation made a profit but whether members received any dividends or profit. The court found that North Star's for-profit incorporators had conducted only a minor amount of business with it. The control of the corporation rested with the board of regents of the University of Minnesota. The majority reserved judgment on the question whether it was a purely public charity.

In revisiting the decision four years later in North Star Research Institute v. Hennepin County, 306 Minn. 1, 236 N.W.2d 754 (Minn. 1975), the court interpreted the original decision much more narrowly. It examined whether the Institute was entitled to full property tax exemption. The court rephrased the issue: is a nonprofit corporation engaged in applied research which to a significant degree makes its services available to private enterprises, who pay for the research defined and requested by them on a cost-plus basis and acquire ownership of the information developed as a result of the undertaking, entitled to tax-exempt status under the provisions of Minnesota's Constitution and statutes? The Court concluded that North Star was not entitled to tax exemption as a "purely public charity" within meaning of the state constitution and statute, despite fact that substantial part of research was done for governmental agencies, federal and state.

Minnesota later adopted a six-pronged test, though each prong was not mandatory, to determine whether organizations in Minnesota were eligible for state tax exemption: (1) whether the stated purpose of the undertaking is to be helpful to others without immediate expectation of material reward; (2) whether the entity involved is supported by donations and gifts in whole or in part; (3) whether the recipients of the 'charity' are required to pay for the assistance received in whole or in part; (4) whether the income received from gifts and donations and charges to users produces a profit to the charitable institution; (5) whether the beneficiaries of the 'charity' are restricted or unrestricted and, if restricted, whether the class of persons to whom the charity is made available is one having a reasonable relationship to the charitable objectives; and (6) whether dividends, in form or substance, or assets upon dissolution are available to private interests.

In Under the Rainbow Child Care Center, Inc. v. County of Goodhue, 741 N.W.2d 880 (Minn. 2007), the Minnesota Supreme Court substantially narrowed the availability of property tax exemptions for charities within the state. The case involved a licensed day care center that lost money every year. Rainbow charged market rates to all who sent their children to the day care facility. Its weekly rates were higher than both of the other child care centers in Red Wing, Minnesota for infants, toddlers, and preschool children, who constituted 55 of Rainbow's 70-child licensed capacity. The court held that: (1) a day care organization that does not provide goods or services free or at considerably reduced rates as a substantial part of its operations is not exempt from payment of real property taxes as an institution of purely public charity; (2) the child care center did not satisfy the exemption; and (3) payments made by a governmental entity for goods or services provided to one of its citizens are not considered "donations" for purposes of determining whether the entity providing the goods or services is an institution of purely public charity.

In mentioning the six-part *North Star* test, the court stated that these are not necessarily the only relevant factors, but in all cases the third factor must be present – the recipients of the "charity" must receive the services on a subsidized basis. Rainbow did not provide scholarships to needy families, and its argument that some families received a 20 percent discount through government funding was not sufficient. Rainbow could not count the government's "charity" as its own.

D. DISSOLUTION AND DISTRIBUTION OF ASSETS

2. CHARITABLE TRUSTS: THE DOCTRINE OF CY PRES

Page 110:

After the third paragraph, insert:

6A. A Dog's Life. Leona Helmsley, widow of a real estate mogul, famously said: "We don't pay taxes. Only the little people pay taxes," a practice that led to her serving eighteen months in federal prison. When she was released she got a dog, a Maltese named Trouble. Ms. Helmsley died in 2007. She left a $12 million trust to care for Trouble, who was her biggest beneficiary. This brought death threats against the dog. Her estate, estimated at the time between $4 and $8 billion, was left to the Leona M. and Harry B. Helmsley Charitable Trust. The mission statement of the trust was for "purposes related to the provision of care for dogs." With the support of the New York Attorney General, the trustees petitioned the Manhattan Surrogate's Court to determine if the trust could be used for more than dog-related purposes. The court ruled that the trustees could apply the trust's funds for such charitable purposes and in such amounts as they in their sole discretion determined. The mission statement, which also allowed the trustees to give to other charitable activities, was found to be merely precatory. The body of the trust instrument, which did not contain a restriction for dogs, had the legal effect. In another proceeding, Trouble's trust was reduced to a mere $2 million.[1] See Mike Spector, Crisis on Wall Street: Helmsley Fortune Ruled Not for Dogs Only, Wall St. J., Feb. 26, 2009, at C3. When the Trust announced its first round of grants amounting to $136 million, animals received leftovers – only $1 million. Was the court's decision correct? Is this the same situation as the Buck Trust? Should idiosyncratic purposes be upheld so long as they are lawful? Should there be limits on how much one can give to charity and receive a tax deduction?

F. OTHER NONPROFIT RESTRUCTURING

Page 139:

After the second full paragraph, insert:

The great recession has battered nonprofits with particular severity as donors, foundations, government and endowment portfolios have been affected. Nonprofit bankruptcy has come out of the shadows, because more institutions cannot meet financial obligations or finance their debt, and must turn to the courts for protection, reorganization or dissolution. Performing arts organizations have been particularly hard hit, but bankruptcy has become a last resort for museums, nonprofit housing developers and social services organizations. One of the largest bankruptcies has been that of the National Heritage Foundation, a manager of donor advised funds that ran into problems in promoting controversial and illegal giving techniques. Other charities have examined mergers to survive the recession. See Stephanie Strom, Bankruptcy Now Touching Nonprofits, N.Y. Times, Feb. 20, 2009, at A17; Nicole Wallace, One in Five Charities Considering Mergers to Help Survive Hard Economic Times, Chron. Philanthropy, Mar. 12, 2009, available at http://philanthropy.com/premium/articles/v21/i10/10002702.htm.

---

[1] Section 408 of the Uniform Trust Code provides that a trust may be created to provide for the care of an animal alive during the settlor's lifetime, except to the extent a court determines that the value of the trust property exceeds the amount required for intended use.

CHAPTER 3

OPERATION AND GOVERNANCE

C. FIDUCIARY OBLIGATIONS

2. THE DUTY OF CARE

Page 170:

After the first full paragraph, insert:

7. *Inattentive Directors*. The Smithsonian Institution and the Red Cross, two of the nation's iconic nonprofits, are federally chartered. Their board makeup is determined by Congressional legislation which mandates certain designated notables. The Smithsonian's board of regents consists of the Vice President and Chief Justice of the United States, six members of Congress, and nine others. The board has three business meetings a year and presides over 19 museums, 9 research centers and the National Zoo. Some of the designated board members rarely attend. The Smithsonian has come under criticism from Congress and the press for overly generous compensation and benefits paid to its executives, inadequate controls and a declining financial situation. According to the Smithsonian's Inspector General the board was unaware of compensation practices and the Institution's other problems. Is such a board large and professional enough? Can the board as structured possibly oversee such a vast institution, even if its prominent members had the time and desire to do so?

In June 2007, a report by an independent review committee appointed by the Smithsonian's Regents found that its former CEO, Lawrence Small, who resigned under pressure earlier in the year, received excessive compensation some of which was disguised as a housing allowance for mortgage payments even though he had owned his own home for many years, had no mortgage, and did not use the home extensively for Smithsonian functions. The review committee found that Small and his chief deputy took off 950 days over seven years, with much of this "leave" used to serve on corporate boards where Small earned an additional $5.7 million. The report also concluded that Small's fundraising prowess was exaggerated when compared to his predecessor, and that the Regents did nothing to make him accountable for personal expenses. A second report by the Smithsonian's Governance Committee recommended far-reaching changes to make the Regents more active and responsible fiduciaries, the Smithsonian more transparent, and the creation of systems to enable senior officials to have direct access to the Regents. Both reports are available on the Smithsonian's web site.

7A. *Meddlesome Directors*. The Red Cross, chartered by Congress in 1905, has been criticized in recent years for its response to 9/11 and Hurricane Katrina. It manages the nation's blood supply, a $1 billion business, and has paid over $5 million in fines for safety lapses. Congressional legislation in 1947 provided that the President of the United States appoint seven cabinet secretaries to the 50 person board. The designated members rarely attended meetings, and had no influence on the organization. Thirty-five board members are elected by the 800 local chapters, and they control the board. The Congressional legislation designated the chairman of the board as the "principal officer." The result of the governance structure was constant meddling by the board into Red Cross operations, leading to five presidents or acting presidents in five years. The organization has been secretive about its finances and governance, essentially accountable to no one. Because it is federally chartered, the Red Cross is exempt from state filing requirements, and the Ninth Circuit Court of Appeals held the organization exempt from the federal Freedom of Information Act. Irwin Memorial Blood Bank v. American National Red Cross, 640 F.2d 1051 (9th Cir. 1981).

In October 2006, the Board recommended changes to the Congressional charter, the bylaws and other governing documents, which would bring the governance structure more in line with other organizations. For a criticism that the proposed changes don't go far enough, see William Josephson, American Red Cross Governance, 55 Exempt Org. Tax. Rev. 71 (2006). In May 2007, the American National Red Cross Governance Modernization Act was signed into law. Pub.L. 110-26, 121 Stat. 103. It reduces the board of governors to 20 but not until 2012. All governors are elected by the board. The designated directors become part of an advisory board that meets with the governing board once each year. The responsibilities of the board are to focus on long term strategic planning, monitoring the organization's management and traditional governance concerns. The statute (36 U.S.C. § 300112) creates an office of the ombudsman, which shall submit to the appropriate Congressional committees an annual report concerning any trends and systematic matters that the ombudsman has identified as confronting the organization. The findings specify that the Red Cross is a charity but also that it is an instrumentality of the United States. In May 2007, the Red Cross selected Mark Everson, who was Commissioner of the Internal Revenue Service, as its next president, but Everson was forced to resign later in the year after it was revealed that he had an inappropriate relationship with a subordinate employee.

5. INVESTMENT RESPONSIBILITY

b. Revisions of the Traditional Prudent Person Rule

Page 229:

Delete the first full paragraph and, after the carryover paragraph, insert:

Uniform Prudent Management of Institutional Funds Act (UPMIFA). The Uniform Prudent Management of Institutional Funds Act is a revision of UMIFA. It attempts to: (1) provide modern articulation of the prudence standards for the management and investment of charitable funds and for endowment spending; and (2) incorporate certain recent revisions with respect to charitable trusts, as set forth in the Uniform Prudent Investor Act (UPIA), (see casebook p. 229, 3rd full paragraph) and the Revised Model Nonprofit Corporation Act into the law governing charitable corporations. The revisers' goal was that standards for managing and investing institutional funds would be the same regardless of whether a charity is organized as a trust, corporation or some other entity. However, the rules do not apply to funds managed by trustees that are not charities but corporate or individual trustees. UPMIFA applies to trusts managed by charities.

The major changes from UMIFA are as follows:

- Standard of Conduct in Managing and Investing Institutional Funds (§ 3).

  UPMIFA gives charities updated guidance on prudent investment decisionmaking by incorporating language from the UPIA and specifically spells out many of the factors a charity should take into account in making a prudent investment decision. Section 3 incorporates the general duty to diversify investments and consider the risk and return objectives of the fund.

- Elimination of Historic Dollar Value

  Under UMIFA, a charitable corporation can only spend amounts above "historic dollar value" that it determines to be prudent. Historic dollar value is defined as all contributions to an endowment fund valued at the time of contribution. Over a long period of time historic dollar value can become meaningless. For example, if a donor provides for a bequest in her will, the date of valuation will likely be the donor's date of death. The determination of historic dollar value could vary significantly depending upon when in the market cycle the donor died. A fund actually could be below historic dollar value at the time the charity receives a bequest if the asset had declined between the donor's death and the distribution of the asset from the estate.[1]

  UPMIFA eliminates the historic dollar value limitation on endowment fund spending (§ 4). Subject to the intent of a donor expressed in a gift instrument, a charitable organization may spend any amount that is prudent, consistent with the purposes of the fund, relevant economic factors and the donor's intent that the fund should continue in perpetuity (or for a period specified in the gift instrument). The elimination of the historic dollar value limitation is motivated by the view that a donor's intent to create a fund of long duration that preserves its value is not always best served by a strict adherence to maintaining historic dollar value and, under certain circumstances, dipping below historic dollar value can, in the long-run, better serve such donor intent.

- Donor Intent (§ 4)

  UPMIFA improves the protection of donor intent with respect to expenditures from endowments. When a donor expresses clear intent in a written instrument, the Act requires that the charity follow the donor's instructions.

---

[1]National Conference of Commissioners on Uniform State Laws, Uniform Prudent Management of Institutional Funds Act, Prefatory Note (2006).

When a donor's intent is not so expressed, UPMIFA directs the charity to spend an amount that is prudent consistent with the purposes of the fund, relevant economic factors and the donor's intent that the fund continue in perpetuity.

Subsection (c) of § 4 provides rules of construction to assist charitable organizations in interpreting donor intent. It states that terms in a gift instrument designating a gift as an endowment, or a direction/authorization in the gift instrument to use only "income," "interest," "dividends," or "rents, issues or profits," or "to preserve the principal intact," or similar words create an endowment fund of permanent duration (unless there is additional language limiting duration) but do not otherwise limit spending authority. Under UPMIFA, these rules of construction will be applied retroactively to funds already in existence.

- Optional Presumption of Imprudence (§ 4(d))

UPMIFA includes as an optional provision (to be included at the enacting jurisdiction's option): a presumption of imprudence if a charitable organization spends more than 7 percent of an endowment fund in any one year. The presumption is meant to protect against spending an endowment too quickly.

The comments to § 4 of UPMIFA include as an optional provision requiring notice to the Attorney General for small charitable organizations invading historic dollar value. The provision is meant to curb imprudent spending by small, unsophisticated charitable organizations. In particular, the provision would:

(1)   apply only to charitable organizations with endowment funds valued, in the aggregate, at less than [$2 million] (or another amount established by the enacting jurisdiction); and

(2)   require such organizations to notify the AG (but not obtain its consent) before spending below historic dollar value. The AG would then have the opportunity to review the organization and its spending decision, educate the organization on prudent decision-making for endowment funds and intervene if the AG determines the spending would be imprudent.

- Release or Modification of Restrictions on Management, Investment, or Purpose – Cy Pres and Deviation (UPMIFA § 6).

Generally, the provisions set forth in § 6 are the same as, or clarify, UMIFA's provisions relating to release/modification of institutional fund restrictions with donor or court consent. In particular, UPMIFA clarifies that the doctrines of cy pres and deviation apply to funds held by charitable corporations as well as to funds held by charitable trusts.

However, § 6 also contains a new provision, not included in UMIFA, that would permit a charitable organization to modify a restriction on its own (i.e. without court approval) for small funds [less than $25,000] (or another amount as determined by the enacting jurisdiction) that have existed for a substantial period of time [20 years] (or another time period as determined by the enacting jurisdiction), after giving notice [60 days] (or another notice period as determined by the enacting jurisdiction) to the attorney general. The attorney general may then take action if the proposed modification appears inappropriate. The provision is meant to permit a charitable organization to lift a restriction that may no longer make sense where the cost of a judicial *cy pres* proceeding would be so great as to be prohibitive.

The financial crisis has left many charitable funds and endowments under their historic dollar values. This accelerated efforts by states to enact UPMIFA, because the Act eliminates the historic dollar value limitation on fund expenditures. In July of 2008, 25 states had enacted UPMIFA and legislation had been introduced in eight others. One year later, 34 states had enacted and 14 had introduced the legislation. UPMIFA permits a charitable organization, subject to donor intent, to "appropriate for expenditure or accumulate so much of an endowment fund as the institution determines to be prudent for the uses, benefits, purposes and duration for which the endowment fund is established." Seven criteria guide the institution in such decisions: "1) duration and preservation of the endowment fund; 2) the purposes of the institution and the endowment fund; 3) general economic conditions; 4) the effect of inflation or deflation; 5) the expected total return from income and the appreciation of investments; 6) other resources of the institution; and, 7) the investment policy of the institution." UPMIFA § 4.

For jurisdictions that have not adopted UPMIFA, such as New York, the organization can seek donor permission to release or modify an endowment restriction. Generally, heirs would not have authority to give consent. If the donor is deceased, the organization could seek judicial release of an endowment restriction. In New York the attorney general is a necessary party, and relief is only granted if the organization can establish that without it, the organization will fail or be so diminished it will be substantially different. The relief is treated as a borrowing. The New York City Opera was in such serious financial straits that the attorney general gave approval and a court agreed for the Opera to "borrow" $23.5 million of its total endowment of $33 million to pay off debts and to meet payroll and other needs. See Daniel Wakin, City Opera Taps Into Endowment, N.Y. Times, April 18, 2009, at C2.

The full text of UPMIFA is included in the Statutes, Regulations and Forms Appendix, *infra* this Supplement, at page 82 *et seq.*

c. The Movement to More Sophisticated (and Riskier) Investment Strategies

Page 232:

After the carryover paragraph, insert:

In recent years higher education endowments grew by double digit figures, led by Harvard's which ballooned from a little over $5 billion in 1993 to $36.6 billion at the end of the fiscal year ending June 30, 2008. Yale's grew from $3.1 billion to $22.9 billion in that period. Early in 2008, Senators Baucus and Grassley of the Senate Finance Committee sent letters to over 100 colleges urging them to increase their endowment payout rate from the 4.6% average and use some of the golden horde for tuition relief. However, higher education endowments averaged only 3 percent returns in a difficult environment in fiscal 2008. Then, the bottom dropped out as the financial crisis wreaked havoc on endowment portfolios.

Between July 1 and November 30, 2008, endowments lost $150 billion in assets or 23 percent of their value.[1] Harvard's endowment dropped 22 percent and is projected to decline about 30 percent to $24 billion; Yale's declined 25 percent to $17 billion. Private foundation endowments dropped by a third. These figures may underestimate the decreases as the markets got worse in the first months of 2009 and may not include losses of illiquid (hard to sell), hard to value alternative investments, which were so attractive during the years of growth.

The impact on college and charities has been severe. Ironically, institutions with largest endowments suffered the most. Larger endowment institutions may fund 35 percent or more of their operating budget with the endowment payout. In response to the declines, colleges, museums and other charities froze or delayed construction and expansion projects, cut operating budgets, drew on cash reserves, implemented hiring and salary freezes, ordered layoffs, and a few sued their financial advisors. Many colleges are struggling to preserve financial aid.[2] Several institutions have issued bonds to raise money for expenses or to allow them to hold on to illiquid assets until their price rises. Rating services have cut university credit ratings. On top of this, charitable giving declined 57 percent on an inflation adjusted basis in 2008 compared to the previous year, the largest percentage drop in 50 years.[3] A Council on Foundations study found that 62 percent of foundations

---

[1]Noelle Barton, Decline in Giving Expected to Follow Drop of $150-Billion in Foundation Assets in 2008, Chron. Philanthopy, April 9, 2009, available at http://philanthropy.com/premium/articles/v21/i12/12001703.htm.

[2]The always quotable Senator Chuck Grassley has not retreated from his position that higher educational endowments should increase their payout rates: "Contrary to what colleges might argue, the weak economy makes a strong case for more endowment spending on student aid. If an endowment is a rainy-day fund, it's pouring. Colleges' smart saving and investing could really help students right now." See John Hechinger, College Endowments Plunge, Wall St. J., Jan. 27, 2009, at D3.

[3]Stephanie Strom, Charitable Giving Declines, a New Report Finds, N.Y. Times, June 10, 2009, at A16.

expect to reduce their grantmaking in the next year. For representative articles see, Matthew Kaminski, The Age of Diminishing Endowments, Wall St. J., June 6-7, 2009, at A11; Claire Cain Miller & Geraldine Fabrikant, Beyond the Ivied Halls, Endowments Suffer, Nov. 26, 2008, at B1; Katie Zezima, Data Show College Endowments Lost 23% in 5 Months, Worst Drop Since '70s, N.Y. Times, Jan. 27, 2009, at A17.

Page 234:

After the second paragraph, insert:

   2A. The Biggest Sure Thing: Madoff. The largest and longest running Ponzi scheme ever was created by Bernard Madoff, who collected an estimated $65 billion over thirty years before the inevitable collapse. Madoff's "innovation" was not to promise extraordinary profits — double your money in six months — but steady returns of 10-12 percent. The Foundation for New Era Philanthropy and Greater Ministries International Ponzis (casebook, pages 233-234) preyed on Christian religious organizations and individuals.   Madoff stole from many Jewish foundations and organizations and their wealthy benefactors, who invested based on social contacts.

   The victims included colleges and universities (Yeshiva to the tune of $110 million; New York Law School; Brandeis; Tufts); philanthropists, charities and over one hundred private foundations (including Steven Spielberg's and Elie Weisel's). Most of the private foundations were family foundations, established by wealthy investors. Several were wiped out and required to close. Others scaled back their grants with obvious impact on their beneficiary charities. Charities that focused on human rights, criminal justice and reproductive health were particularly affected. In three cases the bankruptcy trustee has sued to "claw back," that is, retrieve from foundations or their creators funds invested and later redeemed with appreciation from Madoff. Some nonprofits (New York University, for example) invested with hedge funds that fed money into Madoff funds. These "feeder" funds received referral fees for funneling this money, but the charities allege they did not know their investments would wind up with Madoff.

   How could this happen? Constant returns over time are impossible. There was a lack of transparency of Madoff's investment approach. He was unwilling to disclose his investment strategy. The size of Madoff's fund exceeded the total trading in the securities his investors purportedly owned. In fact, Madoff never traded at all. His auditor was a two partner accounting firm located in a suburban strip mall. Who is to blame for so many charities investing in this scheme? For a sampling of the extensive press coverage, see Diane B. Henriques et al., Madoff Scheme Kept Rippling Outward, Crossing Borders, N.Y. Times, Dec. 20, 2008, at 1; Eleanor Laise & Dennis K. Berman, The Madoff Fraud Case: Impact on Jewish Charities Is Catastrophic – Programs for Bone-Marrow Transplants and Human-Rights Campaigns Find Themselves in Peril, Wall Street J., Dec. 16, 2008, at A20; Ben Gose, Charities Calculate Losses in Alleged Ponzi Scheme, Chron. Philanthropy, Dec. 16, 2008, available at http://philanthropy.com/news/updates/index.php?id=6582; Amir Efrati, Criminal Probe Expands to High-

Profile Investors Who Say They Were Stung, Wall St. J., May 18, 2009, at A1. For a list of the foundations that invested with Madoff, see Nicholas Kristoff, Madoff and America's (Poorer) Foundations, N.Y. Times, Jan. 29, 2009, at http://kristof.blogs.nytimes.com/2009/01/29/madoff-and-americas-poorer-foundations/?scp=1-b&sq=&st=nyt.

The downturn in the financial markets revealed other Ponzi schemes and fraudulent investments in which charities had invested. Even before the Madoff exposure, the Bayou Hedge funds collapsed ensnaring the Christian Brothers School of Nashville, which had invested $1.2 million. The bankruptcy trustee was successful in clawing back the redemption of that investment, because the school was on notice when it redeemed that something was wrong at the fund. In re Bayou Group, LLC, 396 B.R. 810 (Bkrtcy.S.D.N.Y. 2008). The University of Pittsburgh and Carnegie Mellon lost the $114 million they invested in Westridge Capital Management, a firm run by two individuals accused of using the firm as a personal piggy bank. The universities had relied on the recommendation of an outside investment consultant and were lured by the promise of big returns on alternative investments, an unregulated category that includes hedge funds and sometimes risky investment strategies. See Paul Fain, 2 Universities Seek Answers After $114-Million Vanishes in an Alleged Swindle, Chron. Higher Educ. Mar. 5, 2009 available at http://chronicle.com/daily/2009/03/122990n.htm.

Page 235:

After the second full paragraph, delete the Problem and insert:

PROBLEM

Congratulations. You have become general counsel of Sturdley College. Brandy Alexander, Sturdley's president, comes to your office to ask your advice. She says: "The College's biggest donor over the years has been the Chevas Riegal Foundation, a $40 million family foundation founded by Chevas and Shirley Riegal. I serve on the Foundation's Board, along with Chevas, Shirley and their two adult children. The Foundation has no separate investment committee and no written investment or asset allocation policy. Chevas oversees the Foundation's investments. In 2003, based largely on advice from one of his wealthy friends and a fellow country club member, Chevas unilaterally decided to invest 90 percent of the Foundation's assets with B. Madoff & Co., which provided a 2-page summary of its investment strategies and consistent 8 to 10 percent returns over the prior ten years. On December 15, 2008, the Foundation learned that the entire investment with Madoff was worthless. Do I and the Foundation's directors have anything to worry about." Before answering, consider the following additional questions:

(a)   Have the Foundation's directors breached their duty of care? What additional facts do you need to know? If there is a breach, what are the legal ramifications?

(b)   Assume that Chevas is also the chair of the finance committee of Sturdley's Board of Trustees, though the committee doesn't meet much. He is considered an investment guru, and the Board always followed his advice. In 2003, Chevas recommended that Sturdley invest $10 million with Bernard Madoff & Co. The Board was informed of the investment, and no one objected. The Madoff investment represents 10 percent of the Sturdley College's endowment's assets. Does the Board have any legal problems?

6. EXECUTIVE COMPENSATION

Page 239:

After the second full paragraph, insert:

Richard Grasso, the former president of the New York Stock Exchange, won his long-running battle with the New York attorney general to keep $139.5 million in executive compensation. Although Mr. Grasso lost in the lower courts, in May 2007 the New York Appellate Division, the intermediate appellate court, in a 3-2 decision dismissed four causes of action against Grasso on the ground that the New York Not-for-Profit Corporation Law (N-PCL) did not specifically authorize the attorney general to bring claims based on the common law powers of the office, as opposed to claims explictly authorized in the statute. The court found that the statute required scienter by an officer or director, and the transaction had to be unlawful as opposed to unreasonable. It rejected efforts to impose a constructive trust on Grasso's compensation. Spitzer v. Grasso, 42 A.D.3d 126, 836 N.Y.S.2d 40 (2007). In late June, 2008, the New York Court of Appeals, the state's highest court, unanimously affirmed. 2008 WL 2510615.

One week after the Court of Appeals' affirmance, the Appellate Division in a 3-1 decision dismissed the remaining claims against Mr. Grasso and Kenneth Langone, the chair of the New York Stock Exchange's compensation committee during the period in controversy. 2008 WL 2595833. The principal issue in this appeal was whether, if a not-for-profit corporation merges into and is succeeded by a for-profit entity (the NYSE merged into Archipelago Holdings and became a public for-profit company), the attorney general continues to have authority to maintain the remaining causes of action when the sole relief sought is the recovery of money that belongs to the for-profit entity and would inure to its benefit and the private parties, who are its owners. The Appellate Division answered no on the ground that the continued participation by the attorney general served no public purpose. The court reasoned that the state must articulate an interest apart from the interests of particular private parties. Andrew Cuomo, the successor as attorney general to Eliot Spitzer, announced that he would not appeal this decision.

Page 242:

After the carryover paragraph, insert:

10. *IRS Executive Compensation Study*. In March, 2007, the IRS released the results of a three-year study of nonprofit executive compensation. For a brief discussion of the report, see *infra* p. 26 this Supplement.

D. ENFORCEMENT OF FIDUCIARY OBLIGATIONS

5. DONORS

Page 261:

After the first full paragraph, insert:

Shortly before trial the Robertson family and Princeton settled their dispute over whether the University misused a gift to its Woodrow Wilson School from Charles and Marie Robertson, parents of the plaintiffs. The legal fees had reached $80 million! Under the settlement Princeton will retain full control of the endowment associated with the Robertson Foundation.[1] The Robertson Foundation eventually will be dissolved and its assets transferred to the University to create an endowed fund. Over a three year period Robertson Foundation funds will be used to reimburse a Robertson family foundation, the Banbury Fund, for the $40 million in legal fees that were paid by the Fund over the course of the litigation. Commencing in 2012, the Robertson Foundation will provide $50 million in funding over ten years for a new foundation to prepare students for careers in government service.

Who won? For a detailed description of the case, see Iris J. Goodwin, Ask Not What Your Charity Can Do for You: Robertson v. Princeton Provides Liberal-Democratic Insights into the Dilemma of Cy Pres Reform, 51 Ariz. L. Rev. 75 (2009).

---

[1] The foundation was a supporting organization under § 509(a)(3). See casebook, pp. 803-820.

CHAPTER 4

REGULATION OF CHARITABLE SOLICITATION

B. CONSTITUTIONAL RESTRICTIONS ON REGULATION

Page 315:

After the first full paragraph, insert:

NOTE: EMBEDDED GIVING

"If you purchase this casebook, the authors will donate one dollar to the Sturdley Home for Decrepit Law Professors." This common marketing tool is called "embedded giving," the practice of building a donation into the purchase of an item.[1] It has moved to the Internet, where search engines such as Good Search.com and web sites donate a percentage of the revenue received to charities. Several legal issues may arise. Some sites allow only registered nonprofits to participate in the program, but others allow the donor to name the cause, which may not be tax exempt at all.[2] Donors cannot be certain their money is going to the supposed beneficiary. Some programs fail to disclose what part of the transaction will go to charity. Charities occasionally are unaware that they are to receive these donations, and have not given permission to use their names. Who gets the charitable deduction -- the donor or the manufacturer? What if the manufacturer or sponsor doesn't turn over the promised percentage to the charity?

Twenty-two states have enacted commercial co-venturer laws to deal with these issues.[3] These statutes generally require state registration, filing of contracts between the charity and manufacturer/sponsor before the inauguration of the program; the terms of the agreement, reporting requirements, and mandatory disclosures to consumers.[4] The problem with state efforts is that enforcement is minimal.

---

[1] Stephanie Strom, Charity's Share From Shopping Raises Concern, N.Y. Times, Dec. 13, 2007, at A1. Kerri Murphy, "Embedded Giving": How Do You Know Where "A Portion of the Proceeds" Are *Really* Going? (2008), paper on file with authors. This approach, also called cause-related marketing, originated in the 1980s with an American Express campaign to restore the Statue of Liberty and Ellis Island.

[2] Igive.com specifies that the user can designate his or her favorite cause in the United States or Canada as the recipient of funds donated by merchants after the user makes a purchase.

[3] New York defines a commercial co-venturer as "[a]ny person who for profit is regularly and primarily engaged in trade or commerce other than in connection with the raising of funds or any other thing of value for a charitable organization and who advertises that the purchase or use of goods, services, entertainment, or any other thing of value will benefit a charitable organization. N.Y. Exec. L § 171-a.

[4] See Cal. Bus. & Prof. Code § 17510 (2007).

PART THREE

TAXATION OF CHARITABLE ORGANIZATIONS

CHAPTER 5

TAX EXEMPTION: CHARITABLE ORGANIZATIONS

C. AFFIRMATIVE REQUIREMENTS FOR CHARITABLE TAX EXEMPTION

2. APPLICATION FOR § 501(C)(3) EXEMPTION

Page 353:

At the end of the first full paragraph, delete the last sentence, and insert:

The initial application user fee for organizations with more than $10,000 in gross receipts is $750, and the fee for group exemption letters is $900. See Rev. Proc. 2009-8, 2009-1 I.R.B. 229.

3. THE MEANING AND SCOPE OF CHARITY

b. Hospitals and Other Health Care Organizations

Page 373:

At the end of the second full paragraph, insert:

On September 29, 2006, the Illinois Department of Revenue issued an administrative ruling concluding that Provena Covenant Medical Center was not entitled to a property tax exemption because it provided inadequate charity care (less than 1 percent of 2002 revenue, according to the ruling). A state trial judge reinstated Provena's exemption in 2007, but on appeal the Illinois Fourth District Court of Appeals upheld the revocation. In an opinion that may have implications beyond the borders of Illinois, the court rejected a broad community benefit test and instead emphasized significant charity care as an essential prerequisite for Illinois property tax exemptions. Among the points made by the court were: (1) the hospital derived virtually all of its revenue from operating income and thus lacked a "charitable identity;" (2) billing a patient who is unable to pay and then writing off the charge as a bad debt is not necessarily charity care; (3) charity care must be measured by average costs, not customary (inflated?) charges; and (4) contractual discounts with payers such as Medicaid and Medicare do not count as charity care. The court also rejected Provena's alternative argument that it qualified for exemption as a religious organization.

The Illinois Supreme Court has granted Provena Covenant's petition to review the Fourth District's ruling. In announcing its decision to appeal, Provena officials characterized the lower court's opinion as incorrect on factual and legal grounds and "misguided." They complained that the ruling "unfairly impugns the proud history of charitable and religious mission service" by the medical center. The full press release is available at http://www.provena.org/covenant.

For discussions of this controversy and other developments in Illinois, see Jennifer Carr & Cara Griffith, The Fight Over Tax-Exempt Hospitals in Illinois, 54 Exempt Org. Tax Rev. 259 (2006); John D. Colombo, The *Provena* Tax Exemption Case: The Demise of Community Benefit?, 55 Exempt Org. Tax Rev. 175 (2007); and John D. Colombo, Provena Covenant Tax Exemption Saga Continues, 62 Exempt Org. Tax Rev. 29 (2008).

Page 375:

In the sixth line of the carryover paragraph, insert "benefit" between "community" and "standard." At the end of the paragraph, insert:

3A. *More Recent Congressional and IRS Scrutiny.* On July 19, 2007, the IRS released an interim report of its findings on the community benefit practices of nonprofit hospitals. The report is based on responses to questionnaires received from 500 hospitals. Not surprisingly, virtually all the hospitals surveyed reported that they provided some community benefits. The largest category was "uncompensated care," but questions remain about what that really means. The interim report was characterized as inconclusive by the IRS because of inconsistent reporting practices and unclear definitions. An executive summary is available at http://www.irs.gov/pub/irs_tege/eo_interim_hospital_report_execsummary_0720 07.pdf. Further analysis of the data will be made before any final report.

Senator Charles Grassley simultaneously released a discussion draft of proposed tax reforms including, among other things, a requirement that § 501(c)(3) hospitals establish written charity care policies; use 5 percent of operating expenses or revenues for charity care; conduct periodic community needs assessments; and control all joint ventures with for-profit partners. The discussion draft is available at http://www.senate.gov/~finance/press/Gpress/ 2007/prg071907a.pdf. In April 2007, Senator Grassley asked the GAO to prepare a report on community benefits provided by nonprofit hospitals and their executive and board compensation.

The drumbeat continued in 2009 with the IRS's release of its study of the community benefit and compensation practices of nonprofit hospitals. Among the conclusions reached by the 191-page report were:

- Nonprofit hospitals vary widely in the amount and type of charitable benefits they provide. Fewer than one-fifth of the hospitals surveyed accounted for 78 percent of the aggregate community benefit expenditures.

- The 500 hospitals surveyed reported spending an average of 9 percent of total revenues on providing "community benefits," such as free care, education and research. Rural hospitals spent less than urban medical centers.

- Most hospitals follow proper procedures in establishing compensation for their executives. The average and median total compensation paid to top officials were $490,000 and $377,000, respectively, with hospitals in high population areas paying the most (the average was $1.4 million in 20 hospitals with the highest compensation).

- The community benefit and reasonable compensation standards have proved difficult for the IRS to administer because they involve application of imprecise legal standards to complex, varied and evolving fact patterns. For example, the IRS conceded that a major limitation of the report was the difference in how hospitals define uncompensated care, with some including Medicare shortfalls (i.e., the difference between the hospital's stated costs and the government reimbursement) and others providing data based on inflated "rack rate" charges rather than actual costs.

The report is available at http://www.irs.gov/charities/article/0,id=203109,00.html.

As this Supplement went to press in June 2009, comprehensive health care reform had moved to the Congressional front burner. Among the possible "revenue raisers" to finance the costs of health care reform was a Senate Finance Committee proposal to replace the community benefit standard with more specific organizational and operational requirements for hospitals. This codification would require § 501(c)(3) hospitals to conduct a community needs analysis, provide a minimum level or charity care, not refuse service based on a patient's inability to pay, and follow certain procedures before instituting collection action against patients. Hospitals found to be critical to the communities they serve or having an independent basis for tax exemption (e.g., because of teaching or research) would be excluded from the charity care requirement. The proposal would include reporting requirements and impose intermediate sanctions (in the form of excise taxes) in situations where revocation of exempt status was viewed as inappropriate or premature.

Not surprisingly, hospital advocates oppose any new statutory regime. In a letter to the Senate Finance Committee, the American Hospital Association defended the community benefit standard, arguing that replacing it with a "hodge-podge of requirements" was either redundant or premature. It urged Congress to defer any action to permit the IRS to collect more information from nonprofit hospitals through new detailed schedules that have been included on the revised Form 990 information return.   See, e.g., Form 990, Schedule H, reprinted *infra* this Supplement at pages 163-166.

For selective press coverage of this ongoing scrutiny of hospitals, see Theo Francis, Nonprofit Hospitals Scrutinized on Care to Needy, Wall St. J., July 20, 2007, at A5; John Carreyrou & Barbara Martinez, Nonprofit Hospitals, Once for the Poor, Strike it Rich, Wall St. Journal, April 4, 2008, at A1; and Robert Pear, Hospitals Mobilizing to Fight Proposed Charity Care Rules, N.Y. Times, June 1, 2009, at A11.

Page 399:

At the bottom of the page, insert:

g. Credit Counseling Organizations

Internal Revenue Code: § 501(q)

Credit counseling organizations (CCOs) assist people in financial distress to gain control over their finances. At their best, they provide free or low-cost education on financial management, counsel individuals on how to reduce debt and avoid bankruptcy, and help negotiate and structure debt repayment plans. At their worst, CCOs use deceptive advertising, engage in fraudulent business practices, pay excessive salaries, and exploit vulnerable consumers. The earliest nonprofit CCOs were sponsored by an odd coalition of credit card companies, government, private philanthropy and labor unions. They initially limited their services to low-income clients, eventually broadening their client base to the general public. See generally PPA 2006 Technical Explanation at 312-316.

CCOs were first granted tax-exempt status as § 501(c)(4) social welfare organizations. Rev. Rul. 65-299, 1965-2 C.B. 165. Those that engaged in public education and provided counseling to low-income clients achieved § 501(c)(3) exemption as charitable or educational organizations. Rev. Rul. 69-441, 1969-2 C.B. 115. The IRS denied charitable exemptions to CCOs that did not restrict their services to the poor or charged fees but, after losing several court cases, it retreated and began approving § 501(c)(3) exemption to CCOs that provided free public education even if they served the general public and charged nominal fees for debt management plans. See, e.g., Consumer Credit Counseling Services of Alabama, Inc. v. United States, 44 AFTR 2d (RIA) 5122 (D.D.C. 1978).

Nonprofit CCOs began to proliferate in the 1990s as a result of the American culture of excessive debt and stricter new consumer protection laws from which nonprofits were exempted. Although they were hard to distinguish from for-profit businesses, most of these new breed CCOs obtained tax-exempt status despite their high fees, excessive salaries, shady relationships with for-profit affiliates, and little or no public education or service to the poor. The IRS and other regulators gradually took notice, as did the New York Times, which highlighted industry abuses in a front-page expose. Jennifer Bayot, Not-for-Profit Credit Counselors

Are Targets of an I.R.S. Inquiry, N.Y.Times, Oct. 14, 2003, at A1. These developments, along with changes to the Bankruptcy Code requiring individuals seeking debt protection to certify that they received counseling from an approved nonprofit CCO, spurred Congress to conduct its own investigation on several fronts.

The pivotal questions for Congressional tax committees were whether the IRS already had sufficient tools to deny or revoke exemption to abusive CCOs; whether problems were better addressed outside the tax code by consumer protection legislation; or, as proposed by the Senate Finance Committee staff in its 2004 "discussion draft" of exempt organization tax reforms, whether § 501(c)(3) exemption standards should be tightened. The Panel on the Nonprofit Sector strongly opposed any attempt "to narrow the broad range of missions embraced by charitable organizations or mandate the methods or programs that may be used to further exempt purposes." Panel on the Nonprofit Sector, Strengthening Transparency, Governance, Accountability of Charitable Organizations: A Supplement to the Final Report (April 2006) at 25. Although the Panel was quick to condemn CCOs that had no charitable or educational mission, it feared the ripple effect ramifications of micro-managing tax exemption standards to correct a problem that it believed was better handled outside the tax law. In PPA 2006, however, Congress disagreed and enacted detailed statutory requirements that CCOs must satisfy (in addition to prior law) to qualify for exemption under either § 501(c)(3) or § 501(c)(4). I.R.C. § 501(q).

An organization that provides credit counseling services as a substantial purpose generally will be eligible for exemption under § 501(c)(3) or § 501(c)(4) only if it:

1.   Provides credit counseling services tailored to the specific needs and circumstances of consumers.

2.   Makes no loans to debtors (other than loans with no fees or interest) and does not negotiate the making of loans on behalf of debtors.

3.   Provides services for the purpose of improving any consumer's credit record, history or rating only to the extent the services are incidental to credit counseling and does not charge separately stated fees for such services.

4.   Does not refuse to provide services to a consumer because of inability to pay, the ineligibility of the consumer for debt management plan enrollment, or the unwillingness of the consumer to enroll in a debt management plan.

5.   Establishes and implements a policy to require that any fees charged to a consumer are reasonable, allows for fee waivers if the consumer is unable to pay, and, except as provided by state law, prohibits charging fees based in whole or in part on a percentage of the consumer's debt,

payments by the consumer to be made under a debt management plan, or projected or actual savings to the consumer from the plan.

6.   Has a governing board controlled by persons who are broadly representative of the public, with not more than 20 percent of the voting power vested in persons employed by the organization or who will benefit financially from its activities, and not more than 49 percent of the voting power of which is vested in persons who are employed by the organization or who will benefit financially from its activities, other than through receipt of reasonable directors' fees.

7.   Receives no income from providing referrals to others for financial services and pays no amount to others for obtaining referrals from consumers; and

8.   Does not own more than 35 percent of certain for-profit entities in the business of credit repair, lending money, providing debt management plan services, and the like.

I.R.C. § 501(q)(1).

And there's more – additional requirements for CCOs seeking to qualify as either charities or social welfare organizations. Section 501(c)(3) status will be granted only to CCOs that do not solicit contributions from consumers during the initial counseling process or when the consumer is receiving services from the organization; and the organization's aggregate revenue from creditors that is attributable to debt management plan services does not exceed 50 percent of total revenues, with higher percentages during a three-year transition period. I.R.C. § 501(q)(2). CCOs seeking exemption as a § 501(c)(4) social welfare organization must apply for exemption under the same "notice" rules in § 508 generally applicable to charities. I.R.C. § 501(q)(3).

These new rules could serve as a model for more wide-ranging refinements of charitable tax exemption standards for other sub-sectors, such as health care and education, if and when Congress desires to act. The legislative history suggests that some of the new requirements for CCOs affect "core issues," such as providing services without regard to ability to pay and having an independent board, that should be relevant in evaluating qualification of other organizations for tax exemption. PPA 2006 Technical Explanation at 318, n. 435.

4. THE PUBLIC POLICY LIMITATION

Page 426:

At the end of the first full paragraph, insert:

On rehearing, the Ninth Circuit in an 8-7 decision, reversed the three-judge panel and upheld the Kamehameha Schools' Hawaiian-only admissions policy. In ruling that applicants with no Hawaiian ancestry could be denied admission without violating federal civil rights laws, the majority pointed to unique factors in the history of Hawaii and the remedial mission of the schools to counteract significant educational deficits of Native Hawaiian children. Doe v. Kamehameha Schools/Bernice Pauahi Bishop Estate, 470 F.3d 827 (9th Cir. 2006).

It was widely assumed that the Supreme Court would grant certiorari in this case because of its implications on affirmative action programs, but in May 2007 the Kamehameha Schools announced that they had settled the suit. The terms of the settlement were not disclosed.

After the last paragraph, insert:

In 2008, Bob Jones University posted on its web site a "Statement About Race at BJU" in which it acknowledged past failures in allowing institutional policies to be shaped by "the segregationist ethos of American culture." The University said it was "profoundly sorry" for these failures and for allowing "institutional policies to remain in place that were racially hurtful." The full statement is available at http://www.bju.edu/welcome/who-we-are/race-statement.php. According to its web site, Bob Jones University's student body now represents various ethnicities and cultures, and the university solicits financial support through separately incorporated § 501(c)(3) entities for two scholarship funds for minority applicants.

D. INUREMENT, PRIVATE BENEFIT AND INTERMEDIATE SANCTIONS

3. INTERMEDIATE SANCTIONS ON EXCESS BENEFIT TRANSACTIONS

Page 490:

After the carryover paragraph, insert:

In March 2008, the IRS issued final regulations on the circumstances under which exemptions will be revoked on inurement or private benefit grounds. The final version sets forth the same general factors as the proposed regulations but clarifies several areas with new or modified examples. Several examples emphasize whether an organization has implemented safeguards that are reasonably calculated to prevent excess benefit transactions. See Treas. Reg. § 1.501(c)(3)-1(f)(2)(iv) Examples 4 & 5. The full text of the final regulations is included in the Statutes, Regulations and Forms Appendix, *infra* this Supplement, at page 118 *et seq*.

Page 492:

At the beginning of the second full paragraph, change "Disguised Benefits" to "Disregarded Benefits"

Page 495:

After the third full paragraph, insert:

The Pension Protection Act of 2006 increased the dollar limit on organization managers for participation in excess benefit transactions from $10,000 to $20,000 per transaction. I.R.C. § 4958(d)(2).

Page 496:

At the end of the fourth full paragraph, insert:

On appeal in *Caracci*, the Fifth Circuit reversed and rendered judgment for the taxpayers. Caracci v. Commissioner, 456 F.3d 444 (5th Cir. 2006). The court's opinion was a scathing critique of the IRS's valuation analysis, finding a "cascade of errors" made by the government's appraiser, who had no prior experience in the home healthcare industry and spent only two days in Mississippi scrutinizing the transactions, one of which was devoted to retrieving lost luggage in his hotel room. By contrast, the court noted that the taxpayer's expert was a director of a major accounting firm with extensive industry experience who spent eight weeks preparing his appraisal. The government's case also was weakened after the IRS admitted that its initial deficiency notices, which it had insisted were correct for four years, were excessive. The Fifth Circuit held that the Tax Court erred in failing to recognize that this concession shifted the burden of proof on the remaining deficiency to the IRS.

The *Caracci* case stands as an early testimonial to the value of an authoritative appraisal when a disqualified person is confronted with an intermediate sanctions controversy involving a nonprofit to for-profit conversion.

IRS Executive Compensation Study. In March, 2007, the IRS released the results of its study of nonprofit executive compensation. During this three-year project, the Service sent letters to over 1,000 organizations and examined 722 of them, including large and small public charities and a sample of private foundations. The principal focus was on compliance, such as whether compensation was properly reported on annual information returns and whether organizations were complying with the intermediate sanctions and private foundation self-dealing rules.

The only illuminating findings in the report related to reporting issues, such as mistakes on Form 990's. Recommendations were for more education and guidance, including training for IRS agents, to reduce reporting errors and provide sufficient information to enable the IRS to identify excess benefit transactions and self-dealing.   The   report   is   available   at   http://www.irs.gov/pub/irs-tege/exec._comp_final.pdf and is reprinted at 56 Exempt Org. Tax Rev. 99 (2007).

Page 497:

After the second full paragraph, insert:

Special Rules for Donor-Advised Funds and Supporting Organizations.   The Pension Protection Act of 2006 did not include most of the proposals discussed in the text, but it did expand the application of the intermediate sanctions rules to certain situations involving donor-advised funds (see *infra* this Supplement, pages 57-58) and supporting organizations (see *infra* this Supplement, pages 48-49).

E. LIMITATIONS ON LOBBYING AND POLITICAL CAMPAIGN ACTIVITY

5. POLITICAL CAMPAIGN LIMITATIONS

Page 532:

Delete the Revenue Rulings beginning at the bottom of the page through the top of page 540, and replace them with the following:

Revenue Ruling 2007-41
2007-25 I.R.B. 1421 (2007).

Organizations that are exempt from income tax under section 501(a) of the Internal Revenue Code as organizations described in section 501(c)(3) may not participate in, or intervene in (including the publishing or distributing of statements), any political campaign on behalf of (or in opposition to) any candidate for public office.

ISSUE

In each of the 21 situations described below, has the organization participated or intervened in a political campaign on behalf of (or in opposition to) any candidate for public office within the meaning of section 501(c)(3)?

LAW

Section 501(c)(3) provides for the exemption from federal income tax of organizations organized and operated exclusively for charitable or educational purposes, no substantial part of the activities of which is carrying on propaganda, or otherwise attempting to influence legislation (except as otherwise provided in section 501(h)), and which does not participate in, or intervene in (including the publishing or distributing of statements), any political campaign on behalf of (or in opposition to) any candidate for public office.

Section 1.501(c) (3)-1(c)(3)(I) of the Income Tax Regulations states that an organization is not operated exclusively for one or more exempt purposes if it is an "action" organization.

Section 1.501(c)(3)-1(c)(3)(iii) of the regulations defines an "action" organization as an organization that participates or intervenes, directly or indirectly, in any political campaign on behalf of or in opposition to any candidate for public office. The term "candidate for public office" is defined as an individual who offers himself, or is proposed by others, as a contestant for an elective public office, whether such office be national, State, or local. The regulations further provide that activities that constitute participation or intervention in a political campaign on behalf of or in opposition to a candidate include, but are not limited to, the publication or distribution of written statements or the making of oral statements on behalf of or in opposition to such a candidate.

Whether an organization is participating or intervening, directly or indirectly, in any political campaign on behalf of or in opposition to any candidate for public office depends upon all of the facts and circumstances of each case. For example, certain "voter education" activities, including preparation and distribution of certain voter guides, conducted in a non-partisan manner may not constitute prohibited political activities under section 501(c)(3) of the Code. Other so-called "voter education" activities may be proscribed by the statute. Rev. Rul. 78-248, 1978-1 C.B. 154, contrasts several situations illustrating when an organization that publishes a compilation of candidate positions or voting records has or has not engaged in prohibited political activities based on whether the questionnaire used to solicit candidate positions or the voters guide itself shows a bias or preference in content or structure with respect to the views of a particular candidate. See also Rev. Rul. 80-282, 1980-2 C.B. 178, amplifying Rev. Rul. 78-248 regarding the timing and distribution of voter education materials.

The presentation of public forums or debates is a recognized method of educating the public. See Rev. Rul. 66-256, 1966-2 C.B. 210 (nonprofit organization formed to conduct public forums at which lectures and debates on social, political, and international matters are presented qualifies for exemption from federal income tax under section 501(c)(3)). Providing a forum for candidates is not, in and of itself, prohibited political activity. See Rev. Rul. 74-574, 1974-2 C.B. 160 (organization operating a broadcast station is not participating in political campaigns on behalf of public candidates by providing reasonable amounts of air time equally available to all legally qualified candidates for election to public office in compliance with the reasonable access provisions of the Communications Act of 1934). However, a forum for candidates could be operated in a manner that would show a bias or preference for or against a particular candidate. This could be done, for example, through biased questioning procedures. On the other hand, a forum held for the purpose of educating and informing the voters, which provides fair and impartial treatment of candidates, and which does not promote or advance one candidate over another, would not constitute participation or intervention in any political campaign on behalf of or in opposition to any candidate for public office. See Rev. Rul. 86-95, 1986-2 C.B. 73 (organization that proposes to educate voters by conducting a series of public forums in congressional districts during congressional election campaigns is not participating in a political campaign on behalf of any candidate due to the neutral form and content of its proposed forums).

ANALYSIS OF FACTUAL SITUATIONS

The 21 factual situations appear below under specific subheadings relating to types of activities. In each of the factual situations, all the facts and circumstances are considered in determining whether an organization's activities result in political campaign intervention. Note that each of these situations involves only one type of activity. In the case of an organization that combines one or more types of activity, the interaction among the activities may affect the determination of whether or not the organization is engaged in political campaign intervention.

Voter Education, Voter Registration and Get Out the Vote Drives

Section 501(c)(3) organizations are permitted to conduct certain voter education activities (including the presentation of public forums and the publication of voter education guides) if they are carried out in a non-partisan manner. In addition, section 501(c)(3) organizations may encourage people to participate in the electoral process through voter registration and get-out-the-vote drives, conducted in a non-partisan manner. On the other hand, voter education or registration activities conducted in a biased manner that favors (or opposes) one or more candidates is prohibited.

Situation 1. B, a section 501(c)(3) organization that promotes community involvement, sets up a booth at the state fair where citizens can register to vote. The signs and banners in and around the booth give only the name of the organization, the date of the next upcoming statewide election, and notice of the opportunity to register. No reference to any candidate or political party is made by the volunteers staffing the booth or in the materials available at the booth, other than the official voter registration forms which allow registrants to select a party affiliation. *B* is not engaged in political campaign intervention when it operates this voter registration booth.

Situation 2. C is a section 501(c)(3) organization that educates the public on environmental issues. Candidate *G* is running for the state legislature and an important element of her platform is challenging the environmental policies of the incumbent. Shortly before the election, *C* sets up a telephone bank to call registered voters in the district in which Candidate *G* is seeking election. In the phone conversations, *C*'s representative tells the voter about the importance of environmental issues and asks questions about the voter's views on these issues. If the voter appears to agree with the incumbent's position, *C*'s representative thanks the voter and ends the call. If the voter appears to agree with Candidate *G*'s position, *C*'s representative reminds the voter about the upcoming election, stresses the importance of voting in the election and offers to provide transportation to the polls. *C* is engaged in political campaign intervention when it conducts this get-out-the-vote drive.

Individual Activity by Organization Leaders

The political campaign intervention prohibition is not intended to restrict free expression on political matters by leaders of organizations speaking for themselves, as individuals. Nor are leaders prohibited from speaking about important issues of public policy. However, for their organizations to remain tax exempt under section 501(c)(3), leaders cannot make partisan comments in official organization publications or at official functions of the organization.

Situation 3. President *A* is the Chief Executive Officer of Hospital *J*, a section 501(c)(3) organization, and is well known in the community. With the permission of five prominent healthcare industry leaders, including President *A*, who have personally endorsed Candidate *T*, Candidate *T* publishes a full page ad in the local newspaper listing the names of the five leaders. President *A* is identified in the ad as the CEO of Hospital *J*. The ad states, "Titles and affiliations of each individual are provided for identification purposes only." The ad is paid for by Candidate *T*'s campaign committee. Because the ad was not paid for by Hospital *J*, the ad is not otherwise in an official publication of Hospital *J*, and the endorsement is made by President *A* in a personal capacity, the ad does not constitute campaign intervention by Hospital *J*.

Situation 4. President *B* is the president of University *K*, a section 501(c)(3) organization. University K publishes a monthly alumni newsletter that is distributed to all alumni of the university. In each issue, President *B* has a column titled "My Views." The month before the election, President *B* states in the "My Views" column, "It is my personal opinion that Candidate U should be reelected." For that one issue, President *B* pays from his personal funds the portion of the cost of the newsletter attributable to the "My Views" column. Even though he paid part of the cost of the newsletter, the newsletter is an official publication of the university. Because the endorsement appeared in an official publication of University K, it constitutes campaign intervention by University K.

Situation 5. Minister C is the minister of Church L, a section 501(c)(3) organization and Minister C is well known in the community. Three weeks before the election, he attends a press conference at Candidate V's campaign headquarters and states that Candidate V should be reelected. Minister C does not say he is speaking on behalf of Church L. His endorsement is reported on the front page of the local newspaper and he is identified in the article as the minister of Church L. Because Minister C did not make the endorsement at an official church function, in an official church publication or otherwise use the church's assets, and did not state that he was speaking as a representative of Church L, his actions do not constitute campaign intervention by Church L.

Situation 6. Chairman D is the chairman of the Board of Directors of M, a section 501(c)(3) organization that educates the public on conservation issues. During a regular meeting of *M* shortly before the election, Chairman *D* spoke on a number of issues, including the importance of voting in the upcoming election, and concluded by stating, "It is important that you all do your duty in the election and vote for Candidate *W*." Because Chairman *D*'s remarks indicating support for Candidate *W* were made during an official organization meeting, they constitute political campaign intervention by *M*.

Candidate Appearances

Depending on the facts and circumstances, an organization may invite political candidates to speak at its events without jeopardizing its tax-exempt status. Political candidates may be invited in their capacity as candidates, or in their individual capacity (not as a candidate). Candidates may also appear without an invitation at organization events that are open to the public.

When a candidate is invited to speak at an organization event in his or her capacity as a political candidate, factors in determining whether the organization participated or intervened in a political campaign include the following:

- Whether the organization provides an equal opportunity to participate to political candidates seeking the same office;

- Whether the organization indicates any support for or opposition to the candidate (including candidate introductions and communications concerning the candidate's attendance); and

- Whether any political fundraising occurs.

In determining whether candidates are given an equal opportunity to participate, the nature of the event to which each candidate is invited will be considered, in addition to the manner of presentation. For example, an organization that invites one candidate to speak at its well attended annual banquet, but invites the opposing candidate to speak at a sparsely attended general meeting, will likely have violated the political campaign prohibition, even if the manner of presentation for both speakers is otherwise neutral.

When an organization invites several candidates for the same office to speak at a public forum, factors in determining whether the forum results in political campaign intervention include the following:

- Whether questions for the candidates are prepared and presented by an independent nonpartisan panel,

- Whether the topics discussed by the candidates cover a broad range of issues that the candidates would address if elected to the office sought and are of interest to the public,

- Whether each candidate is given an equal opportunity to present his or her view on each of the issues discussed,

- Whether the candidates are asked to agree or disagree with positions, agendas, platforms or statements of the organization, and

- Whether a moderator comments on the questions or otherwise implies approval or disapproval of the candidates.

Situation 7. President E is the president of Society N, a historical society that is a section 501(c)(3) organization. In the month prior to the election, President *E* invites the three Congressional candidates for the district in which Society *N* is located to address the members, one each at a regular meeting held on three successive weeks. Each candidate is given an equal opportunity to address and field questions on a wide variety of topics from the members. Society *N*'s publicity announcing the dates for each of the candidate's speeches and President *E's* introduction of each candidate include no comments on their qualifications or any indication of a preference for any candidate. Society *N*'s actions do not constitute political campaign intervention.

Situation 8. The facts are the same as in *Situation 7* except that there are four candidates in the race rather than three, and one of the candidates declines the invitation to speak. In the publicity announcing the dates for each of the candidate's speeches, Society *N* includes a statement that the order of the speakers was determined at random and the fourth candidate declined the Society's invitation to speak. President E makes the same statement in his opening remarks at each of the meetings where one of the candidates is speaking. Society *N*'s actions do not constitute political campaign intervention.

Situation 9. Minister F is the minister of Church O, a section 501(c)(3) organization. The Sunday before the November election, Minister *F* invites Senate Candidate *X* to preach to her congregation during worship services. During his remarks, Candidate *X* states, "I am asking not only for your votes, but for your enthusiasm and dedication, for your willingness to go the extra mile to get a very large turnout on Tuesday." Minister *F* invites no other candidate to address her congregation during the Senatorial campaign. Because these activities take place during official church services, they are attributed to Church *O*. By selectively providing church facilities to allow Candidate *X* to speak in support of his campaign, Church *O*'s actions constitute political campaign intervention.

Candidate Appearances Where Speaking or Participating as a Non-Candidate

Candidates may also appear or speak at organization events in a non-candidate capacity. For instance, a political candidate may be a public figure who is invited to speak because he or she: (a) currently holds, or formerly held, public office; (b) is considered an expert in a non political field; or (c) is a celebrity or has led a distinguished military, legal, or public service career. A candidate may choose to attend an event that is open to the public, such as a lecture, concert or worship service. The candidate's presence at an organization-sponsored event does not, by itself, cause the organization to be engaged in political campaign intervention. However, if the candidate is publicly recognized by the organization, or if the candidate is invited to speak, factors in determining whether the candidate's appearance results in political campaign intervention include the following:

- Whether the individual is chosen to speak solely for reasons other than candidacy for public office;

- Whether the individual speaks only in a non-candidate capacity;

• Whether either the individual or any representative of the organization makes any mention of his or her candidacy or the election;

• Whether any campaign activity occurs in connection with the candidate's attendance;

• Whether the organization maintains a nonpartisan atmosphere on the premises or at the event where the candidate is present; and

• Whether the organization clearly indicates the capacity in which the candidate is appearing and does not mention the individual's political candidacy or the upcoming election in the communications announcing the candidate's attendance at the event.

Situation 10. Historical society *P* is a section 501(c)(3) organization. Society *P* is located in the state capital. President *G* is the president of Society *P* and customarily acknowledges the presence of any public officials present during meetings. During the state gubernatorial race, Lieutenant Governor *Y*, a candidate, attends a meeting of the historical society. President *G* acknowledges the Lieutenant Governor's presence in his customary manner, saying, "We are happy to have joining us this evening Lieutenant Governor *Y*." President *G* makes no reference in his welcome to the Lieutenant Governor's candidacy or the election. Society *P* has not engaged in political campaign intervention as a result of President *G*'s actions.

Situation 11. Chairman *H* is the chairman of the Board of Hospital *Q*, a section 501(c)(3) organization. Hospital *Q* is building a new wing. Chairman *H* invites Congressman *Z*, the representative for the district containing Hospital *Q*, to attend the groundbreaking ceremony for the new wing. Congressman *Z* is running for reelection at the time. Chairman *H* makes no reference in her introduction to Congressman *Z*'s candidacy or the election. Congressman *Z* also makes no reference to his candidacy or the election and does not do any political campaign fundraising while at Hospital *Q*. Hospital *Q* has not intervened in a political campaign.

Situation 12. University X is a section 501(c)(3) organization. *X* publishes an alumni newsletter on a regular basis. Individual alumni are invited to send in updates about themselves which are printed in each edition of the newsletter. After receiving an update letter from Alumnus *Q*, *X* prints the following: "Alumnus Q, class of 'XX is running for mayor of Metropolis." The newsletter does not contain any reference to this election or to Alumnus *Q*'s candidacy other than this statement of fact. University *X* has not intervened in a political campaign.

Situation 13. Mayor *G* attends a concert performed by Symphony *S*, a section 501(c)(3) organization, in City Park. The concert is free and open to the public. Mayor *G* is a candidate for reelection, and the concert takes place after the primary and before the general election. During the concert, the chairman of *S*'s board addresses the crowd and says, "I am pleased to see Mayor *G* here tonight. Without his support, these free concerts in City Park would not be possible. We will need his help if we want these concerts to continue next year so please support Mayor *G* in November as he has supported us." As a result of these remarks, Symphony *S* has engaged in political campaign intervention.

Issue Advocacy vs. Political Campaign Intervention

Section 501(c)(3) organizations may take positions on public policy issues, including issues that divide candidates in an election for public office. However, section 501(c)(3) organizations must avoid any issue advocacy that functions as political campaign intervention. Even if a statement does not expressly tell an audience to vote for or against a specific candidate, an organization delivering the statement is at risk of violating the political campaign intervention prohibition if there is any message favoring or opposing a candidate. A statement can identify a candidate not only by stating the candidate's name but also by other means such as showing a picture of the candidate, referring to political party affiliations, or other distinctive features of a candidate's platform or biography. All the facts and circumstances need to be considered to determine if the advocacy is political campaign intervention.

Key factors in determining whether a communication results in political campaign intervention include the following:

- Whether the statement identifies one or more candidates for a given public office;

- Whether the statement expresses approval or disapproval for one or more candidates' positions and/or actions;

- Whether the statement is delivered close in time to the election;

- Whether the statement makes reference to voting or an election;

- Whether the issue addressed in the communication has been raised as an issue distinguishing candidates for a given office;

- Whether the communication is part of an ongoing series of communications by the organization on the same issue that are made independent of the timing of any election; and

- Whether the timing of the communication and identification of the candidate are related to a non-electoral event such as a scheduled vote on specific legislation by an officeholder who also happens to be a candidate for public office.

A communication is particularly at risk of political campaign intervention when it makes reference to candidates or voting in a specific upcoming election. Nevertheless, the communication must still be considered in context before arriving at any conclusions.

Situation 14. University *O*, a section 501(c)(3) organization, prepares and finances a full page newspaper advertisement that is published in several large circulation newspapers in State *V* shortly before an election in which Senator *C* is a candidate for nomination in a party primary. Senator *C* represents State *V* in the United States Senate. The advertisement states that S. 24, a pending bill in the United States Senate, would provide additional opportunities for State *V* residents to attend college, but Senator *C* has opposed similar measures in the past. The advertisement ends with the statement "Call or write Senator *C* to tell him to vote for S. 24." Educational issues have not been raised as an issue distinguishing Senator *C* from any opponent. S. 24 is scheduled for a vote in the United States Senate before the election, soon after the date that the advertisement is published in the newspapers. Even though the advertisement appears shortly before the election and identifies Senator *C*'s position on the issue as contrary to *O*'s position, University *O* has not violated the political campaign intervention prohibition because the advertisement does not mention the election or the candidacy of Senator *C*, education issues have not been raised as distinguishing Senator *C* from any opponent, and the timing of the advertisement and the identification of Senator *C* are directly related to the specifically identified legislation University *O* is supporting and appears immediately before the United States Senate is scheduled to vote on that particular legislation. The candidate identified, Senator C, is an officeholder who is in a position to vote on the legislation.

Situation 15. Organization R, a section 501(c)(3) organization that educates the public about the need for improved public education, prepares and finances a radio advertisement urging an increase in state funding for public education in State *X*, which requires a legislative appropriation. Governor *E* is the governor of State *X*. The radio advertisement is first broadcast on several radio stations in State *X* beginning shortly before an election in which Governor *E* is a candidate for re-election. The advertisement is not part of an ongoing series of substantially similar advocacy communications by Organization *R* on the same issue. The advertisement cites numerous statistics indicating that public education in State *X* is under funded. While the advertisement does not say anything about Governor *E*'s position on funding for public education, it ends with "Tell Governor *E* what you think about our under-funded schools." In public appearances and campaign literature, Governor *E*'s opponent has made funding of public education an issue in the campaign by focusing on Governor *E*'s veto of an income tax increase the previous year to increase funding of public education. At the time the advertisement is broadcast, no legislative vote or other major legislative activity is scheduled in the State *X* legislature on state funding of public education. Organization *R* has violated the political campaign prohibition because the advertisement identifies Governor *E*, appears shortly before an election in which Governor *E* is a candidate, is not part of an ongoing series of substantially similar advocacy communications by Organization *R* on the same issue, is not timed to coincide with a non election event such as a legislative vote or other major legislative action on that issue, and takes a position on an issue that the opponent has used to distinguish himself from Governor *E*.

Situation 16. Candidate A and Candidate B are candidates for the state senate in District W of State X. The issue of State X funding for a new mass transit project in District *W* is a prominent issue in the campaign. Both candidates have spoken out on the issue. Candidate A supports funding the new mass transit project. Candidate B opposes the project and supports State X funding for highway improvements instead. P is the executive director of C, a section 501(c)(3) organization that promotes community development in District *W*. At C' s annual fundraising dinner in District W, which takes place in the month before the election in State X, P gives a lengthy speech about community development issues including the transportation issues. P does not mention the name of any candidate or any political party. However, at the conclusion of the speech, P makes the following statement, "For those of you who care about quality of life in District *W* and the growing traffic congestion, there is a very important choice coming up next month. We need new mass transit. More highway funding will not make a difference. You have the power to relieve the congestion and improve your quality of life in District *W*. Use that power when you go to the polls and cast your vote in the election for your state senator." *C* has violated the political campaign intervention as a result of *P*'s remarks at *C*'s official function shortly before the election, in which *P* referred to the upcoming election after stating a position on an issue that is a prominent issue in a campaign that distinguishes the candidates.

Business Activity

The question of whether an activity constitutes participation or intervention in a political campaign may also arise in the context of a business activity of the organization, such as selling or renting of mailing lists, the leasing of office space, or the acceptance of paid political advertising. In this context, some of the factors to be considered in determining whether the organization has engaged in political campaign intervention include the following:

- Whether the good, service or facility is available to candidates in the same election on an equal basis,

- Whether the good, service, or facility is available only to candidates and not to the general public,

- Whether the fees charged to candidates are at the organization's customary and usual rates, and

- Whether the activity is an ongoing activity of the organization or whether it is conducted only for a particular candidate.

Situation 17. Museum K is a section 501(c)(3) organization. It owns an historic building that has a large hall suitable for hosting dinners and receptions. For several years, Museum K has made the hall available for rent to members of the public. Standard fees are set for renting the hall based on the number of people in attendance, and a number of different organizations have rented the hall. Museum K rents the hall on a first come, first served basis. Candidate P rents Museum K's social hall for a fundraising dinner. Candidate P' s campaign pays the standard fee for the dinner. Museum K is not involved in political campaign intervention as a result of renting the hall to Candidate P for use as the site of a campaign fundraising dinner.

Situation 18. Theater L is a section 501(c)(3) organization. It maintains a mailing list of all of its subscribers and contributors. Theater L has never rented its mailing list to a third party. Theater L is approached by the campaign committee of Candidate Q, who supports increased funding for the arts. Candidate Q's campaign committee offers to rent Theater L's mailing list for a fee that is comparable to fees charged by other similar organizations. Theater L rents its mailing list to Candidate Q's campaign committee. Theater L declines similar requests from campaign committees of other candidates. Theater L has intervened in a political campaign.

Web Sites

The Internet has become a widely used communications tool. Section 501(c)(3) organizations use their own web sites to disseminate statements and information. They also routinely link their web sites to web sites maintained by other organizations as a way of providing additional information that the organizations believe is useful or relevant to the public.

A web site is a form of communication. If an organization posts something on its web site that favors or opposes a candidate for public office, the organization will be treated the same as if it distributed printed material, oral statements or broadcasts that favored or opposed a candidate.

An organization has control over whether it establishes a link to another site. When an organization establishes a link to another web site, the organization is responsible for the consequences of establishing and maintaining that link, even if the organization does not have control over the content of the linked site. Because the linked content may change over time, an organization may reduce the risk of political campaign intervention by monitoring the linked content and adjusting the links accordingly.

Links to candidate-related material, by themselves, do not necessarily constitute political campaign intervention. All the facts and circumstances must be taken into account when assessing whether a link produces that result. The facts and circumstances to be considered include, but are not limited to, the context for the link on the organization's web site, whether all candidates are represented, any exempt purpose served by offering the link, and the directness of the links between the organization's web site and the web page that contains material favoring or opposing a candidate for public office.

Situation 19. M, a section 501(c)(3) organization, maintains a web site and posts an unbiased, nonpartisan voter guide that is prepared consistent with the principles discussed in Rev. Rul. 78-248. For each candidate covered in the voter guide, M includes a link to that candidate's official campaign web site. The links to the candidate web sites are presented on a consistent neutral basis for each candidate, with text saying "For more information on Candidate X, you may consult [URL]." M has not intervened in a political campaign because the links are provided for the exempt purpose of educating voters and are presented in a neutral, unbiased manner that includes all candidates for a particular office.

Situation 20. Hospital N, a section 501(c)(3) organization, maintains a web site that includes such information as medical staff listings, directions to Hospital N, and descriptions of its specialty health programs, major research projects, and other community outreach programs. On one page of the web site, Hospital N describes its treatment program for a particular disease. At the end of the page, it includes a section of links to other web sites titled "More Information." These links include links to other hospitals that have treatment programs for this disease, research organizations seeking cures for that disease, and articles about treatment programs. This section includes a link to an article on the web site of O, a major national newspaper, praising Hospital N's treatment program for the disease. The page containing the article on O's web site contains no reference to any candidate or election and has no direct links to candidate or election information. Elsewhere on O's web site, there is a page displaying editorials that O has published. Several of the editorials endorse candidates in an election that has not yet occurred. Hospital N has not intervened in a political campaign by maintaining the link to the article on O's web site because the link is provided for the exempt purpose of educating the public about Hospital N's programs and neither the context for the link, nor the relationship between Hospital N and O nor the arrangement of the links going from Hospital N's web site to the endorsement on O's web site indicate that Hospital N was favoring or opposing any candidate.

Situation 21. Church P, a section 501(c)(3) organization, maintains a web site that includes such information as biographies of its ministers, times of services, details of community outreach programs, and activities of members of its congregation. B, a member of the congregation of Church P, is running for a seat on the town council. Shortly before the election, Church P posts the following message on its web site, "Lend your support to B, your fellow parishioner, in Tuesday's election for town council." Church P has intervened in a political campaign on behalf of B.

HOLDINGS

In situations 2, 4, 6, 9, 13, 15, 16, 18 and 21, the organization intervened in a political campaign within the meaning of section 501(c)(3). In situations 1, 3, 5, 7, 8, 10, 11, 12, 14, 17, 19 and 20, the organization did not intervene in a political campaign within the meaning of section 501(c)(3)

Page 548:

After the fourth full paragraph, insert:

The All Saints Church examination ended in September 2007, when the IRS announced that, although it found the church to have violated the political campaign limitations, it decided not to revoke the church's exemption. In other words, never mind – but don't do it again.

F. PROCEDURAL ISSUES

2. INFORMATION RETURNS AND DISCLOSURE REQUIREMENTS

Page 574:

After the carryover paragraph, insert:

Effective for taxable years beginning after 2006, PPA 2006 added a "notice" requirement for small exempt organizations that under prior law were not required to file Form 990 because their gross receipts normally do not exceed $25,000. To keep them on the IRS's radar screen, these organizations now must file an annual report providing their legal name, mailing and web site address, tax identification number, name and address of a principal officer, and evidence of their continuing basis for exemption from Form 990 filing requirements. Failure to provide this notice for three consecutive years will result in revocation of the organization's exemption unless it shows reasonable cause or is otherwise able to beg for mercy. I.R.C. § 6033(i)(1). Small organizations also must furnish notice to the IRS when their existence is terminated. I.R.C. § 6033(i)(2).

The IRS has developed an "E-postcard" (Form 990-N) for small organizations to use in fulfilling their annual reporting obligation. The E-Postcard is not really a postcard – it is a mandatory electronic filing procedure unless a small organization elects to file a paper copy of the regular Form 990. The notice is due by the fifteenth day of the fifth month after the close of the organization's tax period. Churches and certain church-related affiliates and most government entities are exempt from this requirement. See T.D. 9366, 72 Fed. Reg. 64147.

Page 575:

After the first full paragraph, insert:

Effective for filings after August 17, 2006, Form 990-T unrelated business tax returns of § 501(c)(3) organizations, including churches and some state colleges and universities, must be made available for public inspection, with exceptions for certain proprietary information such as patents or trade secrets. I.R.C. § 6104(d)(1)(A). See I.R.S. Notice 2007-45, 2007-22 I.R.B. 1320, as modified by I.R.S. Notice 2008-49, 2008-20, I.R.B. 979, for interim guidance on how this public inspection requirement will be enforced until regulations are issued and effective.

Page 576:

At the end of the second full paragraph, add:

A reporting requirement for small organizations was included in the Pension Protection Act of 2006.

After the third full paragraph, insert:

Proposed Revisions to Form 990. On June 14, 2007, the IRS unveiled a draft of a revised Form 990 information return. It was responding in part to complaints that the form failed to provide clearly accessible information about executive compensation, endowment funds, governance, complex structures such as joint ventures and subsidiaries, and funds raised versus expenditures to support a charity's mission. Nonprofit watchdogs also craved more data about the major sub-sectors, such as the billing practices of hospitals and the extent of their charity care.

The first version of the redesigned Form 990 was a discussion draft that stimulated great interest – over 3,000 pages of comments were posted on the IRS's web site. In December 2007, the IRS released a "pre-final" version and followed several months later with a draft of the instructions. The "final final" revised 990 and instructions were posted on the IRS's web site in early 2009. The new Form 990 includes an 11-page core form along with 16 schedules many of which will not apply to most organizations. The new Form 990 is based on three guiding principles: (1) enhancing transparency to provide the IRS and the public with a realistic picture of the organization, (2) promoting compliance by accurately reflecting the organization's operations so the IRS may efficiently assess the risk of noncompliance, and (3) minimizing the filing burden.

Highlights of the new form include a summary page providing a snapshot of the organization's key financial, compensation, governance, and operational information; a section dedicated to information about the organization's governance and its compliance with best practices; and schedules focusing on areas of interest to the public, such as political activity, compensation, and noncash contributions, activities outside the United States, gaming activities, and specific sub-sectors such as schools and hospitals. The new form asks many direct questions, such as "enter the number of individuals receiving compensation in excess of $100,000" and "does the organization have a written conflict of interest policy?"

The revised 990 is effective for 2008 tax years – i.e., 2008 calendar years and fiscal years that begin in 2008 and end in 2009. To provide transitional relief for small nonprofits, organizations with less than $1 million in gross receipts and less than $2.5 million in total assets in 2008 tax years may file the simpler Form 990-EZ. For 2009 tax years, the small organization threshold will decrease to less than $500,000 in gross receipts and less than $1.25 million in total assets. Beginning in 2010 tax years, the threshold will be set permanently at less than $200,000 in gross receipts and less than $500,000 in total assets. At the same time, the threshold for filing Form 990-N (for very small organizations) will be raised from $25,000 to $50,000 in gross receipts. See I.R.S. News Release, 2007-204 (Dec. 20, 2007).

The new Form 990 is included in the Statutes, Regulations and Forms Appendix, *infra* this Supplement, at page 132 *et seq.* The instructions are available at http://www.irs.gov/pub/irs-pdf/i990/pdf. A background paper and lots of other materials are available on the IRS's web site at www.irs.gov/pub/irs-tege/background_paper_form_990_redesign.pdf.

CHAPTER 6

COMMERCIAL ACTIVITIES AND UNRELATED BUSINESS INCOME

E. EXCLUSIONS FROM UNRELATED BUSINESS TAXABLE INCOME

5. PAYMENTS FROM CONTROLLED ORGANIZATIONS

Page 684:

After the second full paragraph, insert:

The long pending "fair market value" exception proposal was enacted, but only temporarily and with limited application, as part of PPA 2006. It applies to payments made pursuant to a binding written contract in effect on August 17, 2006 (the date of enactment of PPA 2006) or renewals of these contracts with substantially similar terms. The exception is found in § 512(b)(13)(E), which provides that the general rule in § 512(b)(13) shall apply only to the portion of interest, rent, annuity, or royalty payments received or accrued in a taxable year that exceeds the amount of the specified payment that would have been paid or accrued if the payment had been determined under the arms length standard principles used to patrol transactions between commonly controlled taxpayer under § 482. As a result, if a payment by a controlled subsidiary to its tax-exempt parent exceeds "fair market value," this excess amount is generally included in the parent's unrelated business taxable income. The new provision also includes a 20 percent valuation misstatement penalty on excess payments received by a controlling parent and a new reporting requirement. I.R.C. §§ 512(b)(13)(E)(ii); 6033(h).

Congress directed the Treasury to study this issue and submit a report to the tax-writing committees by January 1, 2009 on the effectiveness of the IRS's administration of the new provision, the results of any audits, and recommendations relating to the tax treatment of payments from controlled to controlling organizations. As of mid-2009, the report was six months overdue. Section 512(b)(13)(E) was scheduled to expire at the end of 2007, but Congress extended the sunset date for two years while we wait for the Treasury to complete its study.

CHAPTER 7

PRIVATE FOUNDATIONS

A. THE UNIVERSE OF PRIVATE FOUNDATIONS

2. THE DISTINCTION BETWEEN PRIVATE FOUNDATIONS AND PUBLIC CHARITIES: HISTORICAL ORIGINS

Page 769:

At the end of Note 2 (For Further Reading), insert:

Joel Fleishman, The Foundation: A Great American Secret (2007).

4. PRIVATE FOUNDATION ALTERNATIVES

b. Donor-Advised Funds

Page 777:

Delete the text (Proposed Legislation) beginning with the second full paragraph of page 777 through the first full paragraph of page 779, and replace it with the following:

NOTE: A NEW REGULATORY REGIME FOR DONOR-ADVISED FUNDS

As discussed in the text, despite their growth and popularity with donors, donor-advised funds have never been defined or regulated by statute. In response to real and perceived abuses, Congress finally took action in the Pension Protection Act of 2006, which provides new and highly technical definitions and makes other sweeping changes to regulate donor-advised funds by requiring more transparency and penalizing donors and related parties who receive personal economic benefits and fund sponsors that make inappropriate distributions. This Note is limited to a broad overview of the new regulatory regime. For those who wish to delve deeper, see *infra* pages 56-60 of this Supplement for more thorough coverage.

New § 4966(d)(2) defines a donor-advised fund as any fund or account that is separately identified by reference to the contributions of a donor or donors; is owned and controlled by a "sponsoring organization," such as a community foundation, and with respect to which a donor or his appointee has or reasonably expects to have advisory rights on distributions or investments. Exceptions are provided for several specialized types of funds, such as those that make distributions to only one charity or make grants to individuals for travel or study and are advised by a committee not controlled by the donor. I.R.C. § 4966(d)(2)(B). These definitions and exceptions have already stimulated controversies and concerns as charities seek to clarify whether some of their endowed funds need to comply with the DAF rules and restrictions.

Donor-advised funds that fit within the new statutory definition may continue to make grants to most public charities upon the donor's recommendations, but their sponsoring organizations will incur penalty taxes if they make grants to individuals or to any entity if the payment is not for a charitable purpose. Certain other distributions, such as grants to most private foundations and certain types of § 509(a)(3) supporting organizations, are permissible only if the fund sponsor exercises a heightened standard of due diligence known as "expenditure responsibility." These grantmaking restrictions are enforced by imposing a 20 percent excise tax on fund sponsors who make "taxable distributions" and a 5 percent tax on fund managers who agree to the distribution. I.R.C. § 4966.

Other provisions are intended to prevent the use of donor-advised funds to provide more than incidental economic benefits to donor-advisors and related parties. First, excise taxes on these prohibited benefits are imposed on persons who recommend donor-advised fund grants or persons receiving benefits and the fund managers who approve such grants. The tax is 125 percent of the prohibited benefit on donor-advisors or benefit recipients and 10 percent (capped at $10,000) on fund managers. I.R.C. § 4967.

Second, the § 4958 intermediate sanctions rules have been extended to grants, loans, compensation and similar payments from donor-advised funds to donors, advisors and related parties. The receipt of any such payments is automatically treated as an excess benefit, and the entire payment (even if reasonable) is subject to a 25 percent excise tax and stiffer second-tier penalties if the amount involved is not repaid to the sponsoring organization (and the restitution amount may not go back into any donor-advised fund). I.R.C. § 4958(c)(2).

Finally, the private foundation excess business holdings rules will be applied to assets held by donor-advised funds; contributions to a donor-advised fund will not be tax-deductible unless sponsoring organizations comply with new gift substantiation rules affirming that they have exclusive legal control over contributed assets; deductions will not be allowed for gifts to donor-advised funds held by Type III supporting organizations that are not functionally integrated with their supported organizations; and sponsors must report annually on their Form 990s the total number of donor-advised funds owned, their aggregate value, and the aggregate contributions and grants made from those funds during the year. I.R.C. §§ 4943(e); 170(f)(18); 6033(k).

PPA 2006 also directs the Treasury to conduct a one-year study of donor-advised funds, focusing on several other questions that were left unaddressed, such as whether donor-advised funds should be subject to a payout requirement and whether a donor's retention of rights and privileges is consistent with the treatment of contributions to donor-advised funds as completed gifts for charitable deduction purposes . The deadline for completion of the study was August 2007, but it had not been issued as of the middle of 2009.

c. Pass-through Foundations and Pooled Common Funds

Pages 779-780:

All citations to I.R.C. § 170(b)(1)(E) should be changed to § 170(b)(1)(F).

B. The Federal Tax Treatment of Private Foundations: An Overview

1. The Tax Definition of a Private Foundation

Page 782:

At the end of the fifth full paragraph, insert:

The IRS has changed the public support testing period under this exception and "Exception 2" (discussed at pages 784-785 of the text) from four to five years, including the year being tested. For more details, see *infra* this Supplement, page 45 *et seq.*

Page 786:

In the bracketed text at the end of the section, insert:

Many new anti-abuse rules were enacted in the Pension Protection Act of 2006. See *infra* this Supplement, pages 47-52 for the details.

3. Private Foundation Excise Taxes

Page 790:

After the carryover paragraph on page 790, insert:

2006 Legislation: Increased Excise Tax Rates. The Pension Protection Act of 2006 doubled all the initial private foundation excise taxes. Effective for tax years beginning after August 17, 2006, the initial penalty rates are: 10 percent for self-dealing; 30 percent for failure to meet the charitable payout requirement; 10 percent for excess business holdings; 10 percent for jeopardy investments; and 20 percent for taxable expenditures.

PPA 2006 also increased the private foundation excise tax dollar limitations and rates for foundation managers as follows:

Act	Dollar Limit	Rate
Self-Dealing	$20,000 per act	5%

Jeopardy Investment	$10,000 (initial tax)	no change
	$20,000 (second-tier tax)	
Taxable Expenditure	$10,000 (initial tax)	5%
	$20,000 (second-tier tax)	

Page 790:

In the second sentence of Problem 1(c), change "four years preceding the current year" to "five years including the current year."

C. AVOIDING PRIVATE FOUNDATION STATUS: THE DETAILS

2. TRADITIONAL PUBLIC CHARITIES: § 509(a)(1)

b. Publicly Supported Organizations

Page 800:

After the second full paragraph, insert:

Elimination of Advance Ruling Process and Public Support Testing Period. Historically, a new § 501(c)(3) organization seeking to qualify as a publicly supported charity was required to obtain an advance ruling from the IRS. If the organization demonstrated to the IRS's satisfaction that it could "reasonably be expected" to meet one of the public support tests in § 170(b)(1)(A)(vi) or § 509(a)(2) during its first five years, it would receive an advance ruling on which donors could rely recognizing its public charity classification. At the end of the five-year advance ruling period, the organization would file a form (Form 8734) to establish that it actually met one of the public support tests. If it did, the IRS issued a final determination letter and the organization's public support would be monitored going forward through information provided on its annual Form 990 information return. If it failed both tests at the end of the advance period, the organization would be reclassified as a private foundation and be subject to the excise tax on net investment income imposed by § 4940 for all five years. After the IRS published notice of the change of status, donors no longer could rely on the advance public charity ruling for charitable contribution deduction purposes.

In September 2008, the IRS issued new regulations eliminating the advance ruling process, changing the public support computation period, and coordinating these changes with Schedule A of the redesigned Form 990. The regulations apply to all exemption applications filed after September 8, 2008, and also to all organizations with applications pending before the IRS on that date, regardless of when they were submitted.

The new regulations eliminate advance public charity classification rulings. If an organization can demonstrate in its exemption application that it "can reasonably be expected" to meet either the one-third public support test or the facts and circumstances test during its first five years, it will be classified as a public charity for all purposes, retain that status for its first five years, and not be subject to any private foundation excise taxes regardless of the level of public support it actually receives during that period. In determining whether an organization can reasonably be expected to meet either of the public support tests of § 170(b)(1)(A)(vi), the regulations provide that the "basic consideration" is whether its organizational structure, current or proposed programs or activities, and actual or intended method of operation are such as can reasonably be expected to attract the type and level of support that is necessary to meet these those tests. The various factors applied under the current (and continuing) ten percent plus facts and circumstances test are considered in making this determination. Treas. Reg. § 1.170A-9T(f)(4)(v)(B).

Beginning with its sixth year, the organization must demonstrate to the IRS (on Schedule A of Form 990, as revised beginning for 2008 tax years) that it actually does meet one of the public support tests, looking to the current tax year and the four immediately preceding years. If it fails to do so, it will be reclassified as a private foundation and be liable for the § 4940 excise tax on investment income and be subject to the other private foundation excise taxes. Treas. Reg. §§ 1.170A-9T(f)(4) & (5).

The 2008 regulations also change the public support computation testing period. Under the old rules discussed in the main text, public support for a current tax year was tested by looking to the four years immediately preceding that year or, alternatively, to the four years immediately preceding the year before the current year – e.g., 2008 public support was tested by looking to 2004 through 2007 or 2003 through 2006. Under the new rules, the public support computation testing period is now a full five years: the current year and the four preceding years. An organization that meets a public support test for any current taxable year is treated as publicly supported for that year and the immediately succeeding taxable year. For example, if an organization using a calendar year meets a public support test for 2011 based on its support for the 2007-2011 computation period, it will be classified as a public charity for 2011 and also 2012 even if it does not meet a public support test for 2008-2012. If it then is unable to meet a public support test for 2013 (based on the 2009-2013 computation period), it will be classified as a private foundation as of the beginning of 2013. Treas. Reg. § 1.170A-9T(f)(4)(i).

The regulations make a few other changes to coordinate the public support tests with the redesigned Form 990. Support must be reported using the organization's overall method of accounting (e.g., cash or accrual). The previous regulations required the cash method for support computation purposes even if the organization used a different method. Under the old rules, organizations that experienced "substantial and material changes" in the sources of support for the current year – i.e., the year being tested – were permitted to use a five-year testing period, including the current year, to measure public support. The new regulations eliminate this exception because it is obsolete now that the general testing period is five years, including the year being tested.

Excerpts from the new regulations are included in the Statutes, Regulations and Forms Appendix, *infra* this Supplement, at pages 116 and 124.

3. "Gross Receipts" and Membership Organizations: § 509(a)(2)

Page 802:

After the first full paragraph, insert:

Changes to Advance Ruling Process and Public Support Testing Period. The changes made by the 2008 regulations discussed above in connection with the public support tests in § 170(b)(1)(A)(vi) also apply to the tests in § 509(a)(2). See Treas. Reg. § 1.509(a)-3T(c)-(e).

Page 803:

In the Problem, add the following new subpart:

(c)   How would the analysis of (b), above, change and what additional information would you need under the temporary regulations issued in 2008?

4. Supporting Organizations: § 509(a)(3)

Page 824:

Delete Section f. (Reform Proposals) and replace it with the following:

f. 2006 Legislation

The Wall Street Journal article at p. 820 of the text shed sunlight on supporting organizations by highlighting their most aggressive abuses. The principal abusers were professional advisors and other "product marketers" who promoted Type III SOs as an attractive alternative to private foundations for donors who wanted public charity tax deduction benefits and less regulation while retaining effective control over a grantmaking entity. The article neglected to mention the many worthy SOs created to support community foundations, religious federations, hospitals, schools, and the like, all of which are legally controlled by one or more public charities. Many of these SOs are formed for valid reasons, such as to insulate charitable assets from liability or facilitate separation of functions in more complex structures such as health care systems. Nonetheless, this article and other anecdotal reports caused Congress to begin considering corrective legislation. Critics argued that SOs should be required to adhere to all or most of the stringent rules on self-dealing and charitable payout applicable to private foundations and that Type III SOs should be eliminated or more closely regulated. Nonprofit sector advocates pointed to the important role played by some Type III SOs, such as those that support public colleges and universities (e.g., to hold and manage technology assets independently so they are not appropriated by state governments), government entities, hospital systems, and foreign charities. See, e.g, Panel on the Nonprofit Sector, Strengthening Transparency, Governance, Accountability of Charitable Organizations: A Final Report to Congress and the Nonprofit Sector 46-47 (June 2005). The debate raged for several years, but a determined Congress finally acted in PPA 2006 by adding an intricate new overlay on what already was a complex regulatory regime.

Types of Support Relationships and New Categories. To set the stage for the statutory snake dance to follow, Congress tidied up the relationship tests in § 509(a)(3)(B) to describe more clearly the three alternative types of permissible relationships between supporting and supported organizations. It also defined "supported" organizations as public charities for whose benefit a supporting organization is organized and operated, or with respect to which a supporting organization performs certain functions or carries out the supported organization's purposes. I.R.C. § 509(f)(3). This adds little to what we already knew, but the key definitions are now in the statute rather than just the regulations.

In refining the relationship test, Congress also singled out for special treatment SOs that have a relationship with supported organizations controlled by the SO's donors. For example, an organization will not qualify as a Type I or Type III SO if it accepts any gift or contribution from any person who alone, or together with related family members and entities, directly or indirectly controls the governing body of the supported organization. I.R.C. § 509(f)(2). This rule is obscured by the lack of any guidance on the definition of control. Regulations yet to be promulgated may clear the fog.

Finally, PPA 2006 introduces a new sub-category of Type III SO – the "functionally integrated" Type III that performs the functions of or carries out the purposes of the organization it supports. I.R.C. § 4943(f)(5)(B). Many of the new anti-abuse rules apply only to Type III SOs that are not functionally integrated, but others apply across the board to all SOs, regardless of their type, and some apply across all types only where donors to the supporting organization control the supported organization.

Automatic Excess Benefit Transaction Rule. Some SOs reportedly were being used to provide economic benefits to the families of their founding donors. Congress's response was overkill – a punitive expansion of the § 4958 intermediate sanctions rules. For transactions occurring after July 25, 2006, all three types of SOs are effectively prohibited from making grants, loans, paying compensation, or making "similar payments"[1] to a "substantial contributor,"[2] a member of the family of a substantial contributor and to certain business entities they control (using a 35 percent test for control). These payments are automatically treated as excess benefit

---

[1]According to the legislative history, "similar payments" include expense reimbursements but not payments made pursuant to a bona fide sale or lease of property with a substantial contributor. Sales and leases may be subject to the general intermediate sanctions rules, however, if the substantial contributor is a disqualified person. PPA 2006 Technical Explanation at 358.

[2]For purposes of this provision, a "substantial contributor" ("SC") is any person (other than a public charity that is not an SO) who contributed or bequeathed an aggregate amount of more than $5,000 to the So if such amount is more than two percent of the total contributions and bequests received before the close of the organization's taxable year in which the contribution or bequest is received from the donor whose status is being tested or, in the case of a trust, its creator. I.R.C. § 4958(c)(3)(C)(i)(I).

transactions, and the substantial contributor who receives them is subject to an excise tax penalty of 25 percent of the full amount of the payment, not merely the excess benefit. In addition, an organization manager who participates in the making of the payment, knowing that it was in one of the forbidden categories, is subject to a tax of 10 percent of the amount paid. The second-tier taxes and other rules of § 4958 also apply to such payments. I.R.C. § 4958(c)(3).

The automatic excess benefit rule also applies to loans by SOs to a § 4958 disqualified person,[3] a category that in some situations may be broader than substantial contributor – e.g., DQPs include officers, directors and other employees with substantial influence whether or not they are substantial contributors to the SO. I.R.C. § 4958(c)(3)(A)(i)(II). The impact is severe because the entire amount of the loan is treated as an excess benefit subject to the 25 percent excise tax imposed by § 4958.

The odd upshot of the automatic excess benefit rule is that SOs are treated more harshly than private foundations in that SOs may not even pay reasonable compensation to substantial contributors and their family members while private foundations are still permitted to do so. Charitable sector advocates have proposed legislation to overturn this odd disconnect and permit SOs to pay reasonable compensation to substantial contributors and reimburse their reasonable and necessary expenses but, as of mid-2009, no action has been taken on this proposal.

Type III Supporting Organizations. Congress decided not to eliminate Type III SOs. It opted instead to add new layers of regulation to those Type IIIs that are most susceptible to abuse by introducing the "functionally integrated" SO, which is not required to make payments to supported organizations but rather engages in activities related to performing the functions of or carrying out their purposes.[4] The Treasury was directed to promulgate regulations to elaborate on this definition and to require Type III SOs that are not functionally integrated to distribute a percentage either of income or assets to the public charities they support in an amount sufficient to ensure that a "significant" amount is paid to the supported organizations. PPA 2006 Technical Explanation at 360.

PPA 2006 also beefs up the responsiveness sub-test by requiring Type III SOs to provide each organization they support with such information as the IRS may require to ensure that the SO is responsive to the needs and demands of the supported organization. I.R.C. § 509(f)(1)(A). The legislative history states that this showing can be satisfied by providing documentation, such as a copy of the SO's governing documents, annual Form 990s and annual reports. Failure to make

---

[3]DQPs of all three types of SOs are now also treated as DQPs with respect to organizations supported by the SO for purposes of § 4958 even if they have no other relationship with or influence over the supported charity. I.R.C. § 4958(f)(1)(D).

[4]The legislative history states that functionally integrated SOs are those that historically were able to satisfy the "integral part" test of the regulations by showing that but for the involvement of the SO, the activities in which they engage in for or on behalf of the supported public charities would have been conducted by those public charities themselves. See Treas. Reg. § 1.509(a)-4(i)(3)(ii), discussed at p. 805 of the main text.

a sufficient showing will be a factor in determining whether the responsiveness test of current law is met. For Type III SOs organized as charitable trusts, a power to enforce the trust will no longer be sufficient to satisfy the responsiveness test. Beginning on August 17, 2007, charitable trusts, like Type III SOs formed as nonprofit corporations, must establish to the IRS's satisfaction that they have a close and continuous relationship with the supported organization such that the trust is responsive to its needs and demands. PPA 2006 General Explanation at 362.

Another significant new limitation prohibits Type III SOs from supporting an organization that is not organized in the United States, with transitional relief delaying the application of this prohibition for three years for existing organizations. I.R.C. § 509(f)(1)(B). The effect is that U.S. charities established principally to provide financial or other assistance to a foreign charity, sometimes referred to as "friends of" organizations) will not qualify as SOs if they do not have broad public support, but they still may be able to qualify as public charities under §§ 170(b)(1)(A)(vi) or 509(a)(2) if either of those public support tests is met.

Excess Business Holdings. PPA 2006 extends the § 4943 excess business holdings rules applicable to private foundations to Type III SOs (other than functionally integrated Type III's) and Type II SOs that accept gifts from persons (other than a public charities that not SOs) who effectively control the governing body of a supported organization of the SO. See pp. 856-860 of the main text and *infra* pp. 53-54 this Supplement for elaboration on the excess business holdings rules.

Grants by Private Foundations to SOs. Another form of punishment included in PPA 2006 adversely affects private foundations that make grants to SOs. Effective August 17, 2006, grants from private nonoperating foundations to Type III SOs (unless functionally integrated), or to Type I and II SOs if a disqualified person with respect to the foundation directly or indirectly controls either the SO or any supported organization of that SO, will not count as a "qualifying distribution" for purposes of the § 4942 private foundation payout requirement. I.R.C. § 4942(g)(4)(A). The Act also authorizes the IRS to define other conditions under which payments by a private foundation to an SO would not be appropriate and thus not count as a qualifying distribution. I.R.C. § 4942(g)(4)(A)(ii)(II). Any amount that does not count as a qualifying distribution under this rule is treated as a taxable expenditure under § 4945. I.R.C. § 4945(d)(4)(A)(ii).

Disclosure. All SOs will be required to file an annual Form 990, regardless of their gross receipts, and indicate whether they are Type I, II or III and identify their supported organizations. They also must demonstrate annually that they are not controlled by one or more disqualified persons and certify that the majority of their governing body is comprised of individuals selected on the basis of their special knowledge or expertise in the SO's particular field or because they represent the community served by the supported public charities. I.R.C. § 6033(l); PPA 2006 Technical Explanation at 359.

Trouble Spots, Interim Guidance and Treasury Study. Several provisions in PPA 2006, such as the restriction on grants by private foundations and donor-advised funds to certain types of SOs, require a donor or grantmaker to be aware of the grantee's specific public charity status. Historically, this information was often unclear or difficult to determine. For example, until recently, IRS determination letters granting tax exemption and Form 990s filed by SOs did not state whether the organization was Type I, II or III, and, until more guidance is forthcoming, donors have no way of knowing with any certainty whether a Type III SO is functionally integrated. Indeed, some public charities are not even sure of their own specific status. All this uncertainty caused many private foundations to suspend making grants to any type of SO for fear that they would not count toward their payout requirement and trigger a taxable expenditure penalty. And some SOs that historically avoided private foundation status under § 509(a)(3) discovered that they had sufficient public support to qualify as public charities under the tests in § 170(b)(1)(A)(vi) or § 509(a)(2), motivating them to seek reclassification to what have become more favorable categories. The IRS was quick to notice this problem and, shortly after PPA 2006 was enacted, it released simplified procedures to permit eligible organizations to submit a written request for reclassification from an SO to a public charity under § 509(a)(1) or § 509(a)(2). I.R.S Ann. 2006-93, 2006-48 I.R.B. 1017. A later notice provides interim guidance for private foundations seeking clarification of a grantee's SO status. I.R.S. Notice 2006-109, 2006-51 I.R.B. 1121.

In 2007, the IRS issued additional guidance on the content of regulations it anticipates proposing for Type III SOs. Advance Notice of Proposed Rulemaking, REG-155929-06 (Aug. 1, 2007). Under this proposal, all Type III SOs still would be required to meet the responsiveness test in Treas. Reg. § 1.509(a)-4(j)(3)(ii). In lieu of the integral part test, functionally integrated Type III's would have to meet the existing "but for" test in Treas. Reg. § 1.509(a)-4(i)(3)(ii) along with a test resembling the qualifying distributions expenditure test for private operating foundations (e.g., a required payout of 85 percent or more of adjusted net income or 5% of net assets) and an assets test requiring use of 65 percent or more of asset value directly in the conduct of activities furthering the exempt purposes of the supported organizations. Non-functionally integrated Type III's would be required to distribute annually to or for the use of their supported organizations an amount equal to at least 5 percent of the aggregate fair market value of all the SO's assets (other than assets used to support the charitable programs of their supported organizations). In addition, non-functionally integrated Type III's coming into existence after the date the regulations are formally proposed could support no more than five publicly supported organizations. Existing Type SOs could support more than five only if they distribute at least 85 percent of their total required payout amount to public charities to which the SO is "responsive." Organizations that fail these proposed tests in any taxable year would be reclassified as private foundations. And, of course, there are more highly technical and specialized rules. The IRS has reviewed many comments on these proposals, but it had not yet issued final regulations as of the middle of 2009.

More to Come? In a signal that it may not be done, Congress directed the Treasury to conduct a study of SOs and donor-advised funds, specifically considering additional issues such as whether charitable deduction benefits are appropriate, what level of payout if any should be required, the advantages and disadvantages of perpetual existence, and the advantages and disadvantages of SOs to the nonprofit sector as compared with private foundations and other giving arrangements. See I.R.S. Notice 2007-21, 2007-9 I.R.B. 611, requesting public comments on these and other questions. Although Treasury was directed to complete the study by August 2007, it had not been released as of the time this Supplement went to press in June 2009.

D. PRIVATE FOUNDATION EXCISE TAXES

1. TAX ON INVESTMENT INCOME

Page 834:

After the first full paragraph, insert:

The Pension Protection Act of 2006 expands the § 4940 "net investment income" tax base to codify regulations and include income from notional principal contracts, annuities and other substantially similar income from ordinary and routine investments. I.R.C. § 4940(c)(2). This change was to ensure that private foundations investing in more sophisticated financial products that were not contemplated when § 4940 was first enacted could not escape tax on forms of investment income that were not specifically enumerated in the Code.

PPA 2006 also expanded the definition of "capital gain net income" to include gain or loss from a disposition of property "used for the production of gross investment income." I.R.C. § 4940(c)(4)(A). This includes property not currently producing income but held for capital gain through appreciation, reversing an old Fifth Circuit decision (the *Zemurray* case cited at p. 833 of the text) which had interpreted "capital gain net income" more narrowly. The legislative history explains that this expanded definition of CGNI is even intended to include gains or losses from the disposition of property used to further an exempt purpose but, once implementing regulations are adopted, such gains need not be recognized if the property was held for exempt use at least one year and it is exchanged for like kind property to be used for exempt purposes under applicable principles for like kind exchanges under § 1031. I.R.C. § 4940(c)(4)(D). See PPA 2006 Technical Explanation at 324.

2. SELF-DEALING: § 4941

Page 839:

After the second full paragraph, insert:

Effective for tax years beginning after August 17, 2006, the initial tax rates on the self-dealer and the foundation manager are increased to five percent of the amount involved. I.R.C. § 4941(a)(1), (2). The dollar limits for management with respect to any one act of self-dealing are increased from $10,000 to $20,000. I.R.C. § 4941(c)(2).

3. CHARITABLE DISTRIBUTION REQUIREMENTS: § 4942

Page 849:

At the end of the second full paragraph, insert:

Effective for tax years beginning after August 17, 2006, the initial tax rate for failure to distribute income is increased from 15 to 30 percent of the undistributed amount. I.R.C. § 4942(a).

Page 850:

At the end of the third full paragraph, insert:

Effective for payments made after August 17, 2006, private foundations may not count as qualifying distributions payments to Type III supporting organizations that are not functionally integrated with the organizations they support, or to all other types of SOs if they or the organizations they support are directly or indirectly controlled by a disqualified person of the private foundation. PPA 2006 also gives the Treasury the authority to define other conditions under which a payment by a private foundation to a supporting organization would not be appropriate and thus not counted as a qualifying distribution. I.R.C. § 4942(g)(4).

4. EXCESS BUSINESS HOLDINGS: § 4943

Page 857:

At the end of the first full paragraph, insert:

Effective for tax years beginning after August 17, 2006, the initial tax rate for excess business holdings is increased to 10 percent of the value of those holdings. I.R.C. § 4943(a)(1).

Page 860:

After the first full paragraph, insert:

Application of Excess Business Holdings Rules to Donor-Advised Funds and Certain Supporting Organizations. During its investigation of donor-advised funds and supporting organizations, Congress concluded that these vehicles were being used by some donors to maximize tax benefits on gifts of interests in closely held businesses and circumvent the excess business holdings rules applicable to private foundations. If these same gifts had been made to a private foundation, the income tax deduction would have been limited to the donor's basis rather than fair market value, and the foundation would have been required to divest its holdings to avoid a § 4943 penalty, possibly diluting the family's control. PPA 2006 attacks these strategies by extending the excess business holdings rules to donor-advised funds and some supporting organizations.

In the case of donor-advised funds, the term "disqualified person" is redefined to include donors, other donor-advisors, members of their families, and 35-percent controlled entities of any of the foregoing. Transitional rules similar to those applicable to private foundations are provided to ease the pain. For example, a donor-advised fund would have five years to divest any new excess business holdings acquired by gift or bequest. See I.R.C. §§ 4943(e); 4943(c)(4)-(6).

PPA 2006 also extends the excess business holdings rules to Type III SOs (other than functionally integrated Type IIIs) and Type II SOs that accept any gift from a person (other than a public charity not including an SO) who controls, alone or with family members and 35-percent controlled entities, the governing body of a supported organization of the SO. I.R.C. §§ 4943(f)(3); 509(f)(2)(B).[1] The legislative history explains that "control" for this purpose includes "the ability to exercise effective control," such as where the SO's supported organization has a five-member board composed of the SO's donor, a family member, the donor's personal attorney, and two independent directors. PPA 2006 Technical Explanation at 361, n. 573. Oddly (or so it seems to the authors), § 4943 was not extended to Type I SOs or functionally integrated Type III SOs.

In applying § 4943 to SOs, the term "disqualified person" is more expansive than the § 4946 definition applicable to private foundations. Borrowing from the intermediate sanctions rules, Congress broadly defined DQP to include persons who can exercise substantial influence over the SO's affairs during the five-year period preceding the transaction, substantial contributors (as defined in § 4958(c)(3)(c)) and persons related to the foregoing, and (accept our apologies in advance) "any organization that is effectively controlled by the same person or persons who control the supporting organization or any organization substantially all of the contributions to which were made by the same person or persons who made substantially all of the contributions to the supporting organization," or members of that person's family. I.R.C. § 4943(f)(4), as interpreted by PPA 2006 Technical Explanation at 360. Congress apparently did not want to leave out any possible suspect!

As with private foundations, affected SOs with present holdings are provided with transitional relief. For an explanation of how some of these stretched out divestiture rules will be resurrected for this purpose, see (only if you have a need to know) PPA 2006 Technical Explanation at 361, n. 572.

---

[1]The IRS may exempt the excess business holdings of any organization from the application of § 4943 if the organization establishes to the IRS's satisfaction that the excess holdings are consistent with the organization's exempt purposes. I.R.C. § 4943(f)(2). A custom tailored exemption provides that excess business holdings do not include the holdings of any Type III SO if, as of November 18, 2005 and at all times thereafter, the holdings are held for the benefit of the community pursuant to a directive by a state attorney general or other appropriate state official with jurisdiction over the organization. I.R.C. § 4943(f)(6).

5. JEOPARDY INVESTMENTS: § 4944

Page 861:

At the end of the first full paragraph, insert:

Effective for tax years beginning after August 17, 2006, the initial tax rates for jeopardy investments are increased to 10 percent of the amount so invested.

Page 862:

At the end of the first full paragraph, insert:

Effective for tax years beginning after August 17, 2006, the initial tax rate on the foundation and on foundation managers is increased to 10 percent, and the dollar limits for management are increased to $10,000 (initial tax) and $20,000 (second-tier tax). I.R.C. §§ 4944(a), (c)(2).

6. TAXABLE EXPENDITURES: § 4945

Page 863:

At the end of the first full paragraph, insert:

Effective for distributions and expenditures after August 17, 2006, the initial tax rates are increased to 20 percent (on the foundation) and 5 percent (on management) and the dollar limits for management are increased to $10,000 (initial tax) and $20,000 (second-level tax). I.R.C. §§ 4945(a), (c)(2).

Page 866:

After the second full paragraph, insert:

Grants to Supporting Organizations. PPA 2006 adds grants to certain supporting organizations to the list of taxable expenditures. See I.R.C. § 4945(d)(4) and *supra* this Supplement page 50.

Page 873:

After the carryover paragraph, insert:

F. REGULATION OF DONOR-ADVISED FUNDS

Internal Revenue Code: §§ 170(f)(18); 4943(e)(1)-(3); 4958(c)(2), (d)(1)(E), (d)(7)-(8); 4966; 4967.

1. DEFINITIONS

Two key definitions – "sponsoring organization" and "donor advised fund" – launch the new regulatory regime. A "sponsoring organization" is generally a public charity that is not a governmental entity and maintains one or more DAFs. I.R.C. § 4966(d)(1). Examples are community foundations and other public charities with donor-advised fund programs as well as funds sponsored by financial services firms such as Fidelity, Vanguard and Schwab. A "donor-advised fund" ("DAF") is any separately identified fund or account owned and controlled by a sponsoring organization ("SPORG") where the donor or any person appointed by the donor has or reasonably expects to have advisory privileges over either distributions or investments of amounts held in the fund by reason of the donor's status as a donor. I.R.C. § 4966(d)(2)(A). The legislative history elaborates on the DAF definition, making it clear that a donor to a DAF, or any person appointed or designated by the donor, must have or reasonably expect to have, advisory privileges with respect to the distribution or investment of amounts held in the fund by reason of the donor's status as such. The presence of an "advisory privilege" may be evident from a written document, such as a fund agreement, or by a pattern of reciprocal conduct between the donor and the SPORG. The privilege need not have existed at the time of the original contribution – e.g., it could arise later when the donor gives advice that is regularly followed by the SPORG. A DAF must be separately identified by reference to contributions of a donor or donors – e.g., naming the fund after a donor or a related family member – or by treating it on the SPORG's books as attributable to funds contributed by a specific donor or donors. An organization's general funds, or restricted or other earmarked funds that pool contributions of multiple donors, are not treated as a DAF.

Two types of funds commonly used by public charities are excluded from the DAF definition. The first exception is for funds that benefit a single designated organization or governmental entity. I.R.C. § 4966(d)(2)(B)(I). This exception excludes from DAF status an endowment fund owned and controlled by a SPORG even if it is named after its principal donor and the donor has advisory privileges with respect to the distribution of amounts held in the fund to such organization.

The second exception is for funds where the donor or his designee offers advice on grants to individuals for travel, study or similar purposes provided that:

(1)   the advisory privileges are performed exclusively by the donor-advisor in that person's capacity as a member of a committee all of the members of which are appointed by the SPORG;

(2)   the committee is not controlled by the donor or donor-advisor or any person related to them; and

(3)   all grants from the fund are awarded on an objective and nondiscriminatory basis pursuant to a procedure approved in advance by the SPORG's board, and such procedure meets the requirements of § 4945(g) (relating to grants to individuals by private foundations).

I.R.C. § 4966(d)(2)(B).

The Treasury is granted authority to grant additional exemptions for funds advised by a committee not controlled by the donor or any person appointed by the donor to advise on distributions from the fund, or if the fund benefits a single identified charitable purpose, such as a fund formed to aid individuals affected by a particular natural or civic disaster. I.R.C. § 4966(d)(2)(C).

2. TAXABLE DISTRIBUTIONS

Effective for tax years beginning after August 17, 2006, § 4966 imposes excise taxes of 20 percent (on the SPORG) and 5 percent with a $10,000 cap (on any "fund manager" who knowingly agrees to the distribution) on the amount of certain "taxable distributions." The "fund managers" who may be subject to the taxable distributions penalty are officers, directors, trustees or persons having similar responsibilities who agree to the making of a taxable distribution. I.R.C. § 4966(a)(2). This new tax effectively prohibits certain DAF grants altogether and requires "expenditure responsibility" (a more rigorous standard of due diligence that is borrowed for this purpose from the private foundation excise tax regime) for certain other types of distributions.

DAFs are still permitted to make distributions to most public charities other than supporting organizations, their sponsoring organizations, other DAFs, and supporting organizations that are not "disqualified" SOs.[1] A "taxable distribution" is any grant from a DAF to:

(1)   an individual;

(2)   any entity if the distribution is not for a charitable purpose; or

(3)   unless the SPORG exercises expenditure responsibility, to "disqualified" SOs and most private grantmaking foundations.

I.R.C. § 4966(c)(1). It seems appropriate at this point to remind readers not to blame the messenger.

3. INTERMEDIATE SANCTIONS

In another response to concerns that some donor-advised funds were providing personal benefits to their donor-advisors and others, Congress extended the § 4958 intermediate sanctions rules to various types of potentially abusive transactions.

The first new rule effectively precludes any grant, loan, payment of compensation, or "other similar payment" by a DAF to a donor, donor-advisor, or

---

[1]A "disqualified" SO is any Type III SO that is not functionally integrated or any Type I, II or functionally integrated SO if the DAF's donor or designated donor-advisor and persons related to them directly or indirectly control the organization that the SO supports. I.R.C. § 4966(d)(4).

persons related to them, by treating those entire payments (and not just the excess benefit portion) as excess benefit transactions under § 4958 and thus subject to a 25 percent excise tax. I.R.C. §§ 4958(c)(2), (f)(7). Bona fide sales or leases of property are not subject to this automatic excess benefit transaction rule, nor are payments of compensation by a SPORG to a person who is both a donor with respect to a DAF and a service provider with respect to the SPORG unless the payment (e.g., a grant, loan or compensation) is viewed as a payment from the DAF and not from the SPORG. Amounts repaid as a result of correcting an excess benefit transaction under this rule may not be held in any DAF but most go into the SPORG's general funds.

In situations not already covered by the automatic excess benefit transaction rule, the generally applicable intermediate sanctions rules are extended to transactions between a DAF and its disqualified persons, with the DQP category under § 4958 expanded for this purpose to include donors and donor-advisors with respect to a DAF. I.R.C. § 4958(f)(1)(E). In addition, an "investment advisor" and persons related to investment advisors are treated as DQPs with respect to a SPORG for which the advice is provided. I.R.C. § 4958(f)(1)(F). "Investment advisors" means any person (other than an employee of a SPORG) compensated by the SPORG for managing the investments of, or providing investment advice with respect to, assets maintained in DAFs owned by the SPORG. I.R.C. § 4958(f)(8). The effect of this rule is to subject investment advisors who receive excess benefits (query how to determine "excess" in this well-compensated industry) to § 4958 intermediate sanctions penalties even if they otherwise are not DQPs because they are not in a position to exercise influence with respect to the SPORG.

4. PROHIBITED BENEFITS

For tax years beginning after August 17, 2006, an excise tax is imposed on the advice of any donor, donor-advisor, family member, or 35-percent controlled entity of a donor or donor-advisor that results in a more than incidental benefit from the grantee as a result of recommended distributions from a DAF. The tax is 125 percent of the amount of the prohibited benefit and is imposed on any person who advises as to the distribution or benefits from it. Any fund manager of a SPORG who approves a distribution from a DAF knowing that it would result in more than an incidental benefit to the persons listed above will be subject to an excise tax equal to 10 percent of the amount of the benefit, not to exceed $10,000 for any one distribution. I.R.C. § 4967(a)(2), (b)(2). To prevent double penalties for the same offense, the excise tax on prohibited benefits will not apply if a § 4958 intermediate sanctions tax has been imposed with respect to the distribution. I.R.C. § 4967(b). There is no requirement to "correct" by repaying the amount of prohibit benefits penalties to the charity.

Examples of prohibited benefits are distributions from a donor-advised fund to pay college tuition for a donor's children (an egregious abuse that few reputable fund sponsors have permitted) or receiving an economic benefit that would have reduced a charitable deduction if the gift had been a direct contribution from the donor (e.g., the value of a dinner at a fundraising event) rather than a recommended grant from a donor-advised fund (e.g., the value of a dinner and entertainment at a charitable fundraising event).

5. EXCESS BUSINESS HOLDINGS RULES

PPA 2006 extends the § 4943 private foundation excess business holdings rules discussed earlier in this chapter (see *supra* this Supplement, pages 53-54) to donor-advised funds. For purposes of this general discussion, it is sufficient to note that the rules to private foundations are imported with some transitional relief for DAFs with existing holdings. Going forward, donors no longer can "park" an interest in a family controlled business indefinitely in a DAF but, like private foundations, DAFs will have five years after receipt of a gift or bequest to divest any excess business holdings and another five years if the DAF can demonstrate hardship. This new provision does not affect business holdings of the SPORG outside of its donor-advised funds.

6. DEDUCTIBILITY OF CONTRIBUTIONS

Contributions to DAFs generally will continue to be tax-deductible for income, gift and estate tax purposes, except income tax deductions are disallowed if the SPORG is a veterans organization, fraternal society, cemetery company or, for all three taxes if the SPORG is a certain type of § 509(a)(3) supporting organization that we have (or should have) come to know as a "Type III SO" that is not functionally integrated with its supported organization. I.R.C. § 170(f)(18)(A).

Contributions to DAFs will be subject to additional substantiation requirements that are the donor's responsibility but, as a practical matter, require the SPORG to state in its contemporaneous written gift acknowledgment that it has exclusive legal control over the contributed assets. I.R.C. § 170(f)(18)(B).

7. REPORTING AND DISCLOSURE

For taxable years ending after August 17, 2006, SPORGs must disclose on their Form 990 information return the number of DAFs they administer, and the aggregate contributions to and grants from the funds during the year. Charities applying for exemption after August 17, 2006 must disclose whether they intend to maintain DAFs and, if so provide information on how the program will be operated – e.g., how they plan to notify donors that the funds are owned by the charity and that distributions may not confer private benefits on donors. I.R.C. § 6033(k).

8. LINGERING POLICY QUESTIONS

Like supporting organizations, donor-advised funds are not out of the woods. PPA 2006 directs the Treasury to conduct a study to consider whether charitable contribution deductions are appropriate for gifts to DAFs; whether DAFs should be subject to a payout requirement; whether retention of advisory rights is consistent with the treatment of transfers as completed gifts; and whether the preceding issues are relevant with respect to other forms of charitable gifts. See I.R.S. Notice 2007-21, inviting public comments on this study by April 7, 2007. Many comments were received, but the eagerly awaited study had not yet been released as of mid-2009.

CHAPTER 8

CHARITABLE CONTRIBUTIONS

A. INTRODUCTION

2. POLICY ISSUES

Page 892:

At the end of Note 2, insert:

The Pension Protection Act of 2006 did not include any provision allowing a charitable contribution deduction for taxpayers who do not itemize deductions or the controversial proposed amendment that would have denied a charitable deduction to itemizers for the first $210 ($420 for joint filers) of their gifts to charity.

Page 893:

After the carryover paragraph, insert:

Beginning in 2011, President Obama's 2009 tax proposals would reinstate the limitation on itemized deductions for married filing jointly taxpayers with adjusted gross income over $250,000 and single filers with AGI over $200,000.

Page 894:

After the carryover paragraph, insert:

President Obama's Proposal to Limit Tax Benefit of Charitable Deduction for Wealthy Donors. Early in his first 100 days, President Obama proposed to limit the tax benefit derived from most itemized deductions, including the charitable deduction, for high-income taxpayers. Under current law, the tax savings from a charitable deduction vary depending on the donor's marginal income tax bracket. For example, assume a taxpayer donates $100,000 cash to a public charity. If that $100,000 otherwise would be taxed at the highest marginal regular tax rate (35 percent in 2009), the deduction saves the donor $35,000 in federal taxes, as compared to $28,000 in tax savings for a taxpayer with a top marginal bracket of 28 percent.

Under the Obama proposal, for tax years beginning after December 31, 2010, the tax benefit of a charitable deduction under the regular income tax would be limited to no more than 28 percent whenever the deduction otherwise would reduce taxable income in the higher brackets (which the Obama administration proposes to increase to 36 percent and 39.6 percent). Taxpayers subject to the alternative minimum tax, which has a broader base but a lower top rate of 28 percent, apparently would be unaffected by the new limitation. The proposal is intended to make the tax system more progressive (and fair?) and raise revenue to help finance health care reform.

It may be too soon to declare this proposal "dead on arrival," but it has received a chilly response from legislators and howls of protest from the charitable sector, especially charities that rely on large gifts from wealthy donors.

B. Charitable Contributions: Basic Principles

1. Qualified Donees

b. International Giving

Page 899:

After Note 3, insert:

2A. *International Grantmaking.* The Pension Protection Act of 2006 included several provisions restricting international grantmaking through donor-advised funds and supporting organizations. In the case of donor-advised funds, a grant to a foreign charity will trigger a taxable distributions penalty unless the SPORG exercises expenditure responsibility in accordance with the rules in § 4945(h). According to the legislative history, an alternative approach would be for the SPORG to make a good faith determination, known in private foundation parlance as an "equivalency determination," that the foreign grantee would qualify as a public charity if it were organized in the United States. See PPA 2006 Technical Explanation at 349, n. 526. See page 899 of the casebook for procedures used by private foundations to make these "equivalency determinations."

PPA 2006 also effectively precludes any § 509(a)(3) support relationship with a foreign charity by requiring that to qualify as a supporting organization, the supported organization must be organized in the United States. I.R.C. § 509(f)(1)(B)(I). Transitional relief of up to three years is provided for relationships as of August 17, 2006. I.R.C. § 509(f)(1)(B)(ii).

3. What is a Charitable Gift?

b. Intangible Religious Benefits

Page 927:

Delete the 2002 opinion in Sklar v. Commissioner, and replace it with the following more recent opinion:

Sklar v. Commissioner

United States Court of Appeals, Ninth Circuit, 2008
549 F.3d 1252.

■ WARDLAW, Circuit Judge:

Michael and Marla Sklar ("the Sklars") appeal from a decision of the Tax Court affirming the disallowance of deductions they claimed for tuition and fees paid to their children's Orthodox Jewish day schools. We have jurisdiction pursuant to 26 U.S.C. § 7482(a)(1), and we affirm.

I. FACTUAL AND PROCEDURAL BACKGROUND

A. Taxpayers

The Sklars are Orthodox Jews who in 1995 had five school-aged children. Rather than send their children to public school to meet California State educational requirements, the Sklars enrolled each of their children in one of two Orthodox Jewish day schools, Emek Hebrew Academy ("Emek") and Yeshiva Rav Isacsohn Torath Emeth Academy ("Yeshiva Rav"). They did so "because of their sincerely and deeply held religious belief that as Jews they have a religious obligation to provide their children with an Orthodox Jewish education in an Orthodox Jewish environment." In 1995, the Sklars paid a total of $27,283 to Emek and Yeshiva Rav which included $24,093 for tuition, $1300 for registration fees, $1715 for other mandatory fees, and $175 for an after school Mishna program at Emek.[1] During 1995, Emek and Yeshiva Rav each were exempt from federal income tax under I.R.C. § 501(c)(3), which provides tax exempt status for certain institutions "organized and operated exclusively for religious, charitable, ... or educational purposes," among others. Both schools also qualified as organizations described in I.R.C. § 170(b)(1)(A), which allows donors to deduct charitable donations to qualifying institutions.

Both schools provided daily exposure to Jewish heritage and values. Their goals included educating their students in Jewish heritage and values, as well as the tenets of the Jewish faith. To this end, time was allocated in the school day for prayers and religious studies, students were required to adhere to Orthodox Jewish dress codes, and boys and girls attended classes separately.

A child's day at each school included specified hours devoted to courses in religious studies and specified hours devoted to secular studies. The length of time that each student participated in secular classes, as opposed to religious studies, and the length of the total school day varied with the gender and grade level of the particular student.

Quality secular education that fulfilled the mandatory education requirements of the State of California also was a goal of both schools. Emek sought to provide a thorough and well-balanced curriculum in both religious and secular studies so that every student could succeed "in the most rigorous yeshiva [(Jewish)] high schools and other institutions of higher learning." Yeshiva Rav sought to prepare

---

[1] Mishna is the study of Jewish oral law.

its students for matriculation to yeshiva high schools and to attend a college or seminary.

During the school years in issue, the Sklars paid tuition and mandatory fees to Emek and Yeshiva Rav for their children's education. To ensure payment, the Sklars, like other parents, were required to contract with each school to pay, and to give to each school postdated checks covering, the tuition for the upcoming school year. Both schools provided tuition discounts to families based on financial need, if documented by detailed financial information submitted to the schools' scholarship committees, but the Sklars did not seek or receive such assistance. Although an Orthodox Rabbinic ruling precluded either school from expelling students from the Jewish studies program during the school year, nonpayment of tuition could result in expulsion from secular studies and the schools' refusal to allow the children to register for classes in the subsequent school year.

B. The Prior Litigation

In 1993, the Sklars learned of a confidential closing agreement[2] the Internal Revenue Service ("IRS") had executed with the Church of Scientology that purportedly allowed deductions for certain religious educational services such as auditing and training. The Sklars subsequently amended their tax returns for 1991 and 1992, and filed a return for 1993, including new deductions for a portion of the tuition they had paid to their children's schools. See Sklar, 125 T.C. at 288. The IRS allowed these deductions, apparently under the impression that the Sklars were Scientologists. See id. The Sklars claimed similar deductions in 1994, but these were disallowed. Id. at 288-89. The IRS Notice of Deficiency explained that because the costs were for personal tuition expenses, they were not deductible. The Sklars pursued an unsuccessful petition for redetermination before the Tax Court regarding their 1994 deductions, which subsequently came before us. Judge Reinhardt, writing for our Court in an opinion joined by Judge Pregerson, upheld the Tax Court's denial of the deduction. See Sklar v. Comm'r (Sklar I) 282 F.3d 610 (9th Cir.2002), amending and superseding Sklar v. Comm'r, 279 F.3d 697 (9th Cir.2002).

In *Sklar I,* the Sklars made virtually identical arguments to those they assert here, based predominantly on their theories that a portion of their tuition payments are tax deductible because they received in exchange only intangible religious benefits and the Scientology Closing Agreement is an unconstitutional establishment of religion from which they should also benefit.

The *Sklar I* panel soundly rejected the Sklars' argument that certain 1993 amendments to the Tax Code rendered their tuition payments deductible as

---

[2]Under § 7121 of the Internal Revenue Code, the IRS is authorized to execute "closing agreements." A closing agreement is "an agreement in writing with any person relating to the liability of such person (or of the person or estate for whom he acts) in respect of any internal revenue tax for any taxable period." I.R.C. § 7121(a), see also 26 C.F.R. § 301.7121-1. Such closing agreements are intended to be "final and conclusive, and, except upon a showing of fraud or malfeasance, or misrepresentation of a material fact," shall not be reopened or annulled. I.R.C. § 7121(b).

payments to exclusively religious organizations for which the Sklars received only intangible religious benefits. 282 F.3d at 612-14. Specifically, the panel noted that the amendments addressed "clearly procedural provisions" and that the deduction the Sklars alleged would be "of doubtful constitutional validity." Id. at 613.

Next, the *Sklar I* panel held that the IRS was compelled to disclose the contents of its Closing Agreement with the Church of Scientology, at least to the extent it fell under I.R.C. § 6104(a)(1)(A), see 282 F.3d at 614-18, and that such disclosure was necessary as a practical matter because the agreement affects "not just one taxpayer or a discrete group of taxpayers, but a broad and indeterminate class of taxpayers with a large and constantly changing membership." Id. at 617. Further, the panel held "where a closing agreement sets out a new policy and contains rules of general applicability to a class of taxpayers, disclosure of at least the relevant part of that agreement is required in the interest of public policy." Id. In *Sklar I*, the panel therefore rejected the argument that the closing agreement made with the Church of Scientology, or at least the portion establishing rules or policies that are applicable to Scientology members generally, is not subject to public disclosure. The IRS is simply not free to enter into closing agreements with religious or other tax-exempt organizations governing the deductions that will be available to their members and to keep such provisions secret from the courts, the Congress, and the public. Id. at 618. The *Sklar I* panel nevertheless opined, without resolving the issue, that the Tax Court's ruling that the Closing Agreement was irrelevant to the deductibility of the Sklars' tuition payments was "in all likelihood correct." Id. It continued:

> The Tax Court concluded that the Sklars were not similarly situated to the members of the Church of Scientology who benefitted from the closing agreement. While we have no doubt that certain taxpayers who belong to religions other than the Church of Scientology would be similarly situated to such members, we think it unlikely that the Sklars are. Religious education for elementary or secondary school children does not appear to be similar to the "auditing" and "training" conducted by the Church of Scientology. Id. at 618 n. 13; see also Hernandez v. Comm'r, 490 U.S. 680, 684-85, 109 S.Ct. 2136, 104 L.Ed.2d 766 (1989) (describing "auditing" and "training").

The *Sklar I* panel then turned to the Sklars' Establishment Clause and administrative consistency arguments. Although it was not required to decide those issues because the Sklars had "failed to show that their tuition payments constitute a partially deductible 'dual payment' under the Tax Code," Sklar I, 282 F.3d at 620, the panel noted that had it been required to do so, it would have first concluded that the IRS policy constitutes an unconstitutional denominational preference under Larson v. Valente, 456 U.S. 228, 102 S.Ct. 1673, 72 L.Ed.2d 33 (1982). See Sklar I, 282 F.3d at 618-19. The panel reasoned that the denominational preference embodied in the Closing Agreement was unconstitutional because it "cannot be justified by a compelling governmental interest." Id. However, the panel indicated it would not be willing to extend that preference to other religious organizations for three reasons: First, an extension of the preference would amount to state sponsorship of all religions, which the panel doubted

"Congress or any agency of the government would intend." Id. at 619-20. Second, an extension of the preference would be "of questionable constitutional validity under Lemon," because administering the policy "could require excessive government entanglement with religion." [5] Id. at 620, 91 S.Ct. 2105. Third, the requested policy appeared to violate I.R.C. § 170. Id.

The panel also indicated it would reject the Sklars' administrative consistency claim because it "seriously doubted" that the Sklars were similarly situated to the Scientologists.[6] The panel further stated that even if the Sklars were similarly situated, "because the treatment they seek is of questionable statutory and constitutional validity under § 170 of the IRC, under *Lemon*, and under *Hernandez,* we would not hold that the unlawful policy set forth in the closing agreement must be extended to all religious organizations." Id. at 620, 91 S.Ct. 2105.

Finally, relying on United States v. American Bar Endowment, 477 U.S. 105, 106 S.Ct. 2426, 91 L.Ed.2d 89 (1986), the *Sklar I* panel rejected the argument that the Sklars' tuition payments were deductible as a "dual payment" or "quid pro quo payment," a payment made in part as consideration for goods and services and in part for charitable purposes. In *American Bar Endowment,* the Supreme Court held that the taxpayer must satisfy a two-part test to be entitled to the § 170 deduction for a quid pro quo payment:

> First, the payment is deductible only if and to the extent it exceeds the market value of the benefit received. Second, the excess payment must be made with the intention of making a gift.

477 U.S. at 117, 106 S.Ct. 2426 (internal citation and quotation marks omitted). The *Sklar I* panel held that the Sklars failed to introduce evidence demonstrating both "that any dual tuition payments they may have made exceeded the market value of the secular education their children received," 282 F.3d at 621, or "that they intended to make a *gift* by contributing such 'excess payment.' " Id. The panel also suggested that for the purpose of demonstrating the first part of the *American Bar Endowment* test, the "market value" for the tuition payments would be the cost of a comparable secular education offered by private schools, evidence the Sklars had failed to introduce, perhaps, because of the "practical realities of the high cost of education." Id.

---

[5] In Hernandez v. Commissioner, 490 U.S. 680, 109 S.Ct. 2136, 104 L.Ed.2d 766 (1989), the Supreme Court rejected the claim that payments made to the Church of Scientology for purely religious education and training were deductible as gifts or contributions under I.R.C. § 170. Id. at 692-94, 109 S.Ct. 2136. Among other reasons it gave for its decision, the Court explained that "the deduction petitioners seek might raise problems of entanglement between church and state." Id. at 694, 109 S.Ct. 2136; see also infra Part II.B (discussing § 170 and Hernandez).

[6] Judge Silverman, concurring, concluded that the question of whether the Sklars were "similarly situated" to the Scientologists had "no bearing on whether the tax code permits the Sklars to deduct the costs of their children's religious education as a charitable contribution." Sklar I, 282 F.3d at 622. Rather, he concluded that the Sklars were absolutely barred from taking the deduction by the Internal Revenue Code and Supreme Court precedent. See id. at 622-23.

C. The Current Litigation

On their 1995 tax return, the Sklars claimed $15,000 in deductions for purported charitable contributions that comprised a portion of their five children's tuition at Emek and Yeshiva Rav. The deduction was based on their estimate that 55% of the tuition payments were for purely religious education, an estimate supported by letters submitted two years later (in 1997) that were drafted by each of the schools at the Sklars' request. Sklar, 125 T.C. at 288-89.

The IRS disallowed the $15,000 deduction. The IRS also determined the Sklars had "failed to meet the substantiation requirements of Internal Revenue Code Section 170(f)(8) with respect to the disallowed $15,000.00 of claimed charitable contributions." The Sklars petitioned the Tax Court for a redetermination of deficiency, asserting that (1) the tuition and fee payments to exclusively religious schools are deductible under a dual payment analysis to the extent the payments exceeded the value of the secular education their children received (a question left somewhat open in *Sklar I*); (2) Sections 170(f)(8) and 6115 of the Internal Revenue Code, as enacted in 1993, authorized the deduction of tuition payments for religious education made to exclusively religious schools (an issue all but foreclosed by *Sklar I*); and (3) that the 1993 Closing Agreement between the Commissioner and the Church of Scientology constitutionally and administratively requires the IRS to allow other taxpayers to take the same charitable deductions for tuition payments to their religious schools (a question the panel discussed at length but declined to decide in *Sklar I*). Before the Tax Court, the Sklars and the IRS stipulated that in 1993 the IRS had executed a confidential closing agreement with the Church of Scientology, settling several outstanding issues between the IRS and the Church of Scientology. See id. at 298. Under this agreement, members of the Church of Scientology were authorized to deduct as charitable contributions at least 80% of the fees for qualified religious services provided by the Church of Scientology. See id. at 298-99.

The Tax Court again rejected the Sklars' arguments, holding that the tuition and fee payments to the Jewish Day Schools were not deductible under any of the Sklars' theories.[7] [The court then summarized the Tax Court's holdings. Ed.]

II. DISCUSSION

* * *

B. The Sklars' 1995 Tuition Payments Are Not Deductible as Charitable Contributions Under the Internal Revenue Code

Section 170 of the Internal Revenue Code allows taxpayers to deduct "any charitable contribution," defined as "a contribution or gift to or for the use of" certain eligible entities enumerated in § 170(c), including those exclusively

---

[7]The Tax Court also ruled that the Sklars were not liable for an accuracy-related penalty the IRS had imposed under I.R.C. § 6662, an issue not before us on this appeal.

organized for religious purposes and educational purposes. I.R.C. § 170(a)(1), (c). "[T]o ensure that the payor's primary purpose is to assist the charity and not to secure some benefit," we require such contributions to be "made for detached and disinterested motives." Graham v. Comm'r, 822 F.2d 844, 848 (9th Cir.1987). Therefore, "quid pro quo" payments, where the taxpayer receives a benefit in exchange for the payment, are generally not deductible as charitable contributions. See Hernandez v. Comm'r, 490 U.S. 680, 689-91, 109 S.Ct. 2136, 104 L.Ed.2d 766 (1989). In keeping with this framework, tuition payments to parochial schools, which are made with the expectation of a substantial benefit, or quid pro quo, "have long been held not to be charitable contributions under § 170." Id. at 693, 109 S.Ct. 2136; see also DeJong v. Comm'r, 309 F.2d 373, 376 (9th Cir.1962) ("The law is well settled that tuition paid for the education of the children of a taxpayer is a family expense, not a charitable contribution to the educating institution.").

In *Hernandez*, the Supreme Court considered "whether taxpayers may deduct as charitable contributions payments made to branch churches of the Church of Scientology"[8] in return for services known as "auditing" and "training." 490 U.S. at 684, 109 S.Ct. 2136. Both are considered forms of religious education. "Auditing" involves a form of spiritual counseling whereby a person gains spiritual awareness in one-on-one sessions with an auditor. By participating in "training," a person studies the tenets of Scientology, gains spiritually, and may seek to become an auditor. Members of the Church of Scientology sought to deduct payments for auditing and training as charitable contributions for religious services. The Court held that such payments for religious educational services "do not qualify as 'contribution[s] or gift[s].' " Id. at 691, 109 S.Ct. 2136. Rather, "[t]hese payments were part of a quintessential quid pro quo exchange: in return for their money, petitioners received an identifiable benefit, namely, auditing and training sessions." Id. The Court reasoned " '[t]he sine qua non of a charitable contribution is a transfer of money or property without adequate consideration. " Id. (quoting American Bar Endowment, 477 U.S. at 118, 106 S.Ct. 2426).

The Court further rejected the taxpayers' argument that a quid pro quo analysis was not even appropriate, because the payments for auditing and training services resulted in receipt of a purely religious benefit. Id. at 692-93, 109 S.Ct. 2136. The Court first found no support in the language of § 170, which makes "no special preference for payments made in the expectation of gaining religious benefits or access to a religious service." Id. at 693, 109 S.Ct. 2136. Second, the Court reasoned that accepting the taxpayers' "deductibility proposal would expand the charitable contribution deduction far beyond what Congress has provided." Id. at 693, 109 S.Ct. 2136. For example, "some taxpayers might regard their tuition payments to parochial schools as generating a religious benefit or as securing access to a religious service," which would be incorrect because "such payments ... have

---

[8]In Hernandez, the Commissioner had stipulated before the Tax Court that "the branch churches of Scientology are religious organizations entitled to receive tax-deductible charitable contributions under the relevant sections of the Code." 490 U.S. at 686, 109 S.Ct. 2136. This stipulation isolated the statutory issue of "whether payments for auditing or training sessions constitute 'contribution[s] or gift[s]' under § 170." Id. Similarly, the parties to the current litigation stipulated before the Tax Court "that an agreement dated October 1, 1993, between the Commissioner and the Church of Scientology settled several longstanding issues." 125 T.C. at 298.

long been held not to be charitable contributions under § 170." Id. Finally, the Court noted that "the deduction petitioners seek might raise problems of entanglement between church and state" because it would "inexorably force the IRS and reviewing courts to differentiate 'religious' benefits from 'secular' ones." Id. at 694, 109 S.Ct. 2136. While declining to pass on the constitutionality of such hypothetical inquiries, the Court noted that " 'pervasive monitoring' for 'the subtle or overt presence of religious matter' is a central danger against which we have held the Establishment Clause guards." Id. (quoting Aguilar v. Felton, 473 U.S. 402, 413, 105 S.Ct. 3232, 87 L.Ed.2d 290 (1985)). Thus, the Hernandez decision clearly forecloses the Sklars' argument that there is an exception in the Code for payments for which one receives purely religious benefits.

1. The 1993 Amendments to the Tax Code Did Not Overrule Hernandez

To circumvent Hernandez's clear holding, the Sklars resurrect their *Sklar I* argument that the 1993 amendments to IRS §§ 170(f)(8) and 6115 overruled the Court's holding in *Hernandez* that only gifts or contributions may be deducted under § 170. According to the Sklars, the 1993 amendments provide for the deduction of tuition payments for which they receive only intangible religious benefits. We agree with the Tax Court that the Sklar's interpretation of the 1993 amendments is misguided.

Amended §170(f)(8) requires the taxpayer to "substantiate[ ] the contribution by a contemporaneous written acknowledgment of the contribution by the donee organization." I.R.C. § 170(f)(8)(A). This acknowledgment must include an estimate of the value of any goods or services the donor received in exchange, "or, if such goods or services consist solely of intangible religious benefits, a statement to that effect." I.R.C. § 170(f)(8)(B)(iii). The amendment also defines an "intangible religious benefit" as one "which is provided by an organization organized exclusively for religious purposes and which generally is not sold in a commercial transaction outside the donative context." Id. As the Tax Court correctly held, *Sklar,* 125 T.C. at 296-97, and as we have previously suggested, Sklar I, 282 F.3d at 613, this amendment creates an exception only to the new substantiation requirement created by § 170(f)(8)(A). Nothing in the amendment's language suggests that Congress intended to expand the types of payments that are deductible contributions. As the *Sklar I* panel explained:

> Given the clear holding of *Hernandez* and the absence of any direct evidence of Congressional intent to overrule the Supreme Court on this issue, we would be extremely reluctant to read an additional and significant substantive deduction into the statute based on what are clearly procedural provisions regarding the documentation of tax return information, particularly where the deduction would be of doubtful constitutional validity.

The second pertinent 1993 amendment requires donee organizations to disclose limitations on the deductibility of certain quid pro quo payments to the donors of such payments. See I.R.C. § 6115. Amended § 6115(a) requires any organization that "receives a quid pro quo contribution in excess of $75" to provide the donor with a written statement declaring that the deductible portion of the contribution cannot include "the value of the goods or services provided by the organization," along with "a good faith estimate of the value of such goods or services." However, § 6115(b) explains:

> *For purposes of this section,* the term "quid pro quo contribution" means a payment made partly as a contribution and partly in consideration for goods or services provided to the payor by the donee organization. A quid pro quo contribution does not include any payment made to an organization, organized exclusively for religious purposes, in return for which the taxpayer receives solely an intangible religious benefit that generally is not sold in a commercial transaction outside the donative context.

I.R.C. § 6115(b) (emphasis added). The Sklars read the exemption from the disclosure requirement for organizations organized exclusively for religious purposes which provide solely an intangible religious benefit completely out of context. The *Sklar I* panel explained why the Sklars' reading of the exemption is unsupportable:

> [Section] 6115 requires that tax-exempt organizations inform taxpayer-donors that they will receive a tax deduction only for the amount of their donation above the value of any goods or services received in return for the donation and requires donee organizations to give donors an estimate of this value, exempting *from this estimate requirement* contributions for which solely intangible religious benefits are received.

282 F.3d at 613.

Nor does the legislative history of these amendments even mention *Hernandez*, and the House Report specifically states that, although the new requirements apply only to quid pro quo contributions for *commercial* benefits, "[n]o inference is intended ... [regarding] whether or not any contribution outside the scope of the bill's substantiation or reporting requirements is deductible (in full or in part) under the present-law requirements of section 170." H.R.Rep. No. 103-111, at 786 n. 170 (1993), reprinted in 1993 U.S.C.C.A.N. 378, 1017 n. 170. Thus, the House Report confirms that Congress intended to preserve the status quo ante, and hardly serves as support for the Sklars' argument.[10]

To put to rest the Sklars' statutory claim, we now hold that neither the plain language of the 1993 amendments nor the accompanying legislative history indicates

---

[10]In light of certain well-established deductible payments to religious organizations in exchange for intangible religious benefits, such as pew rents and church dues, see Hernandez, 490 U.S. at 701-02, 109 S.Ct. 2136, it seems plausible that Congress contemplated these sorts of contributions in amending §§ 170(f)(8) and 6115 in a manner that did not impose the arduous task of valuing the intangible religious benefits, such as the ability to participate in religious celebrations, that donors receive in exchange for these contributions.

any substantive change to Hernandez's holding that payment for religious education to religious organizations is not deductible. We agree with the observation of both the Tax Court and the *Sklar I* panel that had Congress intended to overrule judicial precedent and to provide charitable contributions for tuition and fee payments to religious organizations that provide religious education, it would have expressed its intention more clearly. See 282 F.3d at 613, 125 T.C. at 296-97.

2. The Tuition Payments Were Not "Dual Payment" Contributions

The Tax Court correctly concluded that no part of the Sklar's tuition payments is deductible under a "dual payment" analysis. See Sklar, 125 T.C. at 290-94, 299-300. In *American Bar Endowment,* the Supreme Court considered the question of the extent to which payments to organizations that bear the "dual character" of a purchase and a contribution are deductible under § 170. 477 U.S. at 116-18, 106 S.Ct. 2426. IRS Revenue Ruling 67-246 had set forth a two-part test for determining the extent to which such payments are deductible:

> First, the payment is deductible only if and to the extent it exceeds the market value of the benefit received. Second, the excess payment must be "made with the intention of making a gift."

Id. at 117, 106 S.Ct. 2426 (quoting Rev. Rul. 67-246, 1967-2 Cum. Bull. 104, 105 (1967)). The Court held that Revenue Ruling 67-246 embodied the proper standard, reasoning: "The *sine qua non* of a charitable contribution is a transfer of money or property without adequate consideration. The taxpayer, therefore, must at a minimum demonstrate that he purposely contributed money or property in excess of the value of any benefit he received in return." Id. at 118, 106 S.Ct. 2426.

* * *

The Sklars again have failed to meet their burden of satisfying either prong of the two-part test for a dual payment, and we seriously doubt that they could ever make the showing that would support a "dual payment" deduction for tuition for combined religious and secular education.[11] In *Sklar I,* the panel concluded that the Sklars failed to satisfy the requirements for partial deductibility of their tuition payments. Our analysis has not changed, despite the Sklars' effort to introduce evidence as to market value.

First, the *Sklar I* panel reasoned that the Sklars "failed to show that they intended to make a *gift* by contributing any such 'excess payment.'" 282 F.3d at 621. In fact, the Sklars have never even *argued* – not in *Sklar I,* not before the Tax Court and not before us – that they intended to make a gift as a portion of their tuition payment. Indeed, the record is to the contrary. In their brief, the Sklars explain at length that they pay the tuition and fees to send their children to Orthodox Jewish schools because it is a religious imperative of Orthodox Judaism. They "sent

---

[11]Indeed, the Tax Court expressed skepticism as to whether a dual payment analysis would ever be appropriate in this context. See 125 T.C. at 293 ("[M]ore fundamentally, the record speaks to whether a dual payments analysis applies in this case at all.").

their children to Yeshiva Rav Isacsohn and Emek in 1995 because of their sincerely and deeply held religious belief that as Jews they have a religious obligation to provide their children with an Orthodox Jewish education in an Orthodox Jewish environment." Because they paid for religious education out of their own deeply held religious views, and because the record demonstrates that throughout the school day-during recess, lunch and secular, as well as religious, classes-the schools inculcate their children with their religion's lifestyle, heritage, and values, the Sklars have actually demonstrated the absence of the requisite charitable intent.

Second, the *Sklar I* panel reasoned that "the Sklars have not shown that any dual tuition payments they may have made exceeded the market value of the secular education their children received." Id. The panel stated that the Sklars needed to present evidence that their total payments exceeded "[t]he market value [of] the cost of a comparable secular education offered by private schools." Id. Before the Tax Court, the Sklars introduced expert testimony asserting that "Catholic schools are the most reasonable comparison benchmarks for the schools attended by the Sklar children." Based on his estimation of tuition paid for Archdiocesan Catholic schools[12] in Los Angeles County in 1995, the Sklars' expert concluded that the market value of the secular education the Sklars' children received was between $1483 and $1724, such that in 1995 the Sklars made "excess payments" of almost $5000 per child. The Sklars' expert also included tuition data for other Los Angeles schools in his report. The Tax Court correctly concluded that the evidence in the record indicated: "(1) Some schools charge more tuition than Emek and Yeshiva Rav Isacsohn, and some charge less; and (2) the amount of tuition petitioners paid is unremarkable and is not excessive for the substantial benefit they received in exchange; i.e., an education for their children." 125 T.C. at 293-94. Before us, the Sklars have failed to demonstrate-or even argue on appeal-that the Tax Court's factual findings as to the data set forth in their expert's report are clearly erroneous.

Thus, the Tax Court did not err by concluding that the Sklars failed to show that any part of their tuition fees was a charitable deduction, subject to a dual payment analysis. We conclude that under *Hernandez* and the Internal Revenue Code, their tuition and fee payments must be treated like any other quid pro quo transaction, even if some part of the benefit received was religious in nature. *See* 490 U.S. at 691-94, 109 S.Ct. 2136. We therefore agree with the Tax Court that the Sklars' tuition is not deductible, in whole or in part, under § 170.

C. The 1993 Closing Agreement Does Not Constitutionally and Administratively Require the IRS To Allow Charitable Deductions for the Sklars' Tuition Payments to Religious Schools

---

[12]The flaws in the expert report itself are too numerous to mention, but we point out only one: the archdiocesan schools are subsidized in large measure by the parishes in the Archdiocese in order to force down the costs of education and to afford all Catholic children the opportunity to attend Catholic schools. Thus, by choosing archdiocesan schools as the basis for his comparative market value, the Sklars' expert guaranteed that the tuition and fees paid to the Sklars' schools would greatly exceed the tuition at the archdiocesan Catholic schools.

[In this part of the opinion, the court rejected the Sklars' arguments that, since the IRS allowed similar deductions for members of the Church of Scientology under a closing agreement, the disallowance of deductions for Orthodox Jewish religious education violates the Establishment Clause and principles of administrative consistency. They also argued that the Scientology closing agreement constitutionally and administratively precluded the IRS from disallowing their deductions for school tuition and fees, which they contended were are "jurisprudentially indistinguishable" from the auditing and training provided by the Church of Scientology.

Like the Tax Court and Ninth Circuit panel in *Sklar I*, the court found that the Sklars were not similarly situated to the Scientologists because "tuition and fee payments to schools that provide secular and religious education as part of one curriculum are quite different from payments to organizations that provide exclusively religious services." It also rejected the claims of unconstitutional denominational preference and administrative inconsistency because "[t]o conclude otherwise would be tantamount to rewriting the Tax Code, disregarding Supreme Court precedent, only to reach a conclusion directly at odds with the Establishment Clause-all in the name of the Establishment Clause." The court was concerned that if it allowed the deductions claimed by the Sklars, the "logic" of such a holding "would extend to all members of religious organizations who benefit from educational services that are in whole or part religious in nature." Eds.]

CONCLUSION

The Tax Court correctly affirmed the IRS's disallowance of deductions the Sklars claimed for tuition and fees paid to their children's Orthodox Jewish day schools. The decision of the Tax Court is AFFIRMED.

5. SUBSTANTIATION AND COMPLIANCE RULES

Page 940:

After the first full paragraph, insert:

Substantiation of Gifts of Less than $250. Beginning in 2007, donors are subject to stricter substantiation rules for cash gifts of less than $250. They must have a reliable written record, such as a bank or credit card record (e.g., a cancelled check will suffice) or a written communication from the charity (e-mails are permitted), providing the date and amount of the contribution. A diary or other informal record of small gifts no longer will suffice. I.R.C. § 170(f)(17). The regulations would exempt unreimbursed expenses under $250 for services rendered to charity. For guidance on how to handle these new recordkeeping requirements for gifts made by payroll deduction, see I.R.S. Notice 2006-110, I.R.B. 2006-51 I.R.B. 1127.

C. NONCASH CONTRIBUTIONS

2. ORDINARY INCOME PROPERTY

Page 952:

Delete the Note (Proposed Legislation) on pages 952-953, and replace it with the following:

NOTE: 2006 LEGISLATION – CERTAIN GIFTS OF ORDINARY INCOME PROPERTY

IRA Rollovers. PPA 2006 added § 408(d)(8), which is a watered down version of the long-awaited IRA charitable rollover provisions discussed in the text. For 2006 and 2007, individuals age 70-1/2 or older were able to exclude from otherwise taxable gross income IRA distributions of up to $100,000 per year to "50-percent" (primarily public) charities described in § 170 (b)(1)(A). Distributions to § 509(a)(3) supporting organizations and to donor-advised funds (as defined in new § 4966(d)(2)) did not qualify for the exclusion even though those donees are public charities. To prevent double dipping, charitable IRA rollovers that qualify for the exclusion are not tax-deductible under § 170. Distributions had to be made directly from the IRA plan administrator to the charity and, for those who care (the donor likely will), they count toward the IRA minimum distribution requirements. Unlike earlier proposals, IRA distribution to split-interest vehicles such as charitable remainder trusts do not qualify for the exclusion.

The IRA rollover exclusion was set to expire at the end of 2007 but, as part of economic stimulus legislation enacted in October 2008, Congress extended the rollover opportunity for another two years (2008 and 2009). Efforts continue to make the exclusion permanent and expand its benefits.

Qualified Artistic Contributions. A proposal to allow writers, artists, musicians and other creative talent to deduct the fair market value of recently created works donated to charity was not included in PPA 2006.

Food and Book Inventory. The enhanced charitable deduction for food and book inventory, which generally allows noncorporate business taxpayers to deduct the lesser of the fair market value of the contributed inventory or twice the taxpayer's basis (instead of just basis) was included in PPA 2006, but just for two years, through 2007. See I.R.C. § 170(e)(3)(C) (food); § 170(e)(3)(D) (books to public schools). To be eligible, donated food must be "apparently wholesome." For contributions of book inventory, PPA 2006 extends a provision adding public schools to the list of eligible donees. These provisions were set to expire at the end of 2007, but Congress has extended them through the end of 2009.

3. TANGIBLE PERSONAL PROPERTY

Pages 956-957:

Delete the third and fourth full paragraphs, and replace them with the following:

Clothing and Household Items. The Pension Protection Act of 2006 added new § 170(f)(16), which provides several new rules limiting charitable deduction for contributions of clothing and household items. First, a deduction will be permitted only if the donated item is in "good used condition or better," and the IRS may deny by regulations a deduction for any clothing or household item which has "minimal monetary value" (used undergarments are an example cited in the legislative history). These limitations do not apply, however, to any contribution of a single item of clothing or a household item for which a deduction of more than $500 is claimed if the taxpayer includes with his return a qualified appraisal with respect to the donated property. For purposes of these new limits, "household items" are defined to include furniture, furnishings, electronics, appliances, linens, and other similar items, but not food, paintings, antiques, other art objects, jewelry and gems, and collectibles. I.R.C. § 170(f)(16)(D).

An earlier proposal to require the IRS to publish an annual list of clothing and household items and assign values to listed items was dropped from the final bill as enacted.

Page 957:

After the second full paragraph, insert:

Congress enacted a modified version of the taxidermy property provision as part of PPA 2006. For contributions after July 25, 2006 by the person "who prepared, stuffed or mounted" taxidermy property or paid for the preparation, stuffing, or mounting, the charitable deduction is limited to the lesser of the donor's basis or the fair market value of the property. In determining basis, only the cost of preparing, stuffing, or mounting (and not indirect costs, such as expenses of the safari or hunting trip) are taken into account. I.R.C. §§ 170(e)(1)(B)(iv); 170(f)(5). The more complex valuation procedures described in the text were dropped from the legislation as enacted.

Page 958:

After the carryover paragraph, insert:

PPA 2006 included the provision for recapture of tax benefits for property not held for exempt use in substantially the same form as described in the text. See I.R.C. §§ 170(e)(1)(B)(i)(II); 170(e)(7). The recapture rule applies to contributions made after September 1, 2006. As noted in the text, donors can avoid the recapture rule on an early disposition if an officer of the charity certifies that the donated property was exempt use property. The Tax Technical Corrections Act of 2007 added to the certification exception a requirement that an officer of the donee must certify that the donee's exempt use was "substantial." I.R.C. § 170(e)(7)(D).

5. PARTIAL INTERESTS (NOT IN TRUST)

Page 962:

At the end of the Note, insert:

PPA 2006 included an elaborate new anti-abuse provision targeting fractional interest gifts. For gifts made after August 17, 2006, no income or gift tax charitable deduction is allowed for contributions of fractional interests in tangible personal property unless, immediately before the gift, the entire interest in the property is held by the taxpayer or the taxpayer and the donee. The IRS is authorized to issue regulations providing an exception where all persons owning an interest in the property make proportional contributions of an undivided portion of their respective amounts. I.R.C. § 170(o)(1).

When a donor makes subsequent gifts of a fractional interest, which is common with gifts of art, the fair market value of that gift for charitable deduction purposes must be the lesser of: (1) the value used at the time of the initial contribution, or (2) the fair market value at the time the subsequent gift is made. I.R.C. § 170(o)(2). As initially enacted, this valuation rule for subsequent gifts was be problematic when the final fraction was transferred by bequest. For example, assume Donor contributes to Museum a 10 percent interest in a work of art worth $5 million and claims a $500,000 charitable income tax deduction. Seven years later, when the art is worth $20 million, Donor dies, bequeathing the remaining 90 percent interest to Museum. Donor's estate would include the $18 million value of his 90 percent interest, but the estate tax charitable deduction would be limited to $4.5 million (90 percent of the original $5 million value). In the Tax Technical Corrections Act of 2007, Congress removed the subsequent gifts valuation rule for estate and gift tax purposes, permitting a charitable deduction for the fair market value as of the decedent's estate tax valuation date.

Two other rules have diminished the allure of fractional interest gifts. First, a charity receiving a fractional interest gift must have "significant physical possession" of the property for a period of time corresponding substantially to the charity's percentage interest in the item and use it in a manner related to its exempt purposes. Violations of this rule will cause the donor's tax deduction to be recaptured under a complex formula. Second, if the donor does not contribute his entire interest within ten years of the date of the initial fractional interest gift (or by the date of death, if sooner), the donor's previous charitable deductions will be recaptured and a penalty equal to 10 percent of the amount recaptured will be imposed. I.R.C. § 170(o)(3).

Art lovers (including several in Congress) and museums, contending that lifetime art gifts have decreased and are threatened with extinction, have strongly objected to this legislation, and efforts are ongoing to have it modified or repealed.

6. QUALIFIED CONSERVATION CONTRIBUTIONS

Page 964:

After the second full paragraph, insert:

The proposals discussed in the text were enacted in substantially the same form as part of PPA 2006. See I.R.C. § 170(b)(1)(E) (increasing percentage limitations and carryovers for contributions of real property for conservation purposes, but only for contributions by individuals made in 2006 and 2007) and I.R.C. §§ 170(h)(4); 170(f)(13) (contributions of facade easements in registered historic districts).

7. VALUATION AND APPRAISAL REQUIREMENTS

Page 965:

After the second full paragraph, insert:

PPA 2006 clarified and codified the qualified appraisal requirement and added a more elaborate definition of "qualified appraiser," including minimum education and experience requirements and penalties on appraisers as well as donors. I.R.C. § 170(f)(11)(E). The IRS followed up in 2008 with detailed proposed regulations on appraisal standards. See Prop. Reg. § 1.170A-15 through -18.

Page 966:

At the end of the carryover paragraph, insert:

PPA 2006 tightened the donee information return requirement. For Form 8282's filed after September 1, 2006, donees must report dispositions of contributed assets within three rather than two years of the contribution. Donees also must provide a description of how they used the asset, whether the use was related to the organization's exempt purpose or function and, if it was, the donee must include the detailed written certification required by § 170(e)(7)(D).

After the first full paragraph, insert:

For tax returns filed after August 17, 2006, PPA 2006 lowers the thresholds for imposing accuracy-related penalties on taxpayers who claim a deduction for donated property for which a qualified appraisal is required. The 20 percent penalty for a substantial valuation misstatement is now imposed when the claimed value is 150 percent (instead of 200 percent) or more than the correct value. I.R.C. § 6662(e)(1). The 40 percent penalty for a gross valuation misstatement is imposed when the claimed value is 200 percent (instead of 400 percent) or more than the correct value. I.R.C. § 6662(h)(2). For estate and gift tax purposes, a valuation misstatement is "substantial" if the claimed value is 65 percent or less of the correct value and is "gross" if the claimed value is 40 percent or less of the correct amount. I.R.C. § 6662(g). PPA 2006 also eliminates the reasonable cause exception for certain gross misstatements and imposes new penalties on appraisers whose appraisals result in substantial or gross valuation misstatements.   I.R.C. §§ 6664(c)(2); 6695A.

PART FOUR

MUTUAL BENEFIT AND PRIVATE MEMBERSHIP ORGANIZATIONS

CHAPTER 10

SPECIAL PROBLEMS OF PRIVATE MEMBERSHIP ASSOCIATIONS

F. PRIVATE ASSOCIATIONS AND THE CONSTITUTION

1. FREEDOM OF ASSOCIATION

Page 1066:

Delete Note: Frank v. Ivy Club, and replace it with:

NOTE: MALE ONLY FRATERNITIES

The College of Staten Island ("CSI"), a unit of the City University of New York, required student groups to comply with CSI's nondiscrimination policy in order to obtain recognition which would offer a variety of benefits including the use of CSI's facilities, insurance, and rights to use of the CSI name. Chi Iota was a social fraternity that did not admit women. Although the fraternity identified itself as a Jewish organization devoted to "the inculcation of the traditional values of men's college social fraternities, community service and the expression of Jewish culture," most of its members were non-practicing Jews. It welcomed non-Jewish members, and several current members were not Jewish. Many of the fraternity's activities involved nonmembers.

Chi Iota was denied college recognition, because it failed to comply with CSI's nondiscrimination policy by discriminating against women. The fraternity filed suit alleging it was an intimate association and being forced to admit women would be an unconstitutional burden on its associational rights. The district court, applying a strict scrutiny standard, granted a preliminary injunction because CSI's policy affected a constitutionally protected interest. The Court of Appeals for the Second Circuit reversed. Chi Iota v. City University of New York, 502 F.3d 136 (2d Cir. 2007). Rather than apply a categorical strict scrutiny approach in dealing with association-rights cases, the court asked whether a balancing of all pertinent facts justified the state intrusion on the particular associational freedom. It measured the degree of the fraternity's associational interest by examining its size, purpose, selectivity and whether others were excluded from critical aspects of the relationship.

The court found the size limitation was the product of circumstances and not a desire to maintain intimacy. The fraternity did employ care in selecting members, but upon a graduation it lost contact with its members and had to replace them. Most of those who attended the first recruitment rush were invited back. Chi Iota's purposes were inclusive, broad public minded goals that did not depend for their promotion on close-knit bonds. The fraternity involved nonmembers in several crucial aspects of its existence and gave parties to which nonmembers were encouraged to attend. The court held that the college's denial of recognition was not a substantial imposition on the fraternity's rights of association because the state had a substantial interest in prohibiting sex discrimination, which was no less compelling because federal antidiscrimination statutes exempted fraternities.

PART FIVE

OTHER LEGAL ISSUES AFFECTING NONPROFIT ORGANIZATIONS

CHAPTER 11

ANTITRUST AND NONPROFITS

B. Health Care

Page 1110:

After the carryover paragraph, insert:

In August 2007, the Federal Trade Commissioners unanimously found that the merged entity violated section 7 of the Clayton Act by creating a highly concentrated market, increasing prices and harming consumers. However, the Commission vacated the Administrative Law Judge's divestment order, noting that divestiture after a long period of time is more difficult with a greater risk of unforeseen costs and failure. It imposed an injunction that required Evanston Northwestern to negotiate its hospital contracts separately without sharing information among its hospitals and giving payors the option of renegotiating existing contracts. The Commissioners stated "ENH's [Evanston Northwestern Healthcare] non-profit status did not affect its efforts to raise prices after the merger, and *** does not suffice to rebut complaint counsel's evidence of anticompetitive effects." In re Northwestern Healthcare Corp., 2007 WL 2286195 (No. 9315, August 6, 2007). For a discussion of the decision, see Barak D. Richman, Antitrust and Nonprofit Hospital Mergers: A Return to Basics, 156 U. Pa. L. Rev. 121, 149-150 (2007).

STATUTES, REGULATIONS AND FORMS APPENDIX

[This Appendix includes the full text of the Uniform Prudent Management of Institutional Funds Act ("UPMIFA"), selective statutory text for major Internal Revenue Code provisions affecting nonprofit organizations that were added by the Pension Protection Act of 2006, final treasury regulations on the interaction of the private benefit and inurement limitations with the § 4958 intermediate sanctions penalty regime, excerpts from new regulations on public charity classification ruling procedures and testing periods, and the new Form 990. New or revised Internal Revenue Code language is in italics.]

Uniform Prudent Management of Institutional Funds Act

SECTION 1. SHORT TITLE. This [act] may be cited as the Uniform Prudent Management of Institutional Funds Act.

SECTION 2. DEFINITIONS. In this [act]:

(1) "Charitable purpose" means the relief of poverty, the advancement of education or religion, the promotion of health, the promotion of a governmental purpose, or any other purpose the achievement of which is beneficial to the community.

(2) "Endowment fund" means an institutional fund or part thereof that, under the terms of a gift instrument, is not wholly expendable by the institution on a current basis. The term does not include assets that an institution designates as an endowment fund for its own use.

(3) "Gift instrument" means a record or records, including an institutional solicitation, under which property is granted to, transferred to, or held by an institution as an institutional fund.

(4) "Institution" means:

(A) a person, other than an individual, organized and operated exclusively for charitable purposes;

(B) a government or governmental subdivision, agency, or instrumentality, to the extent that it holds funds exclusively for a charitable purpose; or

(C) a trust that had both charitable and noncharitable interests, after all noncharitable interests have terminated.

(5) "Institutional fund" means a fund held by an institution exclusively for charitable purposes. The term does not include:

(A) program-related assets;

(B) a fund held for an institution by a trustee that is not an institution; or

(C) a fund in which a beneficiary that is not an institution has an interest, other than an interest that could arise upon violation or failure of the purposes of the fund.

(6) "Person" means an individual, corporation, business trust, estate, trust, partnership, limited liability company, association, joint venture, public corporation, government or governmental subdivision, agency, or instrumentality, or any other legal or commercial entity.

(7) "Program-related asset" means an asset held by an institution primarily to accomplish a charitable purpose of the institution and not primarily for investment.

(8) "Record" means information that is inscribed on a tangible medium or that is stored in an electronic or other medium and is retrievable in perceivable form.

SECTION 3. STANDARD OF CONDUCT IN MANAGING AND INVESTING INSTITUTIONAL FUND

(a) Subject to the intent of a donor expressed in a gift instrument, an institution, in managing and investing an institutional fund, shall consider the charitable purposes of the institution and the purposes of the institutional fund.

(b) In addition to complying with the duty of loyalty imposed by law other than this [act], each person responsible for managing and investing an institutional fund shall manage and invest the fund in good faith and with the care an ordinarily prudent person in a like position would exercise under similar circumstances.

(c) In managing and investing an institutional fund, an institution:

(1) may incur only costs that are appropriate and reasonable in relation to the assets, the purposes of the institution, and the skills available to the institution; and

(2) shall make a reasonable effort to verify facts relevant to the management and investment of the fund.

(d) An institution may pool two or more institutional funds for purposes of management and investment.

(e) Except as otherwise provided by a gift instrument, the following rules apply:

(1) In managing and investing an institutional fund, the following factors, if relevant, must be considered:

(A) general economic conditions;

(B) the possible effect of inflation or deflation;

(C) the expected tax consequences, if any, of investment decisions or strategies;

(D) the role that each investment or course of action plays within the overall investment portfolio of the fund;

(E) the expected total return from income and the appreciation of investments;

(F) other resources of the institution;

(G) the needs of the institution and the fund to make distributions and to preserve capital; and

(H) an asset's special relationship or special value, if any, to the charitable purposes of the institution.

(2) Management and investment decisions about an individual asset must be made not in isolation but rather in the context of the institutional fund's portfolio of investments as a whole and as a part of an overall investment strategy having risk and return objectives reasonably suited to the fund and to the institution.

(3) Except as otherwise provided by law other than this [act], an institution may invest in any kind of property or type of investment consistent with this section.

(4) An institution shall diversify the investments of an institutional fund unless the institution reasonably determines that, because of special circumstances, the purposes of the fund are better served without diversification.

(5) Within a reasonable time after receiving property, an institution shall make and carry out decisions concerning the retention or disposition of the property or to rebalance a portfolio, in order to bring the institutional fund into compliance with the purposes, terms, and distribution requirements of the institution as necessary to meet other circumstances of the institution and the requirements of this [act].

(6) A person that has special skills or expertise, or is selected in reliance upon the person's representation that the person has special skills or expertise, has a duty to use those skills or that expertise in managing and investing institutional funds.

SECTION 4.   APPROPRIATION FOR EXPENDITURE OR ACCUMULATION OF ENDOWMENT FUND; RULES OF CONSTRUCTION.

(a) Subject to the intent of a donor expressed in the gift instrument [and to subsection (d)], an institution may appropriate for expenditure or accumulate so much of an endowment fund as the institution determines is prudent for the uses, benefits, purposes, and duration for which the endowment fund is established. Unless stated otherwise in the gift instrument, the assets in an endowment fund are donor-restricted assets until appropriated for expenditure by the institution. In making a determination to appropriate or accumulate, the institution shall act in good faith, with the care that an ordinarily prudent person in a like position would exercise under similar circumstances, and shall consider, if relevant, the following factors:

(1) the duration and preservation of the endowment fund;

(2) the purposes of the institution and the endowment fund;

(3) general economic conditions;

(4) the possible effect of inflation or deflation;

(5) the expected total return from income and the appreciation of investments;

(6) other resources of the institution; and

(7) the investment policy of the institution.

(b) To limit the authority to appropriate for expenditure or accumulate under subsection (a), a gift instrument must specifically state the limitation.

(c) Terms in a gift instrument designating a gift as an endowment, or a direction or authorization in the gift instrument to use only "income", "interest", "dividends", or "rents, issues, or profits", or "to preserve the principal intact", or words of similar import:

(1) create an endowment fund of permanent duration unless other language in the gift instrument limits the duration or purpose of the fund; and

(2) do not otherwise limit the authority to appropriate for expenditure or accumulate under subsection (a).

[(d) The appropriation for expenditure in any year of an amount greater than seven percent of the fair market value of an endowment fund, calculated on the basis of market values determined at least quarterly and averaged over a period of not less than three years immediately preceding the year in which the appropriation for expenditure is made, creates a rebuttable presumption of imprudence. For an endowment fund in existence for fewer than three years, the fair market value of the endowment fund must be calculated for the period the endowment fund has been in existence. This subsection does not:

(1) apply to an appropriation for expenditure permitted under law other than this [act] or by the gift instrument; or

(2) create a presumption of prudence for an appropriation for expenditure of an amount less than or equal to seven percent of the fair market value of the endowment fund.]

[SECTION 5. DELEGATION OF MANAGEMENT AND INVESTMENT FUNCTIONS.

(a) Subject to any specific limitation set forth in a gift instrument or in law other than this [act], an institution may delegate to an external agent the management and investment of an institutional fund to the extent that an institution could prudently delegate under the circumstances. An institution shall act in good faith, with the care that an ordinarily prudent person in a like position would exercise under similar circumstances, in:

(1) selecting an agent;

(2) establishing the scope and terms of the delegation, consistent with the purposes of the institution and the institutional fund; and

(3) periodically reviewing the agent's actions in order to monitor the agent's performance and compliance with the scope and terms of the delegation.

(b) In performing a delegated function, an agent owes a duty to the institution to exercise reasonable care to comply with the scope and terms of the delegation.

(c) An institution that complies with subsection (a) is not liable for the decisions or actions of an agent to which the function was delegated.

(d) By accepting delegation of a management or investment function from an institution that is subject to the laws of this state, an agent submits to the jurisdiction of the courts of this state in all proceedings arising from or related to the delegation or the performance of the delegated function.

(e) An institution may delegate management and investment functions to its committees, officers, or employees as authorized by law of this state other than this [act].]

SECTION 6. RELEASE OR MODIFICATION OF RESTRICTIONS ON MANAGEMENT, INVESTMENT, OR PURPOSE

(a) If the donor consents in a record, an institution may release or modify, in whole or in part, a restriction contained in a gift instrument on the management, investment, or purpose of an institutional fund. A release or modification may not allow a fund to be used for a purpose other than a charitable purpose of the institution.

(b) The court, upon application of an institution, may modify a restriction contained in a gift instrument regarding the management or investment of an institutional fund if the restriction has become impracticable or wasteful, if it impairs the management or investment of the fund, or if, because of circumstances not anticipated by the donor, a modification of a restriction will further the purposes of the fund. The institution shall notify the [Attorney General] of the application, and the [Attorney General] must be given an opportunity to be heard. To the extent practicable, any modification must be made in accordance with the donor's probable intention.

(c) If a particular charitable purpose or a restriction contained in a gift instrument on the use of an institutional fund becomes unlawful, impracticable, impossible to achieve, or wasteful, the court, upon application of an institution, may modify the purpose of the fund or the restriction on the use of the fund in a manner consistent with the charitable purposes expressed in the gift instrument. The institution shall notify the [Attorney General] of the application, and the [Attorney General] must be given an opportunity to be heard.

(d) If an institution determines that a restriction contained in a gift instrument on the management, investment, or purpose of an institutional fund is unlawful, impracticable, impossible to achieve, or wasteful, the institution, [60 days] after notification to the [Attorney General], may release or modify the restriction, in whole or part, if:

(1) the institutional fund subject to the restriction has a total value of less than [$25,000];

(2) more than [20] years have elapsed since the fund was established; and

(3) the institution uses the property in a manner consistent with the charitable purposes expressed in the gift instrument.

SECTION 7. REVIEWING COMPLIANCE. Compliance with this [act] is determined in light of the facts and circumstances existing at the time a decision is made or action is taken, and not by hindsight.

SECTION 8. APPLICATION TO EXISTING INSTITUTIONAL FUNDS. This [act] applies to institutional funds existing on or established after [the effective date of this act]. As applied to institutional funds existing on [the effective date of this act] this [act] governs only decisions made or actions taken on or after that date.

SECTION 9. RELATION TO ELECTRONIC SIGNATURES IN GLOBAL AND NATIONAL COMMERCE ACT. This [act] modifies, limits, and supersedes the Electronic Signatures in Global and National Commerce Act, 15 U.S.C. Section 7001 et seq., but does not modify, limit, or supersede Section 101 of that act, 15 U.S.C. Section 7001(a), or authorize electronic delivery of any of the notices described in Section 103 of that act, 15 U.S.C. Section 7003(b).

SECTION 10. UNIFORMITY OF APPLICATION AND CONSTRUCTION. In applying and construing this uniform act, consideration must be given to the need to promote uniformity of the law with respect to its subject matter among states that enact it.

SECTION 11. EFFECTIVE DATE. This [act] takes effect . . . .

SECTION 12. REPEAL. The following acts and parts of acts are repealed:

* * *

    (a) [The Uniform Management of Institutional Funds Act]

INTERNAL REVENUE CODE OF 1986

§ 170. Charitable, etc., contributions and gifts.

* * *

(b) Percentage limitations.--

    (1) Individuals.--In the case of an individual, the deduction provided in subsection (a) shall be limited as provided in the succeeding subparagraphs.

* * *

    (E) Contributions of qualified conservation contributions.--

        (i) In general.--Any qualified conservation contribution (as defined in subsection (h)(1)) shall be allowed to the extent the aggregate of such contributions does not exceed the excess of 50 percent of the taxpayer's contribution base over the amount of all other charitable contributions allowable under this paragraph.

        (ii) Carryover.--If the aggregate amount of contributions described in clause (i) exceeds the limitation of clause (i), such excess shall be treated (in a manner consistent with the rules of subsection (d)(1)) as a charitable contribution to which clause (i) applies in each of the 15 succeeding years in order of time.

        (iii) Coordination with other subparagraphs. — For purposes of applying this subsection and subsection (d)(1), contributions described in clause (i) shall not be treated as described in subparagraph (A), (B), (C), or (D) and such subparagraphs shall apply without regard to such contributions.

        (iv) Special rule for contribution of property used in agriculture or livestock production.--

            (I) In general.--If the individual is a qualified farmer or rancher for the taxable year for which the contribution is made, clause (i) shall be applied by substituting "100 percent" for "50 percent".

            (II) Exception.--Subclause (I) shall not apply to any contribution of property made after the date of the enactment of this subparagraph which is used in agriculture or livestock production (or available for such production) unless such contribution is subject to a restriction that such property remain available for such production. This subparagraph shall be applied separately with respect to property to which subclause (I) does not apply by reason of the preceding sentence prior to its application to property to which subclause (I) does apply.

        (v) Definition.--For purposes of clause (iv), the term "qualified farmer or rancher" means a taxpayer whose gross income from the trade or business of farming (within the meaning of section

2032A(e)(5)) is greater than 50 percent of the taxpayer's gross income for the taxable year.

(vi) Termination.--This subparagraph shall not apply to any contribution made in taxable years beginning after December 31, 2007.

(F) **Certain private foundations.**--The private foundations referred to in subparagraph (A)(vii) and subsection (e)(1)(B) are--

(i) a private operating foundation (as defined in section 4942(j)(3)),

(ii) any other private foundation (as defined in section 509(a)) which, not later than the 15th day of the third month after the close of the foundation's taxable year in which contributions are received, makes qualifying distributions (as defined in section 4942(g), without regard to paragraph (3) thereof), which are treated, after the application of section 4942(g)(3), as distributions out of corpus (in accordance with section 4942(h)) in an amount equal to 100 percent of such contributions, and with respect to which the taxpayer obtains adequate records or other sufficient evidence from the foundation showing that the foundation made such qualifying distributions, and

(iii) a private foundation all of the contributions to which are pooled in a common fund and which would be described in section 509(a)(3) but for the right of any substantial contributor (hereafter in this clause called "donor") or his spouse to designate annually the recipients, from among organizations described in paragraph (1) of section 509(a), of the income attributable to the donor's contribution to the fund and to direct (by deed or by will) the payment, to an organization described in such paragraph (1), of the corpus in the common fund attributable to the donor's contribution; but this clause shall apply only if all of the income of the common fund is required to be (and is) distributed to one or more organizations described in such paragraph (1) not later than the 15th day of the third month after the close of the taxable year in which the income is realized by the fund and only if all of the corpus attributable to any donor's contribution to the fund is required to be (and is) distributed to one or more of such organizations not later than one year after his death or after the death of his surviving spouse if she has the right to designate the recipients of such corpus.

(G) **Contribution base defined.**--For purposes of this section, the term "contribution base" means adjusted gross income (computed without regard to any net operating loss carryback to the taxable year under section 172).

(2) Corporations.--In the case of a corporation--

(A) In general.--The total deductions under subsection (a) for any taxable year (other than for contributions to which subparagraph (B) applies) shall not exceed 10 percent of the taxpayer's taxable income.

(B) Qualified conservation contributions by certain corporate farmers and ranchers.--

(i) **In general.**--*Any qualified conservation contribution (as defined in subsection (h)(1))--*

(I) *which is made by a corporation which, for the taxable year during which the contribution is made, is a qualified farmer or rancher (as defined in paragraph (1)(E)(v)) and the stock of which is not readily tradable on an established securities market at any time during such year, and*

(II) *which, in the case of contributions made after the date of the enactment of this subparagraph, is a contribution of property which is used in agriculture or livestock production (or available for such production) and which is subject to a restriction that such property remain available for such production, shall be allowed to the extent the aggregate of such contributions does not exceed the excess of the taxpayer's taxable income over the amount of charitable contributions allowable under subparagraph (A).*

(ii) **Carryover.**--*If the aggregate amount of contributions described in clause (i) exceeds the limitation of clause (i), such excess shall be treated (in a manner consistent with the rules of subsection (d)(2)) as a charitable contribution to which clause (i) applies in each of the 15 succeeding years in order of time.*

(iii) **Termination.**--*This subparagraph shall not apply to any contribution made in taxable years beginning after December 31, 2007.*

(C) **Taxable income.**--*For purposes of this paragraph, taxable income shall be computed without regard to--*

(i) *this section,*

(ii) *part VIII (except section 248),*

(iii) *any net operating loss carryback to the taxable year under section 172,*

(iv) *section 199, and*

(v) *any capital loss carryback to the taxable year under section 1212(a)(1).*

* * *

(d) Carryovers of excess contributions.--

* * *

(2) Corporations.--

(A) In general.--Any contribution made by a corporation in a taxable year (hereinafter in this paragraph referred to as the "contribution year") in excess of the amount deductible for such year under *subsection (b)(2)(A)* shall be deductible for each of the 5 succeeding taxable years in order of time, but only to the extent of the lesser of the two following amounts: (i) the excess of the maximum amount deductible for such succeeding taxable year under *subsection (b)(2)(A)* over the sum of the contributions made in such year plus the aggregate of the excess contributions which were made in taxable years before the contribution year and which are deductible under this subparagraph for such succeeding taxable year; or (ii) in the case of the first succeeding taxable year, the amount of such excess contribution, and in the case of the second, third, fourth, or fifth succeeding taxable year, the portion of such excess contribution not deductible under this subparagraph for any taxable year intervening between the contribution year and such succeeding taxable year.

(B) Special rule for net operating loss carryovers.--For purposes of subparagraph (A), the excess of--

(i) the contributions made by a corporation in a taxable year to which this section applies, over

(ii) the amount deductible in such year under the limitation in *subsection (b)(2)(A)*, shall be reduced to the extent that such excess reduces taxable income (as computed for purposes of the second sentence of section 172(b)(2)) and increases a net operating loss carryover under section 172 to a succeeding taxable year.

(e) Certain contributions of ordinary income and capital gain property.--

(1) General rule.--The amount of any charitable contribution of property otherwise taken into account under this section shall be reduced by the sum of–

* * *

(B) in the case of a charitable contribution--

(i) of tangible personal property--

(I) if the use by the donee is unrelated to the purpose or function constituting the basis for its exemption under section 501 (or, in the case of a governmental unit, to any purpose or function described in subsection (c)), or

(II) which is applicable property (as defined in paragraph (7)(C)) which is sold, exchanged, or otherwise disposed of by the donee before the last day of the taxable year in which the contribution was made and with respect to which the donee has not made a certification in accordance with paragraph (7)(D),

(ii) to or for the use of a private foundation (as defined in section 509(a)), other than a private foundation described in subsection (b)(1)(E),

(iii) of any patent, copyright (other than a copyright described in section 1221(a)(3) or 1231(b)(1)(C)), trademark, trade name, trade secret, know-how, software (other than software described in section

197(e)(3)(A)(i)), or similar property, or applications or registrations of such property, or

  (iv) of any taxidermy property which is contributed by the person who prepared, stuffed, or mounted the property or by any person who paid or incurred the cost of such preparation, stuffing, or mounting,

the amount of gain which would have been long-term capital gain if the property contributed had been sold by the taxpayer at its fair market value (determined at the time of such contribution).

For purposes of applying this paragraph (other than in the case of gain to which section 617(d)(1), 1245(a), 1250(a), 1252(a) or 1254(a) applies), property which is property used in the trade or business (as defined in section 1231(b)) shall be treated as a capital asset. For purposes of applying this paragraph in the case of a charitable contribution of stock in an S corporation, rules similar to the rules of Section 751 shall apply in determining whether gain on such stock would have been long-term capital gain if such stock were sold by the taxpayer.

* * *

(3) Special rule for certain contributions of inventory and other property.-

* * *

(C) Special rule for contributions of food inventory.—

* * *

  (iv) Termination. — This subparagraph shall not apply to contributions made after December 31, *2007.*

  (D) Special rule for contributions of book inventory to public schools.--

* * *

  (iv) Termination.--This subparagraph shall not apply to contributions made after December 31, *2007.*

* * *

(7) Recapture of deduction on certain dispositions of exempt use property.--

  (A) In general.--In the case of an applicable disposition of applicable property, there shall be included in the income of the donor of such property for the taxable year of such donor in which the applicable disposition occurs an amount equal to the excess (if any) of--

   (i) the amount of the deduction allowed to the donor under this section with respect to such property, over

(ii) the donor's basis in such property at the time such property was contributed.

(B) Applicable disposition.--*For purposes of this paragraph, the term "applicable disposition" means any sale, exchange, or other disposition by the donee of applicable property--*

(i) after the last day of the taxable year of the donor in which such property was contributed, and

(ii) before the last day of the 3-year period beginning on the date of the contribution of such property, unless the donee makes a certification in accordance with subparagraph (D).

(C) Applicable property.--*For purposes of this paragraph, the term "applicable property" means charitable deduction property (as defined in section 6050L(a)(2)(A))--*

(i) which is tangible personal property the use of which is identified by the donee as related to the purpose or function constituting the basis of the donee's exemption under section 501, and

(ii) for which a deduction in excess of the donor's basis is allowed.

(D) Certification.--*A certification meets the requirements of this subparagraph if it is a written statement which is signed under penalty of perjury by an officer of the donee organization and--*

(i) which–

(I) *certifies that the use of the property by the donee was substantial and related to the purpose or function constituting the basis for the donee's exemption under section 501, and*

(II) *describes how the property was used and how such use furthered such purpose or function, or*

(ii) which--

(I) *states the intended use of the property by the donee at the time of the contribution, and*

(II) *certifies that such intended use has become impossible or infeasible to implement.*

(f) Disallowance of deduction in certain cases and special rules.--

* * *

(11) Qualified appraisal and other documentation for certain contributions.--

* * *

(E) Qualified appraisal and appraiser.--For purposes of this paragraph--

(i) Qualified appraisal.--The term "qualified appraisal" means, with respect to any property, an appraisal of such property which--

(I) is treated for purposes of this paragraph as a qualified appraisal under regulations or other guidance prescribed by the Secretary, and

(II) is conducted by a qualified appraiser in accordance with generally accepted appraisal standards and any regulations or other guidance prescribed under subclause (I).

(ii) Qualified appraiser.--Except as provided in clause (iii), the term "qualified appraiser" means an individual who--

(I) has earned an appraisal designation from a recognized professional appraiser organization or has otherwise met minimum education and experience requirements set forth in regulations prescribed by the Secretary,

(II) regularly performs appraisals for which the individual receives compensation, and

(III) meets such other requirements as may be prescribed by the Secretary in regulations or other guidance.

(iii) Specific appraisals.--An individual shall not be treated as a qualified appraiser with respect to any specific appraisal unless--

(I) the individual demonstrates verifiable education and experience in valuing the type of property subject to the appraisal, and

(II) the individual has not been prohibited from practicing before the Internal Revenue Service by the Secretary under section 330(c) of title 31, United States Code, at any time during the 3-year period ending on the date of the appraisal.

* * *

(13) Contributions of certain interests in buildings located in registered historic districts.--

(A) In general.--No deduction shall be allowed with respect to any contribution described in subparagraph (B) unless the taxpayer includes with the return for the taxable year of the contribution a $500 filing fee.

(B) Contribution described.--A contribution is described in this subparagraph if such contribution is a qualified conservation contribution (as defined in subsection (h)) which is a restriction with respect to the exterior of a building described in subsection (h)(4)(C)(ii) and for which a deduction is claimed in excess of $10,000.

(C) Dedication of fee.--Any fee collected under this paragraph shall be used for the enforcement of the provisions of subsection (h).

(14) Reduction for amounts attributable to rehabilitation credit.--In the case of any qualified conservation contribution (as defined in subsection (h)), the amount of the deduction allowed under this section shall be reduced by an amount which bears the same ratio to the fair market value of the contribution as--

(A) the sum of the credits allowed to the taxpayer under section 47 for the 5 preceding taxable years with respect to any building which is a part of such contribution, bears to

(B) the fair market value of the building on the date of the contribution.

(15) Special rule for taxidermy property.--

(A) Basis.--For purposes of this section and notwithstanding section 1012, in the case of a charitable contribution of taxidermy property which is made by the person who prepared, stuffed, or mounted the property or by any person who paid or incurred the cost of such preparation, stuffing, or mounting, only the cost of the preparing, stuffing, or mounting shall be included in the basis of such property.

(B) Taxidermy property.--For purposes of this section, the term "taxidermy property" means any work of art which--

(i) is the reproduction or preservation of an animal, in whole or in part,

(ii) is prepared, stuffed, or mounted for purposes of recreating one or more characteristics of such animal, and

(iii) contains a part of the body of the dead animal.

(16) Contributions of clothing and household items.--

(A) In general.--In the case of an individual, partnership, or corporation, no deduction shall be allowed under subsection (a) for any contribution of clothing or a household item unless such clothing or household item is in good used condition or better.

(B) Items of minimal value.--Notwithstanding subparagraph (A), the Secretary may by regulation deny a deduction under subsection (a) for any contribution of clothing or a household item which has minimal monetary value.

(C) Exception for certain property.--Subparagraphs (A) and (B) shall not apply to any contribution of a single item of clothing or a household item for which a deduction of more than $500 is claimed if the taxpayer includes with the taxpayer's return a qualified appraisal with respect to the property.

(D) Household items.--For purposes of this paragraph--

(i) In general.--The term "household items" includes furniture, furnishings, electronics, appliances, linens, and other similar items.

(ii) Excluded items.--Such term does not include--

(I) food,

(II) paintings, antiques, and other objects of art,

(III) jewelry and gems, and

(IV) collections.

(E) Special rule for pass-thru entities.--*In the case of a partnership or S corporation, this paragraph shall be applied at the entity level, except that the deduction shall be denied at the partner or shareholder level.*

(17) Recordkeeping.--*No deduction shall be allowed under subsection (a) for any contribution of a cash, check, or other monetary gift unless the donor maintains as a record of such contribution a bank record or a written communication from the donee showing the name of the donee organization, the date of the contribution, and the amount of the contribution.*

(18) Contributions to donor advised funds.--*A deduction otherwise allowed under subsection (a) for any contribution to a donor advised fund (as defined in section 4966(d)(2)) shall only be allowed if--*

(A) *the sponsoring organization (as defined in section 4966(d)(1)) with respect to such donor advised fund is not--*

(i) described in paragraph (3), (4), or (5) of subsection (c), or

(ii) a type III supporting organization (as defined in section 4943(f)(5)(A)) which is not a functionally integrated type III supporting organization (as defined in section 4943(f)(5)(B)), and

(B) *the taxpayer obtains a contemporaneous written acknowledgment (determined under rules similar to the rules of paragraph (8)(C)) from the sponsoring organization (as so defined) of such donor advised fund that such organization has exclusive legal control over the assets contributed.*

* * *

(h) Qualified conservation contribution.--

* * *

(4) Conservation purpose defined.--

* * *

(B) Special rules with respect to buildings in registered historic districts.--*In the case of any contribution of a qualified real property interest which is a restriction with respect to the exterior of a building described in subparagraph (C)(ii), such contribution shall not be considered to be exclusively for conservation purposes unless--*

(i) such interest--

    (I) includes a restriction which preserves the entire exterior of the building (including the front, sides, rear, and height of the building), and

    (II) prohibits any change in the exterior of the building which is inconsistent with the historical character of such exterior,

(ii) the donor and donee enter into a written agreement certifying, under penalty of perjury, that the donee--

    (I) is a qualified organization (as defined in paragraph (3)) with a purpose of environmental protection, land conservation, open space preservation, or historic preservation, and

    (II) has the resources to manage and enforce the restriction and a commitment to do so, and

(iii) in the case of any contribution made in a taxable year beginning after the date of the enactment of this subparagraph, the taxpayer includes with the taxpayer's return for the taxable year of the contribution--

    (I) a qualified appraisal (within the meaning of subsection (f)(11)(E)) of the qualified property interest,

    (II) photographs of the entire exterior of the building, and

    (III) a description of all restrictions on the development of the building.

(C) **Certified historic structure.--**For purposes of subparagraph (A)(iv), the term "certified historic structure" means--

    (i) *any building, structure, or land area which* is listed in the National Register, or

    (ii) *any building which* is located in a registered historic district (as defined in section 47(c)(3)(B)) and is certified by the Secretary of the Interior to the Secretary as being of historic significance to the district.

A building, structure, or land area satisfies the preceding sentence if it satisfies such sentence either at the time of the transfer or on the due date (including extensions) for filing the transferor's return under this chapter for the taxable year in which the transfer is made.

* * *

(o) Special rules for fractional gifts.--

    (1) Denial of deduction in certain cases.--

(A) In general.--*No deduction shall be allowed for a contribution of an undivided portion of a taxpayer's entire interest in tangible personal property unless all interest in the property is held immediately before such contribution by--*

(i) *the taxpayer, or*

(ii) *the taxpayer and the donee.*

(B) Exceptions.--*The Secretary may, by regulation, provide for exceptions to subparagraph (A) in cases where all persons who hold an interest in the property make proportional contributions of an undivided portion of the entire interest held by such persons.*

(2) Valuation of subsequent gifts.--*In the case of any additional contribution, the fair market value of such contribution shall be determined by using the lesser of--*

(A) *the fair market value of the property at the time of the initial fractional contribution, or*

(B) *the fair market value of the property at the time of the additional contribution.*

(3) Recapture of deduction in certain cases; addition to tax.--

(A) Recapture.--*The Secretary shall provide for the recapture of the amount of any deduction allowed under this section (plus interest) with respect to any contribution of an undivided portion of a taxpayer's entire interest in tangible personal property –*

(i) *in any case in which the donor does not contribute all of the remaining interest in such property to the donee (or, if such donee is no longer in existence, to any person described in section 170(c)) before the earlier of –*

(I) *the date that is 10 years after the date of the initial fractional contribution, or*

(II) *the date of the death of the donor, and*

(ii) *in any case in which the donor has not, during the period beginning on the date of the initial fractional contribution and ending on the date described in clause (I) –*

(I) *had substantial physical possession of the property, and*

(II) *used the property in a use which is related to a purpose or function constituting the basis for the organizations' exemption under section 501.*

(B) Addition to tax. – *The tax imposed under this chapter for any taxable year for which there is a recapture under subparagraph (A) shall be increased by 10 percent of the amount so recaptured.*

(4) Definitions. – *For purposes of this subsection –*

　　(A) Additional contribution. –*The term "additional contribution" means any charitable contribution by the taxpayer of any interest in property with respect to which the taxpayer has previously made an initial fractional contribution.*

　　(B) Initial fractional contribution. –*The term "initial fractional contribution" means, with respect to any taxpayer, the first charitable contribution of an undivided portion of the taxpayer's entire interest in any tangible personal property.*

* * *

§ 501. Exemption from tax on corporations, certain trusts, etc.

* * *

(q) Special Rules for Credit Counseling Organizations –

　　(1) In general. --*An organization with respect to which the provision of credit counseling services is a substantial purpose shall not be exempt from tax under subsection (a) unless such organization is described in paragraph (3) or (4) of subsection (c) and such organization is organized and operated in accordance with the following requirements:*

　　　　(A) The organization –

　　　　　　(i) provides credit counseling services tailored to the specific needs and circumstances of consumers,

　　　　　　(ii) makes no loans to debtors (other than loans with no fees or interest) and does not negotiate the making of loans on behalf of debtors,

　　　　　　(iii) provides services for the purpose of improving a consumer's credit record, credit history, or credit rating only to the extent that such services are incidental to providing credit counseling services, and

　　　　　　(iv) does not charge any separately stated fee for services for the purpose of improving any consumer's credit record, credit history, or credit rating.

　　　　(B) The organization does not refuse to provide credit counseling services to a consumer due to the inability of the consumer to pay, the ineligibility of the consumer for debt management plan enrollment, or the unwillingness of the consumer to enroll in a debt management plan.

　　　　(C) The organization establishes and implements a fee policy which –

　　　　　　(i) requires that any fees charged to a consumer for services are reasonable,

　　　　　　(ii) allows for the waiver of fees if the consumer is unable to pay, and

(iii) except to the extent allowed by State law, prohibits charging any fee based in whole or in part on a percentage of the consumer's debt, the consumer's payments to be made pursuant to a debt management plan, or the projected or actual savings to the consumer resulting from enrolling in a debt management plan.

(D) At all times the organization has a board of directors or other governing body --

(i) which is controlled by persons who represent the broad interests of the public, such as public officials acting in their capacities as such, persons having special knowledge or expertise in credit or financial education, and community leaders,

(ii) not more than 20 percent of the voting power of which is vested in persons who are employed by the organization or who will benefit financially, directly or indirectly, from the organization's activities (other than through the receipt of reasonable directors" fees or the repayment of consumer debt to creditors other than the credit counseling organization or its affiliates), and

(iii) not more than 49 percent of the voting power of which is vested in persons who are employed by the organization or who will benefit financially, directly or indirectly, from the organization's activities (other than through the receipt of reasonable directors" fees).

(E) The organization does not own more than 35 percent of –

(i) the total combined voting power of any corporation (other than a corporation which is an organization described in subsection (c)(3) and exempt from tax under subsection (a)) which is in the trade or business of lending money, repairing credit, or providing debt management plan services, payment processing, or similar services,

(ii) the profits interest of any partnership (other than a partnership which is an organization described in subsection (c)(3) and exempt from tax under subsection (a)) which is in the trade or business of lending money, repairing credit, or providing debt management plan services, payment processing, or similar services, and

(iii) the beneficial interest of any trust or estate (other than a trust which is an organization described in subsection (c)(3) and exempt from tax under subsection (a)) which is in the trade or business of lending money, repairing credit, or providing debt management plan services, payment processing, or similar services.

(F) The organization receives no amount for providing referrals to others for debt management plan services, and pays no amount to others for obtaining referrals of consumers.

(2) Additional requirements for organizations described in subsection (c)(3)

(A) In general.--*In addition to the requirements under paragraph (1), an organization with respect to which the provision of credit counseling services is a substantial purpose and which is described in paragraph (3) of subsection (c) shall not be exempt from tax under subsection (a) unless such organization is organized and operated in accordance with the following requirements:*

(i) The organization does not solicit contributions from consumers during the initial counseling process or while the consumer is receiving services from the organization.

(ii) The aggregate revenues of the organization which are from payments of creditors of consumers of the organization and which are attributable to debt management plan services do not exceed the applicable percentage of the total revenues of the organization.

(B) Applicable percentage –

(i) In general. – For purposes of subparagraph (A)(ii), the applicable percentage is 50 percent.

(ii) Transition rule. – Notwithstanding clause (i), in the case of an organization with respect to which the provision of credit counseling services is a substantial purpose and which is described in paragraph (3) of subsection (c) and exempt from tax under subsection (a) on the date of the enactment of this subsection, the applicable percentage is –

(I) 80 percent for the first taxable year of such organization beginning after the date which is 1 year after the date of the enactment of this subsection, and

(II) 70 percent for the second such taxable year beginning after such date, and

(III) 60 percent for the third such taxable year beginning after such date.

(3) Additional requirement for organizations described in subsection (c)(4).– *In addition to the requirements under paragraph (1), an organization with respect to which the provision of credit counseling services is a substantial purpose and which is described in paragraph (4) of subsection (c)) shall not be exempt from tax under subsection (a) unless such organization notifies the Secretary, in such manner as the Secretary may by regulations prescribe, that it is applying for recognition as a credit counseling organization.*

(4) Credit counseling services; debt management plan services.--*For purposes of this subsection –*

(A) Credit counseling services.--*The term "credit counseling services" means –*

(i) the providing of educational information to the general public on budgeting, personal finance, financial literacy, saving and spending practices, and the sound use of consumer credit,

(ii) the assisting of individuals and families with financial problems by providing them with counseling, or

(iii) a combination of the activities described in clauses (i) and (ii).

(B) Debt management plan services. – The term "debt management plan services" means services related to the repayment, consolidation, or restructuring of a consumer's debt, and includes the negotiation with creditors of lower interest rates, the waiver or reduction of fees, and the marketing and processing of debt management plans.

§ 509. Private foundation defined.

(a) General rule. For purposes of this title, the term "private foundation" means a domestic or foreign organization described in section 501(c)(3) other than--

* * *

(3) an organization which--

(A) is organized, and at all times thereafter is operated, exclusively for the benefit of, to perform the functions of, or to carry out the purposes of one or more specified organizations described in paragraph (1) or (2),

(B) is --

(i) operated, supervised, or controlled by one or more organizations described in paragraph (1) or (2),

(ii) supervised or controlled in connection with one or more such organizations, or

(iii) operated in connection with one or more such organizations, and

(C) is not controlled directly or indirectly by one or more disqualified persons (as defined in section 4946) other than foundation managers and other than one or more organizations described in paragraph (1) or (2);

(e) Definition of gross investment income. For purposes of subsection (d), the term "gross investment income" means the gross amount of income from interest, dividends, payments with respect to securities loans (as defined in section 512(a)(5)), rents, and royalties, but not including any such income to the extent included in computing the tax imposed by section 511. *Such term shall also include income from sources similar to those in the preceding sentence.*

(f) Requirements for supporting organizations. –

(1) Type III supporting organizations. – For purposes of subsection (a)(3)(B)(iii), an organization shall not be considered to be operated in connection with any organization described in paragraph (1) or (2) of subsection (a) unless such organization meets the following requirements:

(A) Responsiveness. For each taxable year beginning after the date of the enactment of this subsection, the organization provides to each supported organization such information as the Secretary may require to ensure that such organization is responsive to the needs or demands of the supported organization.

(B) Foreign supported organizations. –

*(i) In general.–*The organization is not operated in connection with any supported organization that is not organized in the United States.

(ii) Transition rule for existing organizations.– If the organization is operated in connection with an organization that is not organized in the United States on the date of the enactment of this subsection, clause (i) shall not apply until the first day of the third taxable year of the organization beginning after the date of the enactment of this subsection.

(2) Organizations controlled by donors –

*(A) In general.–*For purposes of subsection (a)(3)(B), an organization shall not be considered to be –

(i) operated, supervised, or controlled by any organization described in paragraph (1) or (2) of subsection (a), or

(ii) operated in connection with any organization described in paragraph (1) or (2) of subsection (a), if such organization accepts any gift or contribution from any person described in subparagraph (B).

*(B) Person described.–*A person is described in this subparagraph if, with respect to a supported organization of an organization described in subparagraph (A), such person is –

(i) a person (other than an organization described in paragraph (1), (2), or (4) of section 509(a)) who directly or indirectly controls, either alone or together with persons described in clauses (ii) and (iii), the governing body of such supported organization,

(ii) a member of the family (determined under section 4958(f)(4)) of an individual described in clause (i), or

(iii) a 35-percent controlled entity (as defined in section 4958(f)(3) by substituting "persons described in clause (i) or (ii) of section 509(f)(2)(B)" for "persons described in subparagraph (A) or (B) of paragraph (1)" in subparagraph (A)(i) thereof).

(3) Supported organization. – For purposes of this subsection, the term "supported organization" means, with respect to an organization described in subsection (a)(3), an organization described in paragraph (1) or (2) of subsection (a) –

(A) for whose benefit the organization described in subsection (a)(3) is organized and operated, or

(B) with respect to which the organization performs the functions of, or carries out the purposes of.

§ 512. Unrelated business taxable income.

* * *

(b) **Modifications**. – The modifications referred to in subsection (a) are as follows:

(13) Special rules for certain amounts received from controlled entities –

* * *

(E) Paragraph to apply only to certain excess payments. –

(i) In general. – Subparagraph (A) shall apply only to the portion of a qualifying specified payment received or accrued by the controlling organization that exceeds the amount which would have been paid or accrued if such payment met the requirements prescribed under section 482.

(ii) Addition to tax for valuation misstatements. – The tax imposed by this chapter on the controlling organization shall be increased by an amount equal to 20 percent of the larger of –

(I) such excess determined without regard to any amendment or supplement to a return of tax, or

(II) such excess determined with regard to all such amendments and supplements.

(iii) Qualifying specified payment. – The term "qualifying specified payment" means a specified payment which is made pursuant to –

(I) a binding written contract in effect on the date of the enactment of this subparagraph, or

(II) a contract which is a renewal, under substantially similar terms, of a contract described in subclause (I).

(iv) Termination. – This subparagraph shall not apply to payments received or accrued after December 31, 2007.

(F) Related persons . – The Secretary shall prescribe such rules as may be necessary or appropriate to prevent avoidance of the purposes of this paragraph through the use of related persons.

* * *

§ 4943. Taxes on excess business holdings.

(e) Application of tax to donor advised funds. --

    (1) In general.--For purposes of this section, a donor advised fund (as defined in) shall be treated as a private foundation.

    (2) Disqualified person.--In applying this section to any donor advised fund (as so defined), the term "disqualified person" means, with respect to the donor advised fund, any person who is--

        (A) described in,

        (B) a member of the family of an individual described in subparagraph (A), or

        (C) a 35-percent controlled entity (as defined in by substituting "persons described in subparagraph (A) or (B) of section 4943(e)(2)" for "persons described in subparagraph (A) or (B) of paragraph (1)" in subparagraph (A)(i) thereof).

    (3) Present holdings.--For purposes of this subsection, rules similar to the rules of paragraphs (4), (5), and (6) of subsection (c) shall apply to donor advised funds (as so defined), except that--

        (A) "the date of the enactment of this subsection" shall be substituted for "May 26, 1969" each place it appears in paragraphs (4), (5), and (6), and

        (B) "January 1, 2007" shall be substituted for "January 1, 1970" in paragraph (4)(E).

(f) Application of tax to supporting organizations.--

    (1) In general.--For purposes of this section, an organization which is described in paragraph (3) shall be treated as a private foundation.

    (2) Exception.--The Secretary may exempt the excess business holdings of any organization from the application of this subsection if the Secretary determines that such holdings are consistent with the purpose or function constituting the basis for its exemption under .

    (3) Organizations described.--An organization is described in this paragraph if such organization is–

        (A) a type III supporting organization (other than a functionally integrated type III supporting organization), or

        (B) an organization which meets the requirements of and which is supervised or controlled in connection with one or more organizations described in , but only if such organization accepts any gift or contribution from any person described in .

    (4) Disqualified person.--

(A) In general.--In applying this section to any organization described in paragraph (3), the term "disqualified person" means, with respect to the organization--

   (i) any person who was, at any time during the 5-year period ending on the date described in subsection (a)(2)(A), in a position to exercise substantial influence over the affairs of the organization,

   (ii) any member of the family (determined under) of an individual described in clause (i),

   (iii) any 35-percent controlled entity (as defined in by substituting "persons described in clause (i) or (ii) of section 4943(f)(4)(A)" for "persons described in subparagraph (A) or (B) of paragraph (1)" in subparagraph (A)(i) thereof),

   (iv) any person described in , and

   (v) any organization--

      (I) which is effectively controlled (directly or indirectly) by the same person or persons who control the organization in question, or

      (II) substantially all of the contributions to which were made (directly or indirectly) by the same person or persons described in subparagraph (B) or a member of the family (within the meaning of) of such a person.

(B) Persons described.--A person is described in this subparagraph if such person is--

   (i) a substantial contributor to the organization (as defined in),

   (ii) an officer, director, or trustee of the organization (or an individual having powers or responsibilities similar to those of the officers, directors, or trustees of the organization), or

   (iii) an owner of more than 20 percent of--

      (I) the total combined voting power of a corporation,

      (II) the profits interest of a partnership, or

      (III) the beneficial interest of a trust or unincorporated enterprise,

which is a substantial contributor (as so defined) to the organization.

(5) Type III supporting organization; functionally integrated type III supporting organization.--For purposes of this subsection--

(A) Type III supporting organization.--The term "type III supporting organization" means an organization which meets the requirements of and which is operated in connection with one or more organizations described in .

(B) Functionally integrated type III supporting organization.--The term "functionally integrated type III supporting organization" means a type III supporting organization which is not required under regulations established by the Secretary to make payments to supported organizations (as defined under) due to the activities of the organization related to performing the functions of, or carrying out the purposes of, such supported organizations.

(6) Special rule for certain holdings of type III supporting organizations.-- For purposes of this subsection, the term "excess business holdings" shall not include any holdings of a type III supporting organization in any business enterprise if, as of November 18, 2005, the holdings were held (and at all times thereafter, are held) for the benefit of the community pursuant to the direction of a State attorney general or a State official with jurisdiction over such organization.

(7) Present holdings.--For purposes of this subsection, rules similar to the rules of paragraphs (4), (5), and (6) of subsection (c) shall apply to organizations described in , except that--

(A) "the date of the enactment of this subsection" shall be substituted for "May 26, 1969" each place it appears in paragraphs (4), (5), and (6), and

(B) "January 1, 2007" shall be substituted for "January 1, 1970" in paragraph (4)(E).

* * *

§ 4958. Taxes on excess benefit transactions

* * *

(c) Excess benefit transaction; excess benefit.--For purposes of this section–

* * *

(2) Special rules for donor advised funds.--In the case of any donor advised fund (as defined in section 4966(d)(2))--

(A) the term "excess benefit transaction" includes any grant, loan, compensation, or other similar payment from such fund to a person described in subsection (f)(7) with respect to such fund, and

(B) the term "excess benefit" includes, with respect to any transaction described in subparagraph (A), the amount of any such grant, loan, compensation, or other similar payment.

(3) Special rules for supporting organizations.--

(A) In general.--In the case of any organization described in section 509(a)(3)

(i) the term "excess benefit transaction" includes--

> *(I) any grant, loan, compensation, or other similar payment provided by such organization to a person described in subparagraph (B), and*

> *(II) any loan provided by such organization to a disqualified person (other than an organization described in paragraph (1), (2), or (4) of section 509(a)), and*

(ii) the term "excess benefit" includes, with respect to any transaction described in clause (i), the amount of any such grant, loan, compensation, or other similar payment.

(B) Person described.--A person is described in this subparagraph if such person is--

(i) a substantial contributor to such organization,

(ii) a member of the family (determined under section 4958(f)(4)) of an individual described in clause (i), or

(iii) a 35-percent controlled entity (as defined in section 4958(f)(3) by substituting "persons described in clause (i) or (ii) of section 4958(c)(3)(B)" for "persons described in subparagraph (A) or (B) of paragraph (1)" in subparagraph (A)(i) thereof).

(C) Substantial contributor.--For purposes of this paragraph--

(i) In general.--The term "substantial contributor" means any person who contributed or bequeathed an aggregate amount of more than $5,000 to the organization, if such amount is more than 2 percent of the total contributions and bequests received by the organization before the close of the taxable year of the organization in which the contribution or bequest is received by the organization from such person. In the case of a trust, such term also means the creator of the trust. Rules similar to the rules of subparagraphs (B) and (C) of section 507(d)(2) shall apply for purposes of this subparagraph.

(ii) Exception.--Such term shall not include any organization described in paragraph (1), (2), or (4) of section 509(a).

(4) **Authority to include certain other private inurement.--**To the extent provided in regulations prescribed by the Secretary, the term "excess benefit transaction" includes any transaction in which the amount of any economic benefit provided to or for the use of a disqualified person is determined in whole or in part by the revenues of 1 or more activities of the organization but only if such transaction results in inurement not permitted under paragraph (3) or (4) of section 501(c), as the case may be. In the case of any such transaction, the excess benefit shall be the amount of the inurement not so permitted.

(d) Special rules.--For purposes of this section–

* * *

(2) Limit for management.--With respect to any 1 excess benefit transaction, the maximum amount of the tax imposed by subsection (a)(2) shall not exceed *$20,000*.

* * *

(f) **Other definitions.**--For purposes of this section--

(1) Disqualified person.--The term "disqualified person" means, with respect to any transaction--

    (A) any person who was, at any time during the 5-year period ending on the date of such transaction, in a position to exercise substantial influence over the affairs of the organization.

    (B) a member of the family of an individual described in subparagraph (A),

    (C) a 35-percent controlled entity,

    (D) any person who is described in subparagraph (A), (B), or (C) with respect to an organization described in section 509(a)(3) and organized and operated exclusively for the benefit of, to perform the functions of, or to carry out the purposes of the applicable tax-exempt organization.

    (E) which involves a donor advised fund (as defined in section 4966(d)(2)), any person who is described in paragraph (7) with respect to such donor advised fund (as so defined), and

    (F) which involves a sponsoring organization (as defined in section 4966(d)(1)), any person who is described in paragraph (8) with respect to such sponsoring organization (as so defined).

* * *

    (6) Correction.--The terms "correction" and "correct" mean, with respect to any excess benefit transaction, undoing the excess benefit to the extent possible, and taking any additional measures necessary to place the organization in a financial position not worse than that in which it would be if the disqualified person were dealing under the highest fiduciary standards, *except that in the case of any correction of an excess benefit transaction described in subsection (c)(2), no amount repaid in a manner prescribed by the Secretary may be held in any donor advised fund.*

    (7) Donors and donor advisors.--*For purposes of paragraph (1)(E), a person is described in this paragraph if such person--*

    (A) is described in section 4966(d)(2)(A)(iii),

    (B) is a member of the family of an individual described in subparagraph (A), or

    (C) is a 35-percent controlled entity (as defined in paragraph (3) by substituting "persons described in subparagraph (A) or (B) of paragraph (7)"

for "persons described in subparagraph (A) or (B) of paragraph (1)" in subparagraph (A)(i) thereof).

(8) Investment advisors.--*For purposes of paragraph (1)(F)--*

    (A) In general.--*A person is described in this paragraph if such person--*

        (i) *is an investment advisor,*

        (ii) *is a member of the family of an individual described in clause (i), or*

        (iii) *is a 35-percent controlled entity (as defined in paragraph (3) by substituting "persons described in clause (i) or (ii) of paragraph (8)(A)" for "persons described in subparagraph (A) or (B) of paragraph (1)" in subparagraph (A)(i) thereof).*

    (B) Investment advisor defined.--*For purposes of subparagraph (A), the term "investment advisor" means, with respect to any sponsoring organization (as defined in section 4966(d)(1)), any person (other than an employee of such organization) compensated by such organization for managing the investment of, or providing investment advice with respect to, assets maintained in donor advised funds (as defined in section 4966(d)(2)) owned by such organization.*

§ 4966. Taxes on taxable distributions.

(a) Imposition of taxes.--

    (1) On the sponsoring organization.--*There is hereby imposed on each taxable distribution a tax equal to 20 percent of the amount thereof. The tax imposed by this paragraph shall be paid by the sponsoring organization with respect to the donor advised fund.*

    (2) On the fund management.--*There is hereby imposed on the agreement of any fund manager to the making of a distribution, knowing that it is a taxable distribution, a tax equal to 5 percent of the amount thereof. The tax imposed by this paragraph shall be paid by any fund manager who agreed to the making of the distribution.*

(b) Special rules.--*For purposes of subsection (a)--*

    (1) Joint and several liability.--*If more than one person is liable under subsection (a)(2) with respect to the making of a taxable distribution, all such persons shall be jointly and severally liable under such paragraph with respect to such distribution.*

    (2) Limit for management.--*With respect to any one taxable distribution, the maximum amount of the tax imposed by subsection (a)(2) shall not exceed $10,000.*

(c) Taxable distribution.--*For purposes of this section--*

    (1) In general.--*The term "taxable distribution" means any distribution from a donor advised fund--*

(A) to any natural person, or

(B) to any other person if--

    (i) such distribution is for any purpose other than one specified in section 170(c)(2)(B), or

    (ii) the sponsoring organization does not exercise expenditure responsibility with respect to such distribution in accordance with section 4945(h).

(2) Exceptions.--Such term shall not include any distribution from a donor advised fund–

    (A) to any organization described in section 170(b)(1)(A) (other than a disqualified supporting organization),

    (B) to the sponsoring organization of such donor advised fund, or

    (C) to any other donor advised fund.

(d) Definitions.--For purposes of this subchapter--

(1) Sponsoring organization.--The term "sponsoring organization" means any organization which--

    (A) is described in section 170(c) (other than in paragraph (1) thereof, and without regard to paragraph (2)(A) thereof),

    (B) is not a private foundation (as defined in section 509(a)), and

    (C) maintains 1 or more donor advised funds.

(2) Donor advised fund.--

    (A) In general.--Except as provided in subparagraph (B) or (C), the term "donor advised fund" means a fund or account--

        (i) which is separately identified by reference to contributions of a donor or donors,

        (ii) which is owned and controlled by a sponsoring organization, and

        (iii) with respect to which a donor (or any person appointed or designated by such donor) has, or reasonably expects to have, advisory privileges with respect to the distribution or investment of amounts held in such fund or account by reason of the donor's status as a donor.

    (B) Exceptions.--The term "donor advised fund" shall not include any fund or account--

        (i) which makes distributions only to a single identified organization or governmental entity, or

(ii) with respect to which a person described in subparagraph (A)(iii) advises as to which individuals receive grants for travel, study, or other similar purposes, if--

(I) such person's advisory privileges are performed exclusively by such person in the person's capacity as a member of a committee all of the members of which are appointed by the sponsoring organization,

(II) no combination of persons described in subparagraph (A)(iii) (or persons related to such persons) control, directly or indirectly, such committee, and

(III) all grants from such fund or account are awarded on an objective and nondiscriminatory basis pursuant to a procedure approved in advance by the board of directors of the sponsoring organization, and such procedure is designed to ensure that all such grants meet the requirements of paragraph (1), (2), or (3) of section 4945(g).

(C) Secretarial authority.--The Secretary may exempt a fund or account not described in subparagraph (B) from treatment as a donor advised fund--

(i) if such fund or account is advised by a committee not directly or indirectly controlled by the donor or any person appointed or designated by the donor for the purpose of advising with respect to distributions from such fund (and any related parties), or

(ii) if such fund benefits a single identified charitable purpose.

(3) Fund manager.--The term "fund manager" means, with respect to any sponsoring organization--

(A) an officer, director, or trustee of such sponsoring organization (or an individual having powers or responsibilities similar to those of officers, directors, or trustees of the sponsoring organization), and

(B) with respect to any act (or failure to act), the employees of the sponsoring organization having authority or responsibility with respect to such act (or failure to act).

(4) Disqualified supporting organization.--

(A) In general.--The term "disqualified supporting organization" means, with respect to any distribution--

(i) any type III supporting organization (as defined in section 4943(f)(5)(A)) which is not a functionally integrated type III supporting organization (as defined in section 4943(f)(5)(B)), and

(ii) any organization which is described in subparagraph (B) or (C) if–

(I) the donor or any person designated by the donor for the purpose of advising with respect to distributions from a donor advised fund (and any related parties) directly or indirectly controls a supported organization (as defined in section 509(f)(3)) of such organization, or

(II) the Secretary determines by regulations that a distribution to such organization otherwise is inappropriate.

(B) Type I and type II supporting organizations.-- An organization is described in this subparagraph if the organization meets the requirements of subparagraphs (A) and (C) of section 509(a)(3) and is--

(i) operated, supervised, or controlled by one or more organizations described in paragraph (1) or (2) of section 509(a), or

(ii) supervised or controlled in connection with one or more such organizations.

(C) Functionally integrated type III supporting organizations.-- An organization is described in this subparagraph if the organization is a functionally integrated type III supporting organization (as defined under section 4943(f)(5)(B)).

§ 4967. Taxes on prohibited benefits

(a) Imposition of taxes.--

(1) On the donor, donor advisor, or related person.--There is hereby imposed on the advice of any person described in subsection (d) to have a sponsoring organization make a distribution from a donor advised fund which results in such person or any other person described in subsection (d) receiving, directly or indirectly, a more than incidental benefit as a result of such distribution, a tax equal to 125 percent of such benefit. The tax imposed by this paragraph shall be paid by any person described in subsection (d) who advises as to the distribution or who receives such a benefit as a result of the distribution.

(2) On the fund management.--There is hereby imposed on the agreement of any fund manager to the making of a distribution, knowing that such distribution would confer a benefit described in paragraph (1), a tax equal to 10 percent of the amount of such benefit. The tax imposed by this paragraph shall be paid by any fund manager who agreed to the making of the distribution.

(b) Exception.--No tax shall be imposed under this section with respect to any distribution if a tax has been imposed with respect to such distribution under section 4958.

(c) Special rules.--For purposes of subsection (a)--

(1) Joint and several liability.--If more than one person is liable under paragraph (1) or (2) of subsection (a) with respect to a distribution described in subsection (a), all such persons shall be jointly and severally liable under such paragraph with respect to such distribution.

*(2) Limit for management.--*With respect to any one distribution described in subsection (a), the maximum amount of the tax imposed by subsection (a)(2) shall not exceed $10,000.

*(d) Person described.--*A person is described in this subsection if such person is described in section 4958(f)(7) with respect to a donor advised fund.

TREASURY REGULATIONS

§ 1.170A-9T(f). Definition of section 170(b)(1)(A)(vi) organization.

* * *

(4) **Definition of normally; general rule--(i) Normally; 33 1/3 percent support test.** An organization meets the 33 1/3 percent support test for its current taxable year and the taxable year immediately succeeding its current year, if, for the current taxable year and the 4 taxable years immediately preceding the current taxable year, the organization meets the 33 1/3 percent support test on an aggregate basis.

(ii) **Normally; facts and circumstances test.** An organization meets the facts and circumstances test for its current taxable year and the taxable year immediately succeeding its current year, if, for the current taxable year and the 4 taxable years immediately preceding the current taxable year, the organization meets the facts and circumstances test on an aggregate basis. In the case of paragraphs (f)(3)(iii)(A) and (B) of this section, facts pertinent to the 5-year period may also be taken into consideration. The combination of factors set forth in paragraphs (f)(3)(iii)(A) through (E) of this section that an organization "normally" must meet does not have to be the same for each 5- year period so long as there exists a sufficient combination of factors to show compliance with the facts and circumstances test.

(iii) **Special rule.** The fact that an organization has normally met the requirements of the 33 1/3 percent support test for a current taxable year, but is unable normally to meet such requirements for a succeeding taxable year, will not in itself prevent such organization from meeting the facts and circumstances test for such succeeding taxable year.

(iv) **Example.** The application of paragraphs (f)(4)(i), (ii), and (iii) of this section may be illustrated by the following example:

Example. (i) X is recognized as an organization described in section 501(c)(3). On the basis of support received during taxable years 2008, 2009, 2010, 2011 and 2012, it meets the 33 1/3 percent support test for taxable year 2012 (the current taxable year). X also meets the 33 1/3 support test for 2013, as the immediately succeeding taxable year.

(ii) In taxable years 2009, 2010, 2011, 2012 and 2013, in the aggregate, X does not receive at least 33 1/3 percent of its support from governmental units referred to in section 170(c)(1), from contributions made directly or indirectly by the general public, or from a combination of these sources. X still meets the 33 1/3 percent support test for taxable year 2013 based on the aggregate support received for taxable years 2008 through 2012.

(iii) In taxable years 2010, 2011, 2012, 2013 and 2014, in the aggregate, X does not receive at least 33 1/3 percent of its support from governmental units referred to in section 170(c)(1), from contributions made directly or indirectly by the general public, or from a combination of these sources. X does not meet the 33 1/3 percent support test for taxable year 2014.

(iv) Based on the aggregate support and other factors listed in paragraphs (f)(3)(iii)(A) through (E) of this section for taxable years 2009, 2010, 2011, 2012, and 2013, X meets the facts and circumstances test for taxable year 2013 and for taxable year 2014 (as the immediately succeeding taxable year). Therefore, X is still an organization described in section 170(b)(1)(A)(vi) for taxable year 2014, even though X did not meet the 33 1/3 percent support test for that year.

(v) Normally; first five years of an organization's existence. (A) An organization meets the 33 1/3 public support test or the facts and circumstances test during its first five taxable years as a section 501(c)(3) organization if the organization can reasonably be expected to meet the requirements of the 33 1/3 percent support test or the facts and circumstances test during that period. With respect to such organization's sixth taxable year, the organization shall be described in section 170(b)(1)(A)(vi) if it meets the 33 1/3 percent support test or the facts and circumstances test under the definitions of normally set forth in paragraphs (f)(4)(i) through (iii) of this section for its sixth taxable year (based on support received in its second through sixth taxable years), or for its fifth taxable year (based on support received in its first through fifth taxable years).

(B) Basic consideration. In determining whether an organization can reasonably be expected (within the meaning of paragraph (f)(4)(v)(A) of this section) to meet the requirements of the 33 1/3 percent support test or the facts and circumstances test during its first five taxable years, the basic consideration is whether its organizational structure, current or proposed programs or activities, and actual or intended method of operation are such as can reasonably be expected to attract the type of broadly based support from the general public, public charities, and governmental units that is necessary to meet such tests. The factors that are relevant to this determination, and the weight accorded to each of them, may differ from case to case, depending on the nature and functions of the organization. The information to be considered for this purpose shall consist of all pertinent facts and circumstances relating to the requirements set forth in paragraph (f)(3) of this section.

(vi) Example. The application of paragraph (f)(4)(v) of this section may be illustrated by the following example:

Example. (i) Organization Y was formed in January 2008, and uses a December 31 taxable year. After September 9, 2008, and before December 31, 2008, Organization Y filed Form 1023 requesting recognition of exemption as an organization described in section 501(c)(3) and in sections 170(b)(1)(A)(vi) and 509(a)(1). In its application, Organization Y established that it can reasonably be expected to operate as a public charity under paragraph (f)(4)(v) of this section. Subsequently, Organization Y received a ruling or determination letter that it is an organization described in section 501(c)(3) and sections 170(b)(1)(A)(vi) and 509(a)(1) effective as of the date of its formation.

(ii) Organization Y is described in sections 170(b)(1)(A)(vi) and 509(a)(1) for its first 5 taxable years (the taxable years ending December 31, 2008, through December 31, 2012).

(iii) Organization Y can qualify as a public charity beginning with the taxable year ending December 31, 2013, if Organization Y can meet the requirements of paragraphs (f)(2) through (3) of this section or § 1.509(a)- 3T(a) through (b) for the taxable years ending December 31, 2009, through December 31, 2013, or for the taxable years ending December 31, 2008, through December 31, 2012.

(5) Determinations on foundation classification and reliance. (i) A ruling or determination letter that an organization is described in section 170(b)(1)(A)(vi) may be issued to an organization. Such determination may be made in conjunction with the recognition of the organization's tax-exempt status or at such other time as the organization believes it is described in section 170(b)(1)(A)(vi). The ruling or determination letter that the organization is described in section 170(b)(1)(A)(vi) may be revoked if, upon examination, the organization has not met the requirements of paragraph (f) of this section. The ruling or determination letter that the organization is described in section 170(b)(1)(A)(vi) also may be revoked if the organization's application for a ruling or determination contained one or more material misstatements of fact or if such application was part of a scheme or plan to avoid or evade any provision of the Internal Revenue Code. The revocation of the determination that an organization is described in section 170(b)(1)(A)(vi) does not preclude revocation of the determination that the organization is described in section 501(c)(3).

(ii) **Status of grantors or contributors.** For purposes of sections 170, 507, 545(b)(2), 642(c), 4942, 4945, 2055, 2106(a)(2), and 2522, grantors or contributors may rely upon a determination letter or ruling that an organization is described in section 170(b)(1)(A)(vi) until the Internal Revenue Service publishes notice of a change of status (for example, in the Internal Revenue Bulletin or Publication 78, "Cumulative List of Organizations described in Section 170(c) of the Internal Revenue Code of 1986," which can be searched at www.irs.gov). For this purpose, grantors or contributors also may rely on an advance ruling that expires on or after June 9, 2008. However, a grantor or contributor may not rely on such an advance ruling or any determination letter or ruling if the grantor or contributor was responsible for, or aware of, the act or failure to act that resulted in the organization's loss of classification under section 170(b)(1)(A)(vi) or acquired knowledge that the Internal Revenue Service had given notice to such organization that it would be deleted from such classification.

§ 1.501(c)(3)-1(d). Exempt purposes – in general. * * *

(iii) **Examples**. The following examples illustrate the requirement of paragraph (d)(1)(ii) of this section that an organization serve a public rather than a private interest:

Example 1. (i) O is an educational organization the purpose of which is to study history and immigration. O's educational activities include sponsoring lectures and publishing a journal. The focus of O's historical studies is the genealogy of one family, tracing the descent of its present members. O actively solicits for membership only individuals who are members of that one family. O's research is directed toward publishing a history of that family that will document the pedigrees of family members. A major objective of O's research is to identify and locate living descendants of that family to enable those descendants to become acquainted with each other.

(ii) O's educational activities primarily serve the private interests of members of a single family rather than a public interest. Therefore, O is operated for the benefit of private interests in violation of the restriction on private benefit in paragraph (d)(1)(ii) of this section. Based on these facts and circumstances, O is not operated exclusively for exempt purposes and, therefore, is not described in section 501(c)(3).

Example 2. (i) O is an art museum. O's principal activity is exhibiting art created by a group of unknown but promising local artists. O's activity, including organized tours of its art collection, promotes the arts. O is governed by a board of trustees unrelated to the artists whose work O exhibits. All of the art exhibited is offered for sale at prices set by the artist. Each artist whose work is exhibited has a consignment arrangement with O. Under this arrangement, when art is sold, the museum retains 10 percent of the selling price to cover the costs of operating the museum and gives the artist 90 percent.

(ii) The artists in this situation directly benefit from the exhibition and sale of their art. As a result, the principal activity of O serves the private interests of these artists. Because O gives 90 percent of the proceeds from its sole activity to the individual artists, the direct benefits to the artists are substantial and O's provision of these benefits to the artists is more than incidental to its other purposes and activities. This arrangement causes O to be operated for the benefit of private interests in violation of the restriction on private benefit in paragraph (d)(1)(ii) of this section. Based on these facts and circumstances, O is not operated exclusively for exempt purposes and, therefore, is not described in section 501(c)(3).

Example 3. (i) O is an educational organization the purpose of which is to train individuals in a program developed by P, O's president. The program is of interest to academics and professionals, representatives of whom serve on an advisory panel to O. All of the rights to the program are owned by Company K, a for-profit corporation owned by P. Prior to the existence of O, the teaching of the program was conducted by Company K. O licenses, from Company K, the right to conduct seminars and lectures on the program and to use the name of the program as part of O's name, in exchange for specified royalty payments. Under the license agreement, Company K provides O with the services of trainers and with course materials on the program. O may develop and copyright new course materials on the program but all such materials must be assigned to Company K without consideration if and when the license agreement is terminated. Company K sets the tuition for the seminars and lectures on the program conducted by O. O has agreed not to become involved in any activity resembling the program or its implementation for 2 years after the termination of O's license agreement.

(ii) O's sole activity is conducting seminars and lectures on the program. This arrangement causes O to be operated for the benefit of P and Company K in violation of the restriction on private benefit in paragraph (d)(1)(ii) of this section, regardless of whether the royalty payments from O to Company K for the right to teach the program are reasonable. Based on these facts and circumstances, O is not operated exclusively for exempt purposes and, therefore, is not described in section 501(c)(3).

(iv) Since each of the purposes specified in subdivision (i) of this subparagraph is an exempt purpose in itself, an organization may be exempt if it is organized and operated exclusively for any one or more of such purposes. If, in fact, an organization is organized and operated exclusively for an exempt purpose or purposes, exemption will be granted to such an organization regardless of the purpose or purposes specified in its application for exemption. For example, if an organization claims exemption on the ground that it is educational, exemption will not be denied if, in fact, it is charitable.

* * *

(f) Interaction with section 4958--(1) Application process. An organization that applies for recognition of exemption under section 501(a) as an organization described in section 501(c)(3) must establish its eligibility under this section. The Commissioner may deny an application for exemption for failure to establish any of section 501(c)(3)'s requirements for exemption. Section 4958 does not apply to transactions with an organization that has failed to establish that it satisfies all of the requirements for exemption under section 501(c)(3). See § 53.4958-2.

(2) Substantive requirements for exemption still apply to applicable tax-exempt organizations described in section 501(c)(3)--(i) In general. Regardless of whether a particular transaction is subject to excise taxes under section 4958, the substantive requirements for tax exemption under section 501(c)(3) still apply to an applicable tax-exempt organization (as defined in section 4958(e) and § 53.4958-2) described in section 501(c)(3) whose disqualified persons or organization managers are subject to excise taxes under section 4958. Accordingly, an organization will no longer meet the requirements for tax-exempt status under section 501(c)(3) if the organization fails to satisfy the requirements of paragraph (b), (c) or (d) of this section. See § 53.4958-8(a).

(ii) Determination of whether revocation of tax-exempt status is appropriate when section 4958 excise taxes also apply. In determining whether to continue to recognize the tax-exempt status of an applicable tax-exempt organization (as defined in section 4958(e) and § 53.4958-2) described in section 501(c)(3) that engages in one or more excess benefit transactions (as defined in section 4958(c) and § 53.4958-4) that violate the prohibition on inurement under section 501(c)(3), the Commissioner will consider all relevant facts and circumstances, including, but not limited to, the following--

(A) The size and scope of the organization's regular and ongoing activities that further exempt purposes before and after the excess benefit transaction or transactions occurred;

(B) The size and scope of the excess benefit transaction or transactions (collectively, if more than one) in relation to the size and scope of the organization's regular and ongoing activities that further exempt purposes;

(C) Whether the organization has been involved in multiple excess benefit transactions with one or more persons;

(D) Whether the organization has implemented safeguards that are reasonably calculated to prevent excess benefit transactions; and

(E) Whether the excess benefit transaction has been corrected (within the meaning of section 4958(f)(6) and § 53.4958-7), or the organization has made good faith efforts to seek correction from the disqualified person(s) who benefited from the excess benefit transaction.

(iii) All factors will be considered in combination with each other. Depending on the particular situation, the Commissioner may assign greater or lesser weight to some factors than to others. The factors listed in paragraphs (f)(2)(ii)(D) and (E) of this section will weigh more heavily in favor of continuing to recognize exemption where the organization discovers the excess benefit transaction or transactions and takes action before the Commissioner discovers the excess benefit transaction or transactions. Further, with respect to the factor listed in paragraph (f)(2)(ii)(E) of this section, correction after the excess benefit transaction or transactions are discovered by the Commissioner, by itself, is never a sufficient basis for continuing to recognize exemption.

(iv) **Examples.** The following examples illustrate the principles of paragraph (f)(2)(ii) of this section. For purposes of each example, assume that O is an applicable tax-exempt organization (as defined in section 4958(e) and § 53.4958-2) described in section 501(c)(3). The examples read as follows:

Example 1. (i) O was created as a museum for the purpose of exhibiting art to the general public. In Years 1 and 2, O engages in fundraising and in selecting, leasing, and preparing an appropriate facility for a museum. In Year 3, a new board of trustees is elected. All of the new trustees are local art dealers. Beginning in Year 3 and continuing to the present, O uses a substantial portion of its revenues to purchase art solely from its trustees at prices that exceed fair market value. O exhibits and offers for sale all of the art it purchases. O's Form 1023, "Application for Recognition of Exemption," did not disclose the possibility that O would purchase art from its trustees.

(ii) O's purchases of art from its trustees at more than fair market value constitute excess benefit transactions between an applicable tax-exempt organization and disqualified persons under section 4958. Therefore, these transactions are subject to the applicable excise taxes provided in that section. In addition, O's purchases of art from its trustees at more than fair market value violate the proscription against inurement under section 501(c)(3) and paragraph (c)(2) of this section.

(iii) The application of the factors in paragraph (f)(2)(ii) of this section to these facts is as follows. Beginning in Year 3, O does not engage primarily in regular and ongoing activities that further exempt purposes because a substantial portion of O's activities consists of purchasing art from its trustees and dealing in such art in a manner similar to a commercial art gallery. The size and scope of the excess benefit transactions collectively are significant in relation to the size and scope of any of O's ongoing activities that further exempt purposes. O has been involved in multiple excess benefit transactions, namely, purchases of art from its trustees at more than fair market value. O has not implemented safeguards that are reasonably calculated to prevent such improper purchases in the future. The excess benefit transactions have not been corrected, nor has O made good faith efforts to seek correction from the disqualified persons who benefited from the excess benefit transactions (the trustees). The trustees continue to control O's Board. Based on the application of the factors to these facts, O is no longer described in section 501(c)(3) effective in Year 3.

Example 2. (i) The facts are the same as in Example 1, except that in Year 4, O's entire board of trustees resigns, and O no longer offers all exhibited art for sale. The former board is replaced with members of the community who are not in the business of buying or selling art and who have skills and experience running charitable and educational programs and institutions. O promptly discontinues the practice of purchasing art from current or former trustees, adopts a written conflicts of interest policy, adopts written art valuation guidelines, hires legal counsel to recover the excess amounts O had paid its former trustees, and implements a new program of activities to further the public's appreciation of the arts.

(ii) O's purchases of art from its former trustees at more than fair market value constitute excess benefit transactions between an applicable tax-exempt organization and disqualified persons under section 4958. Therefore, these transactions are subject to the applicable excise taxes provided in that section. In addition, O's purchases of art from its trustees at more than fair market value violate the proscription against inurement under section501(c)(3) and paragraph (c)(2) of this section.

(iii) The application of the factors in paragraph (f)(2)(ii) of this section to these facts is as follows. In Year 3, O does not engage primarily in regular and ongoing activities that further exempt purposes. However, in Year 4, O elects a new board of trustees comprised of individuals who have skills and experience running charitable and educational programs and implements a new program of activities to further the public's appreciation of the arts. As a result of these actions, beginning in Year 4, O engages in regular and ongoing activities that further exempt purposes. The size and scope of the excess benefit transactions that occurred in Year 3, taken collectively, are significant in relation to the size and scope of O's regular and ongoing exempt function activities that were conducted in Year 3. Beginning in Year 4, however, as O's exempt function activities grow, the size and scope of the excess benefit transactions that occurred in Year 3 become less and less significant as compared to the size and scope of O's regular and ongoing exempt function activities. O was involved in multiple excess benefit transactions in Year 3. However, by discontinuing its practice of purchasing art from its current and former trustees, by replacing its former board with independent members of the community, and by adopting a conflicts of interest policy and art valuation guidelines, O has implemented safeguards that are reasonably calculated to prevent future violations. In addition, O has made a good faith effort to seek correction from the disqualified persons who benefited from the excess benefit transactions (its former trustees). Based on the application of the factors to these facts, O continues to meet the requirements for tax exemption under section 501(c)(3).

Example 3. (i) O conducts educational programs for the benefit of the general public. Since its formation, O has employed its founder, C, as its Chief Executive Officer. Beginning in Year 5 of O's operations and continuing to the present, C caused O to divert significant portions of O's funds to pay C's personal expenses. The diversions by C significantly reduced the funds available to conduct O's ongoing educational programs. The board of trustees never authorized C to cause O to pay C's personal expenses from O's funds. Certain members of the board were aware that O was paying C's personal expenses. However, the board did not terminate C's employment and did not take any action to seek repayment from C or to prevent C from continuing to divert O's funds to pay C's personal expenses. C claimed that O's payments of C's personal expenses represented loans from O to C. However, no contemporaneous loan documentation exists, and C never made any payments of principal or interest.

(ii) The diversions of O's funds to pay C's personal expenses constitute excess benefit transactions between an applicable tax-exempt organization and a disqualified person under section 4958. Therefore, these transactions are subject to the applicable excise taxes provided in that section. In addition, these transactions violate the proscription against inurement under section 501(c)(3) and paragraph (c)(2) of this section.

(iii) The application of the factors in paragraph (f)(2)(ii) of this section to these facts is as follows. O has engaged in regular and ongoing activities that further exempt purposes both before and after the excess benefit transactions occurred. However, the size and scope of the excess benefit transactions engaged in by O beginning in Year 5, collectively, are significant in relation to the size and scope of O's activities that further exempt purposes. Moreover, O has been involved in multiple excess benefit transactions. O has not implemented any safeguards that are reasonably calculated to prevent future diversions. The excess benefit transactions have not been corrected, nor has O made good faith efforts to seek correction from C, the disqualified person who benefited from the excess benefit transactions. Based on the application of the factors to these facts, O is no longer described in section 501(c)(3) effective in Year 5.

Example 4. (i) O conducts activities that further exempt purposes. O uses several buildings in the conduct of its exempt activities. In Year 1, O sold one of the buildings to Company K for an amount that was substantially below fair market value. The sale was a significant event in relation to O's other activities. C, O's Chief Executive Officer, owns all of the voting stock of Company K. When O's board of trustees approved the transaction with Company K, the board did not perform due diligence that could have made it aware that the price paid by Company K to acquire the building was below fair market value. Subsequently, but before the IRS commences an examination of O, O's board of trustees determines that Company K paid less than the fair market value for the building. Thus, O concludes that an excess benefit transaction occurred. After the board makes this determination, it promptly removes C as Chief Executive Officer, terminates C's employment with O, and hires legal counsel to recover the excess benefit from Company K. In addition, O promptly adopts a conflicts of interest policy and new contract review procedures designed to prevent future recurrences of this problem.

(ii) The sale of the building by O to Company K at less than fair market value constitutes an excess benefit transaction between an applicable tax-exempt organization and a disqualified person under section 4958 in Year 1. Therefore, this transaction is subject to the applicable excise taxes provided in that section. In addition, this transaction violates the proscription against inurement under section 501(c)(3) and paragraph (c)(2) of this section.

(iii) The application of the factors in paragraph (f)(2)(ii) of this section to these facts is as follows. O has engaged in regular and ongoing activities that further exempt purposes both before and after the excess benefit transaction occurred. Although the size and scope of the excess benefit transaction were significant in relation to the size and scope of O's activities that further exempt purposes, the transaction with Company K was a one-time occurrence. By adopting a conflicts of interest policy and new contract review procedures and by terminating C, O has implemented safeguards that are reasonably calculated to prevent future violations. Moreover, O took corrective actions before the IRS commenced an examination of O. In addition, O has made a good faith effort to seek correction from Company K, the disqualified person who benefited from the excess benefit transaction. Based on the application of the factors to these facts, O continues to be described in section 501(c)(3).

Example 5. (i) O is a large organization with substantial assets and revenues. O conducts activities that further its exempt purposes. O employs C as its Chief Financial Officer. During Year 1, O pays $2,500 of C's personal expenses. O does not make these payments pursuant to an accountable plan, as described in § 53.4958-4(a)(4)(ii). In addition, O does not report any of these payments on C's Form W-2, "Wage and Tax Statement," or on a Form 1099- MISC, "Miscellaneous Income," for C for Year 1, and O does not report these payments as compensation on its Form 990, "Return of Organization Exempt From Income Tax," for Year 1. Moreover, none of these payments can be disregarded as nontaxable fringe benefits under § 53.4958-4(c)(2) and none consisted of fixed payments under an initial contract under § 53.4958-4(a)(3). C does not report the $2,500 of payments as income on his individual Federal income tax return for Year 1. O does not repeat this reporting omission in subsequent years and, instead, reports all payments of C's personal expenses not made under an accountable plan as income to C.

(ii) O's payment in Year 1 of $2,500 of C's personal expenses constitutes an excess benefit transaction between an applicable tax-exempt organization and a disqualified person under section 4958. Therefore, this transaction is subject to the applicable excise taxes provided in that section. In addition, this transaction violates the proscription against inurement in section 501(c)(3) and paragraph (c)(2) of this section.

(iii) The application of the factors in paragraph (f)(2)(ii) of this section to these facts is as follows. O engages in regular and ongoing activities that further exempt purposes. The payment of $2,500 of C's personal expenses represented only a de minimis portion of O's assets and revenues; thus, the size and scope of the excess benefit transaction were not significant in relation to the size and scope of O's activities that further exempt purposes. The reporting omission that resulted in the excess benefit transaction in Year 1 occurred only once and is not repeated in subsequent years. Based on the application of the factors to these facts, O continues to be described in section 501(c)(3).

Example 6. (i) O is a large organization with substantial assets and revenues. O furthers its exempt purposes by providing social services to the population of a specific geographic area. O has a sizeable workforce of employees and volunteers to conduct its work. In Year 1, O's board of directors adopted written procedures for setting executive compensation at O. O's executive compensation procedures were modeled on the procedures for establishing a rebuttable presumption of reasonableness under § 53.4958-6. In accordance with these procedures, the board appointed a compensation committee to gather data on compensation levels paid by similarly situated organizations for functionally comparable positions. The members of the compensation committee were disinterested within the meaning of § 53.4958- 6(c)(1)(iii). Based on its research, the compensation committee recommended a range of reasonable compensation for several of O's existing top executives (the Top Executives). On the basis of the committee's recommendations, the board approved new compensation packages for the Top Executives and timely documented the basis for its decision in board minutes. The board members were all disinterested within the meaning of § 53.4958-6(c)(1)(iii). The Top Executives were not involved in setting their own compensation. In Year 1, even though payroll expenses represented a significant portion of O's total operating expenses, the total compensation paid to O's Top Executives represented only an insubstantial portion of O's total payroll expenses. During a subsequent examination, the IRS found that the compensation committee relied exclusively on compensation data from organizations that perform similar social services to O. The IRS concluded, however, that the organizations were not similarly situated because they served substantially larger geographic regions with more diverse populations and were larger than O in terms of annual revenues, total operating budget, number of employees, and number of beneficiaries served. Accordingly, the IRS concluded that the compensation committee did not rely on "appropriate data as to comparability" within the meaning of § 53.4958-6(c)(2) and, thus, failed to establish the rebuttable presumption of reasonableness under § 53.4958-6. Taking O's size and the nature of the geographic area and population it serves into account, the IRS concluded that the Top Executives' compensation packages for Year 1 were excessive. As a result of the examination, O's board added new members to the compensation committee who have expertise in compensation matters and also amended its written procedures to require the compensation committee to evaluate a number of specific factors, including size, geographic area, and population covered by the organization, in assessing the comparability of compensation data. O's board renegotiated the Top Executives' contracts in accordance with the recommendations of the newly constituted compensation committee on a going forward basis. To avoid potential liability for damages under state contract law, O did not seek to void the Top Executives' employment contracts retroactively to Year 1 and did not seek correction of the excess benefit amounts from the Top Executives. O did not terminate any of the Top Executives.

(ii) O's payments of excessive compensation to the Top Executives in Year 1 constituted excess benefit transactions between an applicable tax-exempt organization and disqualified persons under section 4958. Therefore, these payments are subject to the applicable excise taxes provided under that section, including second-tier taxes if there is no correction by the disqualified persons. In addition, these payments violate the proscription against inurement under section 501(c)(3) and paragraph (c)(2) of this section.

(iii) The application of the factors in paragraph (f)(2)(ii) of this section to these facts is as follows. O has engaged in regular and ongoing activities that further exempt purposes both before and after the excess benefit transactions occurred. The size and scope of the excess benefit transactions, in the aggregate, were not significant in relation to the size and scope of O's activities that further exempt purposes. O engaged in multiple excess benefit transactions. Nevertheless, prior to entering into these excess benefit transactions, O had implemented written procedures for setting the compensation of its top management that were reasonably calculated to prevent the occurrence of excess benefit transactions. O followed these written procedures in setting the compensation of the Top Executives for Year 1. Despite the board's failure to rely on appropriate comparability data, the fact that O implemented and followed these written procedures in setting the compensation of the Top Executives for Year 1 is a factor favoring continued exemption. The fact that O amended its written procedures to ensure the use of appropriate comparability data and renegotiated the Top Executives' compensation packages on a going-forward basis are also factors favoring continued exemption, even though O did not void the Top Executives' existing contracts and did not seek correction from the Top Executives. Based on the application of the factors to these facts, O continues to be described in section 501(c)(3).

(3) Applicability. The rules in paragraph (f) of this section will apply with respect to excess benefit transactions occurring after March 28, 2008.

§ 1.509(a)-3T. Broadly, publicly supported organizations.

* * *

(c) Normally--(1) In general--(i) Definition. The support tests set forth in section 509(a)(2) are to be computed on the basis of the nature of the organization's normal sources of support. An organization will be considered as normally receiving one third of its support from any combination of gifts, grants, contributions, membership fees, and gross receipts from permitted sources (subject to the limitations described in § 1.509(a)-3(b)) and not more than one third of its support from items described in section 509(a)(2)(B) for its current taxable year and the taxable year immediately succeeding its current year, if, for the current taxable year and the four taxable years immediately preceding the current taxable year, the aggregate amount of the support received during the applicable period from gifts, grants, contributions, membership fees, and gross receipts from permitted sources (subject to the limitations described in § 1.509(a)-3(b)) is more than one third, and the aggregate amount of the support received from items described in section 509(a)(2)(B) is not more than one third, of the total support of the organization for such 5-year period.

(ii) First five years of an organization's existence. See paragraph (d)(1) of this section for the definition of "normally" for organizations in the first five years of their existence.

* * *

(6) Examples. The application of the principles set forth in this paragraph are illustrated by the examples as follows. For purposes of these examples, the term general public is defined as persons other than disqualified persons and other than persons from whom the foundation received gross receipts in excess of the greater of $5,000 or 1 percent of its support in any taxable year, the term gross investment income is as defined in section 509(e), and the term gross receipts is limited to receipts from activities which are not unrelated trades or businesses (within the meaning of section 513).

Example 1. (i) For the years 2008 through 2012, X, an organization exempt under section 501(c)(3) that makes scholarship grants to needy students of a particular city, received support from the following sources:

2008:

Gross receipts (general public)	$35,000
Contributions (substantial contributors)	36,000
Gross investment income	29,000
Total support	100,000

2009:

Gross receipts (general public)	34,000
Contributions (substantial contributors)	35,000
Gross investment income	31,000
Total support	100,000

2010:

Gross receipts (general public)	35,000
Contributions (substantial contributors)	30,000
Gross investment income	35,000
Total support	100,000

2011:

Gross receipts (general public)	33,000
Contributions (substantial contributors)	32,000
Gross investment income	35,000
Total support	100,000

2012:

Gross receipts (general public) 31,000
Contributions (substantial contributors) 39,000
Gross investment income 30,000
Total support $100,000

(ii) In applying section 509(a)(2) to the taxable year 2012, on the basis of paragraph (c)(1)(i) of this section, the total amount of support from gross receipts from the general public ($168,000) for the period 2008 through 2012, was more than one third, and the total amount of support from gross investment income ($160,000) was less than one third, of X's total support for the same period ($500,000). For the taxable years 2012 and 2013, X is therefore considered normally to receive more than one third of its support from the public sources described in section 509(a)(2)(A) and less than one third of its support from items described in section 509(a)(2)(B). The fact that X received less than one third of its support from section 509(a)(2)(A) sources in 2012 and more than one third of its support from items described in section 509(a)(2)(B) in 2011 does not affect its status because it met the normally test over a 5-year period.

Example 2. Assume the same facts as in Example 1 except that in 2012, X also received an unexpected bequest of $50,000 from A, an elderly widow who was interested in encouraging the work of X, but had no other relationship to it. Solely by reason of the bequest, A became a disqualified person. X used the bequest to create 5 new scholarships. Its operations otherwise remained the same. Under these circumstances X could not meet the 5-year support test because the total amount received from gross receipts from the general public ($168,000) would not be more than one-third of its total support for the 5-year period ($550,000). Because A is a disqualified person, her bequest cannot be included in the numerator of the one-third support test under section 509(a)(2)(A). However, based on the factors set forth in paragraph (c)(4) of this section, A's bequest may be excluded as an unusual grant under paragraph (c)(3) of this section. Therefore, X will be considered to have met the support test for the taxable years 2012 and 2013.

Example 3. Y, an organization described in section 501(c)(3), was created by A, the holder of all the common stock in M corporation, B, A's wife, and C, A's business associate. The purpose of Y was to sponsor and equip athletic teams for underprivileged children in the community. Each of the three creators makes small cash contributions to Y. A, B, and C have been active participants in the affairs of Y since its creation. Y regularly raises small amounts of contributions through fundraising drives and selling admission to some of the sponsored sporting events. The operations of Y are carried out on a small scale, usually being restricted to the sponsorship of two to four baseball teams of underprivileged children. In 2009, M recapitalizes and creates a first and second class of 6 percent nonvoting preferred stock, most of which is held by A and B. In 2010, A contributes 49 percent of his common stock in M to Y. A's contribution of M's common stock was substantial and constitutes 90 percent of Y's total support for 2010. A combination of the facts and circumstances described in paragraph (c)(4) of this section preclude A's contribution of M's common stock in 2010 from being excluded as an unusual grant under paragraph (c)(3) of this section for purposes of determining whether Y meets the one-third support test under section 509(a)(2).

Example 4. (i) M is organized in 2009 to promote the appreciation of ballet in a particular region of the United States. Its principal activities consist of erecting a theater for the performance of ballet and the organization and operation of a ballet company. M receives a determination letter that it is an organization described in section 501(c)(3) and that it is a public charity described in section 509(a)(2). The governing body of M consists of 9 prominent unrelated citizens residing in the region who have either an expertise in ballet or a strong interest in encouraging appreciation of the art form.

(ii) In 2010, Z, a private foundation, proposes to makes a grant of $500,000 in cash to M to provide sufficient capital for M to commence its activities. Although A, the creator of Z, is one of the nine members of M's governing body, was one of M's original founders, and continues to lend his prestige to M's activities and fund raising efforts, A does not, directly or indirectly, exercise any control over M. M also receives a significant amount of support from a number of smaller contributions and pledges from other members of the general public. M charges admission to the ballet performances to the general public.

(iii) Although the support received in 2010 will not impact M's status as a public charity for its first 5 taxable years, it will be relevant to the determination of whether M meets the one-third support test under section 509(a)(2) for the 2014 taxable year, using the computation period 2010 through 2014. Within the appropriate timeframe, M may submit a request for a private letter ruling that the $500,000 contribution from Z qualifies as an unusual grant.

(iv) Under the above circumstances, even though A was a founder and member of the governing body of M, M may exclude Z's contribution of $500,000 in 2010 as an unusual grant under paragraph (c)(3) of this section for purposes of determining whether M meets the one-third support test under section 509(a)(2) for 2014.

Example 5. (i) Assume the same facts as Example 4. In 2013, B, a widow, passes away and bequeaths $4 million to M. During 2009 through 2013, B made small contributions to M, none exceeding $10,000 in any year. During 2009 through 2013, M received approximately $550,000 from receipts for admissions and contributions from the general public. At the time of B's death, no person standing in a relationship to B described in section 4946(a)(1)(C) through (G) was a member of M's governing body. B's bequest was in the form of cash and readily marketable securities. The only condition placed upon the bequest was that it be used by M to advance the art of ballet.

(ii) Although the support received in 2013 will not impact M's status as a public charity for its first five taxable years, it will be relevant to the determination of whether M meets the one-third support test under section 509(a)(2) for future years. Within the appropriate timeframe, M may submit a request for a private letter ruling that the $4 million bequest from B qualifies as an unusual grant.

(iii) Under the above circumstances, M may exclude B's bequest of $4 million in 2013 as an unusual grant under paragraph (c)(3) of this section for purposes of determining whether M meets the one-third support test under section 509(a)(2) for 2014 and subsequent years.

Example 6. (i) N is a research organization that was created by A in 2009 for the purpose of carrying on economic studies primarily through persons receiving grants from N and engaging in the sale of economic publications. N received a determination letter that it is described in section 501(c)(3) and that it is a public charity described in 509(a)(2). N's five-member governing body consists of A, A's sons, B and C, and two unrelated economists. In 2009, A made a contribution to N of $100,000 to help establish the organization. During 2009 through 2013, A made annual contributions to N averaging $20,000 a year. During the same period, N received annual contributions from members of the general public averaging $15,000 per year and receipts from the sale of its publications averaging $50,000 per year. In 2013, B made an inter vivos contribution to N of $600,000 in cash and readily marketable securities.

(ii) Although the support received in 2013 will not impact N's status as a public charity for its first 5 taxable years, it will be relevant to the determination of whether N meets the one-third support test under section 509(a)(2) for future years. In determining whether B's contribution of $600,000 in 2013 may be excluded as an unusual grant, the support N received in 2009 through 2013 is relevant in considering the factor described in paragraph (c)(4)(vi) of this section, notwithstanding that N received a determination letter that it is described in section 509(a)(2).

(iii) Based on the application of the factors in paragraphs (c)(4)(i) through (ix) of this section to N's circumstances, in particular the facts that B is a disqualified person described in section 4946(a)(1)(D) and N does not have a representative governing body as described in paragraphs (c)(4)(viii) and (d)(3)(i) of this section, N cannot exclude B's contribution of $600,000 in 2013 as an unusual grant under paragraph (c)(3) of this section for purposes of determining whether N meets the one-third support test under section 509(a)(2) for 2014 and future years.

Example 7. (i) O is an educational organization created in 2009. O received a determination letter that it is described in section 501(c)(3) and that it is a public charity described in section 509(a)(2). The governing body of O has 9 members, consisting of A, a prominent civic leader and 8 other unrelated civic leaders and educators in the community, all of whom participated in the creation of O. During 2009 through 2013, the principal source of income for O has been receipts from the sale of its educational periodicals. These sales have amounted to $200,000 for this period. Small contributions amounting to $50,000 have also been received during the same period from members of the governing body, including A, as well as other members of the general public.

(ii) In 2013, A contributed $750,000 of the nonvoting stock of S, a closely held corporation, to O. A retained a substantial portion of the voting stock of S. By a majority vote, the governing body of O decided to retain the S stock for a period of at least 5 years.

(iii) Although the support received in 2013 will not impact O's status as a public charity for its first 5 taxable years, it will be relevant to the determination of whether O meets the one-third support test under section 509(a)(2) for future years. In determining whether A's contribution of the S stock in 2013 may be excluded as an unusual grant, the support O received in 2009 through 2013 is relevant in considering the factor described in paragraph (c)(4)(vi) of this section, notwithstanding that O received a determination letter that it is described in section 509(a)(2).

(iv) Based on the application of the factors in paragraphs (c)(4)(i) through (ix) of this section to O's circumstances, in particular the facts that A is a foundation manager within the meaning of section 4946(b) and A's contribution is in the form of closely held stock, O cannot exclude A's contribution of the S stock in 2013 as an unusual grant under paragraph (c)(3) of this section for purposes of determining whether O meets the one-third support test under section 509(a)(2) for 2014 and future years.

(d) Definition of normally--first five years of an organization's existence-- (1) In general. An organization meets the one-third support test and the not-more-than-one-third support test during its first five taxable years as a section 501(c)(3) organization if the organization can reasonably be expected to meet the requirements of the one-third support test and the not-more-than-one-third support test during that period. With respect to such organization's sixth taxable year, the organization shall be described in section 509(a)(2) if it meets the one-third support test and the not-more-than-one-third support test under the definition of normally set forth in paragraph (c)(1)(i) of this section for its sixth taxable year (based on support received in its second through sixth taxable years), or for its fifth taxable year (based on support received in its first through fifth taxable years).

(2) Basic consideration. In determining whether an organization can reasonably be expected (within the meaning of paragraph (c)(1)(i) of this section) to meet the one-third support test under section 509(a)(2)(A) and the not-more-than-one-third support test under section 509(a)(2)(B) described in paragraph (c) of this section during its first 5 taxable years, the basic consideration is whether its organizational structure, current or proposed programs or activities, and actual or intended method of operation are such as to attract the type of broadly based support from the general public, public charities, and governmental units that is necessary to meet such tests. The factors that are relevant to this determination, and the weight accorded to each of them, may differ from case to case, depending on the nature and functions of the organization. An organization cannot reasonably be expected to meet the one-third support test and the not-more-than-one-third support test where the facts indicate that an organization is likely during its first five taxable years to receive less than one-third of its support from permitted sources (subject to the limitations of paragraph (b) of this section) or to receive more than one-third of its support from items described in section 509(a)(2)(B).

(3) Factors taken into account. All pertinent facts and circumstances shall be taken into account under paragraph (d)(2) of this section in determining whether the organizational structure, programs or activities, and method of operation of an organization are such as to enable it to meet the tests under section 509(a)(2) during its first five taxable years. Some of the pertinent factors are:

(i) Whether the organization has or will have a governing body which is comprised of public officials, or individuals chosen by public officials acting in their capacity as such, of persons having special knowledge in the particular field or discipline in which the organization is operating, of community leaders, such as elected officials, clergymen, and educators, or, in the case of a membership organization, of individuals elected pursuant to the organization's governing instrument or bylaws by a broadly based membership. This characteristic does not exist if the membership of the organization's governing body is such as to indicate that it represents the personal or private interests of disqualified persons, rather than the interests of the community or the general public.

(ii) Whether a substantial portion of the organization's initial funding is to be provided by the general public, by public charities, or by government grants, rather than by a limited number of grantors or contributors who are disqualified persons with respect to the organization. The fact that the organization plans to limit its activities to a particular community or region or to a special field which can be expected to appeal to a limited number of persons will be taken into consideration in determining whether those persons providing the initial support for the organization are representative of the general public. On the other hand, the subsequent sources of funding which the organization can reasonably expect to receive after it has become established and fully operational will also be taken into account.

(iii) Whether a substantial proportion of the organization's initial funds are placed, or will remain, in an endowment, and whether the investment of such funds is unlikely to result in more than one-third of its total support being received from items described in section 509(a)(2)(B).

(iv) In the case of an organization that carries on fundraising activities, whether the organization has developed a concrete plan for solicitation of funds from the general public on a community or area-wide basis; whether any steps have been taken to implement such plan; whether any firm commitments of financial or other support have been made to the organization by civic, religious, charitable, or similar groups within the community; and whether the organization has made any commitments to, or established any working relationships with, those organizations or classes of persons intended as the future recipients of its funds.

(v) In the case of an organization that carries on community services, such as combating community deterioration in an economically depressed area that has suffered a major loss of population and jobs, whether the organization has a concrete program to carry out its work in the community; whether any steps have been taken to implement that program; whether it will receive any part of its funds from a public charity or governmental agency to which it is in some way held accountable as a condition of the grant or contribution; and whether it has enlisted the sponsorship or support of other civic or community leaders involved in community service programs similar to those of the organization.

(vi) In the case of an organization that carries on educational or other exempt activities for, or on behalf of, members, whether the solicitation for dues-paying members is designed to enroll a substantial number of persons in the community, area, profession, or field of special interest (depending on the size of the area and the nature of the organization's activities); whether membership dues for individual (rather than institutional) members have been fixed at rates designed to make membership available to a broad cross-section of the public rather than to restrict membership to a limited number of persons; and whether the activities of the organization will be likely to appeal to persons having some broad common interest or purpose, such as educational activities in the case of alumni associations, musical activities in the case of symphony societies, or civic affairs in the case of parent-teacher associations.

(vii) In the case of an organization that provides goods, services, or facilities, whether the organization is or will be required to make its services, facilities, performances, or products available (regardless of whether a fee is charged) to the general public, public charities, or governmental units, rather than to a limited number of persons or organizations; whether the organization will avoid executing contracts to perform services for a limited number of firms or governmental agencies or bureaus; and whether the service to be provided is one which can be expected to meet a special or general need among a substantial portion of the general public.

(4) Example. The application of this paragraph (d) may be illustrated by the following example:

Example. (i) Organization X was formed in January 2008 and uses a December 31 taxable year. After September 9, 2008, and before December 31, 2008, Organization X filed Form 1023 requesting recognition of exemption as an organization described in section 501(c)(3) and in section 509(a)(2). In its application, Organization X established that it can reasonably be expected to operate as a public charity under this paragraph (d). Subsequently, Organization X received a ruling or determination letter that it is an organization described in sections 501(c)(3) and 509(a)(2) effective as of the date of its formation.

(ii) Organization X is described in section 509(a)(2) for its first 5 taxable years (for the taxable years ending December 31, 2008, through December 31, 2012).

(iii) Organization X can qualify as a public charity beginning with the taxable year ending December 31, 2013, if Organization X can meet the requirements of § 1.170A-9T(f)(4)(i) through (iii) or paragraphs (a) through (b) of this section for the taxable years ending December 31, 2009, through December 31, 2013, or for the taxable years ending December 31, 2008, through December 31, 2012.

FORM 990

Form **990**

Return of Organization Exempt From Income Tax

Under section 501(c), 527, or 4947(a)(1) of the Internal Revenue Code (except black lung benefit trust or private foundation)

Department of the Treasury
Internal Revenue Service

▶ The organization may have to use a copy of this return to satisfy state reporting requirements.

OMB No. 1545-0047

2008

Open to Public Inspection

A For the 2008 calendar year, or tax year beginning _____, 2008, and ending _____, 20____

B Check if applicable:	Please use IRS label or print or type. See Specific Instruc- tions.	**C** Name of organization		**D** Employer identification number
☐ Address change		Doing Business As		
☐ Name change		Number and street (or P.O. box if mail is not delivered to street address)	Room/suite	**E** Telephone number ( )
☐ Initial return				
☐ Termination		City or town, state or country, and ZIP + 4		
☐ Amended return				**G** Gross receipts $
☐ Application pending				

F Name and address of principal officer:

H(a) Is this a group return for affiliates? ☐ Yes ☐ No
H(b) Are all affiliates included? ☐ Yes ☐ No
If "No," attach a list. (see instructions)

I Tax-exempt status: ☐ 501(c) ( )◀ (insert no.) ☐ 4947(a)(1) or ☐ 527

J Website: ▶

H(c) Group exemption number ▶

K Type of organization: ☐ Corporation ☐ Trust ☐ Association ☐ Other ▶   **L** Year of formation: **M** State of legal domicile:

Part I   Summary

Activities & Governance

1 Briefly describe the organization's mission or most significant activities: ....

....

....

....

2 Check this box ▶ ☐ if the organization discontinued its operations or disposed of more than 25% of its assets.

3 Number of voting members of the governing body (Part VI, line 1a)	**3**	
4 Number of independent voting members of the governing body (Part VI, line 1b)	**4**	
5 Total number of employees (Part V, line 2a)	**5**	
6 Total number of volunteers (estimate if necessary)	**6**	
7a Total gross unrelated business revenue from Part VIII, line 12, column (C).	**7a**	
b Net unrelated business taxable income from Form 990-T, line 34.	**7b**	

Revenue		Prior Year	Current Year
8 Contributions and grants (Part VIII, line 1h)			
9 Program service revenue (Part VIII, line 2g)			
10 Investment income (Part VIII, column (A), lines 3, 4, and 7d)			
11 Other revenue (Part VIII, column (A), lines 5, 6d, 8c, 9c, 10c, and 11e) . .			
12 Total revenue—add lines 8 through 11 (must equal Part VIII, column (A), line 12)			

Expenses			
13 Grants and similar amounts paid (Part IX, column (A), lines 1–3)			
14 Benefits paid to or for members (Part IX, column (A), line 4)			
15 Salaries, other compensation, employee benefits (Part IX, column (A), lines 5–10)			
16a Professional fundraising fees (Part IX, column (A), line 11e)			
b Total fundraising expenses (Part IX, column (D), line 25) ▶			
17 Other expenses (Part IX, column (A), lines 11a–11d, 11f–24f)			
18 Total expenses. Add lines 13–17 (must equal Part IX, column (A), line 25). .			
19 Revenue less expenses. Subtract line 18 from line 12			

Net Assets or Fund Balances		Beginning of Year	End of Year
20 Total assets (Part X, line 16)			
21 Total liabilities (Part X, line 26)			
22 Net assets or fund balances. Subtract line 21 from line 20			

Part II   Signature Block

Under penalties of perjury, I declare that I have examined this return, including accompanying schedules and statements, and to the best of my knowledge and belief, it is true, correct, and complete. Declaration of preparer (other than officer) is based on all information of which preparer has any knowledge.

Sign Here

▶ _____   _____
Signature of officer   Date

_____
Type or print name and title

Paid Preparer's Use Only

Preparer's signature ▶		Date	Check if self-employed ▶ ☐	Preparer's identifying number (see instructions)
Firm's name (or yours if self-employed), address, and ZIP + 4 ▶			EIN ▶	
			Phone no. ▶ ( )	

May the IRS discuss this return with the preparer shown above? (see instructions) . . . . ☐ Yes ☐ No

For Privacy Act and Paperwork Reduction Act Notice, see the separate instructions.   Cat. No. 11282Y   Form **990** (2008)

Part III	**Statement of Program Service Accomplishments** (see instructions)

1   Briefly describe the organization's mission:

----

2   Did the organization undertake any significant program services during the year which were not listed on
the prior Form 990 or 990-EZ? .   .   .   .   ☐ **Yes** ☐ **No**
If "Yes," describe these new services on Schedule O.

3   Did the organization cease conducting, or make significant changes in how it conducts, any program
services? .   .   .   .   ☐ **Yes** ☐ **No**
If "Yes," describe these changes on Schedule O.

4   Describe the exempt purpose achievements for each of the organization's three largest program services by expenses.
Section 501(c)(3) and 501(c)(4) organizations and section 4947(a)(1) trusts are required to report the amount of grants and
allocations to others, the total expenses, and revenue, if any, for each program service reported.

4a (Code: _____) (Expenses $ _____ including grants of $_____) (Revenue $ _____)

4b (Code: _____) (Expenses $ _____ including grants of $_____) (Revenue $ _____)

4c (Code: _____) (Expenses $ _____ including grants of $_____) (Revenue $ _____)

4d Other program services. (Describe in Schedule O.)
(Expenses $ including grants of $) (Revenue $)

4e **Total program service expenses ▶ $**   *(Must equal Part IX, Line 25, column (B).)*

Form **990** (2008)

Part IV	**Checklist of Required Schedules**			

			Yes	No
1	Is the organization described in section 501(c)(3) or 4947(a)(1) (other than a private foundation)? *If "Yes," complete Schedule A*	1		
2	Is the organization required to complete Schedule B, Schedule of Contributors?.	2		
3	Did the organization engage in direct or indirect political campaign activities on behalf of or in opposition to candidates for public office? *If "Yes," complete Schedule C, Part I*	3		
4	**Section 501(c)(3) organizations.** Did the organization engage in lobbying activities? *If "Yes," complete Schedule C, Part II*	4		
5	**Section 501(c)(4), 501(c)(5), and 501(c)(6) organizations.** Is the organization subject to the section 6033(e) notice and reporting requirement and proxy tax? *If "Yes," complete Schedule C, Part III*	5		
6	Did the organization maintain any donor advised funds or any accounts where donors have the right to provide advice on the distribution or investment of amounts in such funds or accounts? *If "Yes," complete Schedule D, Part I*	6		
7	Did the organization receive or hold a conservation easement, including easements to preserve open space, the environment, historic land areas, or historic structures? *If "Yes," complete Schedule D, Part II* . . .	7		
8	Did the organization maintain collections of works of art, historical treasures, or other similar assets? *If "Yes," complete Schedule D, Part III*	8		
9	Did the organization report an amount in Part X, line 21; serve as a custodian for amounts not listed in Part X; or provide credit counseling, debt management, credit repair, or debt negotiation services? *If "Yes," complete Schedule D, Part IV*	9		
10	Did the organization hold assets in term, permanent, or quasi-endowments? *If "Yes," complete Schedule D, Part V*	10		
11	Did the organization report an amount in Part X, lines 10, 12, 13, 15, or 25? *If "Yes," complete Schedule D, Parts VI, VII, VIII, IX, or X as applicable*	11		
12	Did the organization receive an audited financial statement for the year for which it is completing this return that was prepared in accordance with GAAP? *If "Yes," complete Schedule D, Parts XI, XII, and XIII* . . .	12		
13	Is the organization a school described in section 170(b)(1)(A)(ii)? *If "Yes," complete Schedule E*	13		
14a	Did the organization maintain an office, employees, or agents outside of the U.S.?	14a		
b	Did the organization have aggregate revenues or expenses of more than $10,000 from grantmaking, fundraising, business, and program service activities outside the U.S.? *If "Yes," complete Schedule F, Part I*	14b		
15	Did the organization report on Part IX, column (A), line 3, more than $5,000 of grants or assistance to any organization or entity located outside the United States? *If "Yes," complete Schedule F, Part II.*	15		
16	Did the organization report on Part IX, column (A), line 3, more than $5,000 of aggregate grants or assistance to individuals located outside the United States? *If "Yes," complete Schedule F, Part III*	16		
17	Did the organization report more than $15,000 on Part IX, column (A), line 11e? *If "Yes," complete Schedule G, Part I*	17		
18	Did the organization report more than $15,000 total on Part VIII, lines 1c and 8a? *If "Yes," complete Schedule G, Part II*	18		
19	Did the organization report more than $15,000 on Part VIII, line 9a? *If "Yes," complete Schedule G, Part III*	19		
20	Did the organization operate one or more hospitals? *If "Yes," complete Schedule H*	20		
21	Did the organization report more than $5,000 on Part IX, column (A), line 1? *If "Yes," complete Schedule I, Parts I and II*	21	.	
22	Did the organization report more than $5,000 on Part IX, column (A), line 2? *If "Yes," complete Schedule I, Parts I and III*	22		
23	Did the organization answer "Yes" to Part VII, Section A, questions 3, 4, or 5? *If "Yes," complete Schedule J*	23		
24a	Did the organization have a tax-exempt bond issue with an outstanding principal amount of more than $100,000 as of the last day of the year, that was issued after December 31, 2002? *If "Yes," answer questions 24b–24d and complete Schedule K. If "No," go to question 25.*	24a		
b	Did the organization invest any proceeds of tax-exempt bonds beyond a temporary period exception? . .	24b		
c	Did the organization maintain an escrow account other than a refunding escrow at any time during the year to defease any tax-exempt bonds?	24c		
d	Did the organization act as an "on behalf of" issuer for bonds outstanding at any time during the year?	24d		
25a	**Section 501(c)(3) and 501(c)(4) organizations.** Did the organization engage in an excess benefit transaction with a disqualified person during the year? *If "Yes," complete Schedule L, Part I*	25a		
b	Did the organization become aware that it had engaged in an excess benefit transaction with a disqualified person from a prior year? *If "Yes," complete Schedule L, Part I*	25b		
26	Was a loan to or by a current or former officer, director, trustee, key employee, highly compensated employee, or disqualified person outstanding as of the end of the organization's tax year? *If "Yes," complete Schedule L, Part II* . .	26		
27	Did the organization provide a grant or other assistance to an officer, director, trustee, key employee, or substantial contributor, or to a person related to such an individual? *If "Yes," complete Schedule L, Part III*	27		

Form 990 (2008)   Page **4**

Part IV	Checklist of Required Schedules *(continued)*			
			Yes	No
28	During the tax year, did any person who is a current or former officer, director, trustee, or key employee:			
a	Have a direct business relationship with the organization (other than as an officer, director, trustee, or employee), or an indirect business relationship through ownership of more than 35% in another entity (individually or collectively with other person(s) listed in Part VII, Section A)? *If "Yes," complete Schedule L, Part IV*	**28a**		
b	Have a family member who had a direct or indirect business relationship with the organization? *If "Yes," complete Schedule L, Part IV*	**28b**		
c	Serve as an officer, director, trustee, key employee, partner, or member of an entity (or a shareholder of a professional corporation) doing business with the organization? *If "Yes," complete Schedule L, Part IV* . .	**28c**		
29	Did the organization receive more than $25,000 in non-cash contributions? *If "Yes," complete Schedule M*	**29**		
30	Did the organization receive contributions of art, historical treasures, or other similar assets, or qualified conservation contributions? *If "Yes," complete Schedule M*	**30**		
31	Did the organization liquidate, terminate, or dissolve and cease operations? *If "Yes," complete Schedule N, Part I*	**31**		
32	Did the organization sell, exchange, dispose of, or transfer more than 25% of its net assets? *If "Yes," complete Schedule N, Part II*	**32**		
33	Did the organization own 100% of an entity disregarded as separate from the organization under Regulations sections 301.7701-2 and 301.7701-3? *If "Yes," complete Schedule R, Part I*	**33**		
34	Was the organization related to any tax-exempt or taxable entity? *If "Yes," complete Schedule R, Parts II, III, IV, and V, line 1*	**34**		
35	Is any related organization a controlled entity within the meaning of section 512(b)(13)? *If "Yes," complete Schedule R, Part V, line 2*	**35**		
36	**Section 501(c)(3) organizations.** Did the organization make any transfers to an exempt non-charitable related organization? *If "Yes," complete Schedule R, Part V, line 2*	**36**		
37	Did the organization conduct more than 5% of its activities through an entity that is not a related organization and that is treated as a partnership for federal income tax purposes? *If "Yes," complete Schedule R, Part VI*	**37**		

Form **990** (2008)

Form 990 (2008)   Page **5**

Part V	**Statements Regarding Other IRS Filings and Tax Compliance**		
		Yes	No

1a Enter the number reported in Box 3 of Form 1096, Annual Summary and Transmittal of U.S. Information Returns. Enter -0- if not applicable . . . . | **1a** |

  b Enter the number of Forms W-2G included in line 1a. Enter -0- if not applicable . . | **1b** |

  c Did the organization comply with backup withholding rules for reportable payments to vendors and reportable gaming (gambling) winnings to prize winners? . . . . | **1c** |

2a Enter the number of employees reported on Form W-3, Transmittal of Wage and Tax Statements, filed for the calendar year ending with or within the year covered by this return | **2a** |

  b If at least one is reported on line 2a, did the organization file all required federal employment tax returns? | **2b** |

  Note. If the sum of lines 1a and 2a is greater than 250, you may be required to *e-file* this return. (see instructions)

3a Did the organization have unrelated business gross income of $1,000 or more during the year covered by this return? . . . . | **3a** |

  b If "Yes," has it filed a Form 990-T for this year? *If "No," provide an explanation in Schedule O* . . . . | **3b** |

4a At any time during the calendar year, did the organization have an interest in, or a signature or other authority over, a financial account in a foreign country (such as a bank account, securities account, or other financial account)? . . . . | **4a** |

  b If "Yes," enter the name of the foreign country: ▶ ....
See the instructions for exceptions and filing requirements for Form TD F 90-22.1, Report of Foreign Bank and Financial Accounts.

5a Was the organization a party to a prohibited tax shelter transaction at any time during the tax year? . . | **5a** |

  b Did any taxable party notify the organization that it was or is a party to a prohibited tax shelter transaction? | **5b** |

  c If "Yes," to question 5a or 5b, did the organization file Form 8886-T, Disclosure by Tax-Exempt Entity Regarding Prohibited Tax Shelter Transaction? . . . . | **5c** |

6a Did the organization solicit any contributions that were not tax deductible? . . . . | **6a** |

  b If "Yes," did the organization include with every solicitation an express statement that such contributions or gifts were not tax deductible?. . . . . | **6b** |

7 **Organizations that may receive deductible contributions under section 170(c).**

  a Did the organization provide goods or services in exchange for any quid pro quo contribution of more than $75? . . . . | **7a** |

  b If "Yes," did the organization notify the donor of the value of the goods or services provided? . . . . | **7b** |

  c Did the organization sell, exchange, or otherwise dispose of tangible personal property for which it was required to file Form 8282? . . . . | **7c** |

  d If "Yes," indicate the number of Forms 8282 filed during the year . . . . | **7d** |

  e Did the organization, during the year, receive any funds, directly or indirectly, to pay premiums on a personal benefit contract? . . . . | **7e** |

  f Did the organization, during the year, pay premiums, directly or indirectly, on a personal benefit contract? | **7f** |

  g For all contributions of qualified intellectual property, did the organization file Form 8899 as required? . | **7g** |

  h For contributions of cars, boats, airplanes, and other vehicles, did the organization file a Form 1098-C as required?. . . . . | **7h** |

8 **Section 501(c)(3) and other sponsoring organizations maintaining donor advised funds and section 509(a)(3) supporting organizations.** Did the supporting organization, or a fund maintained by a sponsoring organization, have excess business holdings at any time during the year? . . . . | **8** |

9 **Section 501(c)(3) and other sponsoring organizations maintaining donor advised funds.**

  a Did the organization make any taxable distributions under section 4966? . . . . | **9a** |

  b Did the organization make a distribution to a donor, donor advisor, or related person?. . . . . . | **9b** |

10 **Section 501(c)(7) organizations.** Enter:

  a Initiation fees and capital contributions included on Part VIII, line 12 . . . . | **10a** |

  b Gross receipts, included on Form 990, Part VIII, line 12, for public use of club facilities | **10b** |

11 **Section 501(c)(12) organizations.** Enter:

  a Gross income from members or shareholders . . . . | **11a** |

  b Gross income from other sources (Do not net amounts due or paid to other sources against amounts due or received from them.) . . . . | **11b** |

12a **Section 4947(a)(1) non-exempt charitable trusts.** Is the organization filing Form 990 in lieu of Form 1041? | **12a** |

  b If "Yes," enter the amount of tax-exempt interest received or accrued during the year . | **12b** |

Form **990** (2008)

Part VI **Governance, Management, and Disclosure** *(Sections A, B, and C request information about policies not required by the Internal Revenue Code.)*

Section A. Governing Body and Management

		Yes	No
	For each "Yes" response to lines 2–7b below, and for a "No" response to lines 8 or 9b below, describe the circumstances, processes, or changes in Schedule O. See instructions.		
1a	Enter the number of voting members of the governing body **1a**		
b	Enter the number of voting members that are independent **1b**		
2	Did any officer, director, trustee, or key employee have a family relationship or a business relationship with any other officer, director, trustee, or key employee? **2**		
3	Did the organization delegate control over management duties customarily performed by or under the direct supervision of officers, directors or trustees, or key employees to a management company or other person? . **3**		
4	Did the organization make any significant changes to its organizational documents since the prior Form 990 was filed? **4**		
5	Did the organization become aware during the year of a material diversion of the organization's assets? **5**		
6	Does the organization have members or stockholders? **6**		
7a	Does the organization have members, stockholders, or other persons who may elect one or more members of the governing body? **7a**		
b	Are any decisions of the governing body subject to approval by members, stockholders, or other persons? . . **7b**		
8	Did the organization contemporaneously document the meetings held or written actions undertaken during the year by the following:		
a	The governing body? **8a**		
b	Each committee with authority to act on behalf of the governing body? **8b**		
9a	Does the organization have local chapters, branches, or affiliates? **9a**		
b	If "Yes," does the organization have written policies and procedures governing the activities of such chapters, affiliates, and branches to ensure their operations are consistent with those of the organization? **9b**		
10	Was a copy of the Form 990 provided to the organization's governing body before it was filed? All organizations must describe in Schedule O the process, if any, the organization uses to review the Form 990 ...... **10**		
11	Is there any officer, director or trustee, or key employee listed in Part VII, Section A, who cannot be reached at the organization's mailing address? *If "Yes," provide the names and addresses in Schedule O* **11**		

Section B. Policies

		Yes	No
12a	Does the organization have a written conflict of interest policy? *If "No," go to line 13* **12a**		
b	Are officers, directors or trustees, and key employees required to disclose annually interests that could give rise to conflicts? **12b**		
c	Does the organization regularly and consistently monitor and enforce compliance with the policy? *If "Yes," describe in Schedule O how this is done* **12c**		
13	Does the organization have a written whistleblower policy? **13**		
14	Does the organization have a written document retention and destruction policy? **14**		
15	Did the process for determining compensation of the following persons include a review and approval by independent persons, comparability data, and contemporaneous substantiation of the deliberation and decision:		
a	The organization's CEO, Executive Director, or top management official? **15a**		
b	Other officers or key employees of the organization? **15b**		
	Describe the process in Schedule O. (see instructions)		
16a	Did the organization invest in, contribute assets to, or participate in a joint venture or similar arrangement with a taxable entity during the year? **16a**		
b	If "Yes," has the organization adopted a written policy or procedure requiring the organization to evaluate its participation in joint venture arrangements under applicable federal tax law, and taken steps to safeguard the organization's exempt status with respect to such arrangements? **16b**		

Section C. Disclosure

17   List the states with which a copy of this Form 990 is required to be filed ▶--

18   Section 6104 requires an organization to make its Forms 1023 (or 1024 if applicable), 990, and 990-T (501(c)(3)s only) available for public inspection. Indicate how you make these available. Check all that apply.
☐ Own website   ☐ Another's website   ☐ Upon request

19   Describe in Schedule O whether (and if so, how), the organization makes its governing documents, conflict of interest policy, and financial statements available to the public.

20   State the name, physical address, and telephone number of the person who possesses the books and records of the organization: ▶ ---

Form **990** (2008)

Part VII Compensation of Officers, Directors, Trustees, Key Employees, Highest Compensated Employees, and Independent Contractors

Section A. Officers, Directors, Trustees, Key Employees, and Highest Compensated Employees

1a Complete this table for all persons required to be listed. Use Schedule J-2 if additional space is needed.

● List all of the organization's **current** officers, directors, trustees (whether individuals or organizations), regardless of amount of compensation. Enter -0- in columns (D), (E), and (F) if no compensation was paid.

● List the organization's five **current** highest compensated employees (other than an officer, director, trustee, or key employee) who received reportable compensation (Box 5 of Form W-2 and/or Box 7 of Form 1099-MISC) of more than $100,000 from the organization and any related organizations.

● List all of the organization's **former** officers, key employees, and highest compensated employees who received more than $100,000 of reportable compensation from the organization and any related organizations.

● List all of the organization's **former directors or trustees** that received, in the capacity as a former director or trustee of the organization, more than $10,000 of reportable compensation from the organization and any related organizations.

List persons in the following order: individual trustees or directors; institutional trustees; officers; key employees; highest compensated employees; and former such persons.

☐ Check this box if the organization did not compensate any officer, director, trustee, or key employee.

(A) Name and Title	(B) Average hours per week	(C) Position (check all that apply)						(D) Reportable compensation from the organization (W-2/1099-MISC)	(E) Reportable compensation from related organizations (W-2/1099-MISC)	(F) Estimated amount of other compensation from the organization and related organizations
		Individual trustee or director	Institutional trustee	Officer	Key employee	Highest compensated employee	Former			

Form **990** (2008)

Form 990 (2008)   Page **8**

| Part VII | Section A. Officers, Directors, Trustees, Key Employees, and Highest Compensated Employees *(continued)* |

(A) Name and title	(B) Average hours per week	(C) Position (check all that apply)						(D) Reportable compensation from the organization (W-2/1099-MISC)	(E) Reportable compensation from related organizations (W-2/1099-MISC)	(F) Estimated amount of other compensation from the organization and related organizations
		Individual trustee or director	Institutional trustee	Officer	Key employee	Highest compensated employee	Former			

1b Total . . . . ▶

2   Total number of individuals (including those in 1a) who received more than $100,000 in reportable compensation from the organization ▶

		Yes	No
3	Did the organization list any **former** officer, director or trustee, key employee, or highest compensated employee on line 1a? *If "Yes," complete Schedule J for such individual*	3	
4	For any individual listed on line 1a, is the sum of reportable compensation and other compensation from the organization and related organizations greater than $150,000? *If "Yes," complete Schedule J for such individual.*	4	
5	Did any person listed on line 1a receive or accrue compensation from any unrelated organization for services rendered to the organization? *If "Yes," complete Schedule J for such person*	5	

Section B. Independent Contractors

1   Complete this table for your five highest compensated independent contractors that received more than $100,000 of compensation from the organization.

(A) Name and business address	(B) Description of services	(C) Compensation

2   Total number of independent contractors (including those in 1) who received more than $100,000 in compensation from the organization ▶

Form **990** (2008)

Form 990 (2008)   Page **9**

Part VIII	Statement of Revenue					(A) Total revenue	(B) Related or exempt function revenue	(C) Unrelated business revenue	(D) Revenue excluded from tax under sections 512, 513, or 514

Contributions, gifts, grants and other similar amounts

1a	Federated campaigns			1a					
b	Membership dues			1b					
c	Fundraising events			1c					
d	Related organizations			1d					
e	Government grants (contributions)			1e					
f	All other contributions, gifts, grants, and similar amounts not included above			1f					
g	Noncash contributions included in lines 1a-1f: $								
h	**Total.** Add lines 1a–1f . . . . . . ▶								

Program Service Revenue

		Business Code					
2a	....						
b	....						
c	....						
d	....						
e	....						
f	All other program service revenue .						
g	**Total.** Add lines 2a–2f . . . . ▶						

Other Revenue

3	Investment income (including dividends, interest, and other similar amounts) . . . . ▶						
4	Income from investment of tax-exempt bond proceeds ▶						
5	Royalties . . . . ▶						

		(i) Real	(ii) Personal				
6a	Gross Rents . .						
b	Less: rental expenses						
c	Rental income or (loss)						
d	Net rental income or (loss) . . . . ▶						

		(i) Securities	(ii) Other				
7a	Gross amount from sales of assets other than inventory						
b	Less: cost or other basis and sales expenses .						
c	Gain or (loss) . .						
d	Net gain or (loss) . . . . ▶						

8a	Gross income from fundraising events (not including $ .... of contributions reported on line 1c). See Part IV, line 18 . . . . . . a					
b	Less: direct expenses . . . . . b					
c	Net income or (loss) from fundraising events . . ▶					
9a	Gross income from gaming activities. See Part IV, line 19 . . . . . a					
b	Less: direct expenses. . . . . b					
c	Net income or (loss) from gaming activities . . ▶					
10a	Gross sales of inventory, less returns and allowances . . . . a					
b	Less: cost of goods sold . . . b					
c	Net income or (loss) from sales of inventory . . . ▶					

	Miscellaneous Revenue	Business Code				
11a	....					
b	....					
c	....					
d	All other revenue					
e	**Total.** Add lines 11a–11d . . . . ▶					
12	**Total Revenue.** Add lines 1h, 2g, 3, 4, 5, 6d, 7d, 8c, 9c, 10c, and 11e . . . . ▶					

Form **990** (2008)

Part IX	**Statement of Functional Expenses**			

Section 501(c)(3) and 501(c)(4) organizations must complete all columns.

All other organizations must complete column (A) but are not required to complete columns (B), (C), and (D).

Do not include amounts reported on lines 6b, 7b, 8b, 9b, and 10b of Part VIII.	**(A)** Total expenses	**(B)** Program service expenses	**(C)** Management and general expenses	**(D)** Fundraising expenses
1 Grants and other assistance to governments and organizations in the U.S. See Part IV, line 21				
2 Grants and other assistance to individuals in the U.S. See Part IV, line 22				
3 Grants and other assistance to governments, organizations, and individuals outside the U.S. See Part IV, lines 15 and 16 . . .				
4 Benefits paid to or for members				
5 Compensation of current officers, directors, trustees, and key employees				
6 Compensation not included above, to disqualified persons (as defined under section 4958(f)(1)) and persons described in section 4958(c)(3)(B) . .				
7 Other salaries and wages				
8 Pension plan contributions (include section 401(k) and section 403(b) employer contributions) . .				
9 Other employee benefits				
10 Payroll taxes				
11 Fees for services (non-employees):				
a Management				
b Legal				
c Accounting				
d Lobbying				
e Professional fundraising services. See Part IV, line 17				
f Investment management fees				
g Other				
12 Advertising and promotion				
13 Office expenses				
14 Information technology				
15 Royalties				
16 Occupancy				
17 Travel				
18 Payments of travel or entertainment expenses for any federal, state, or local public officials				
19 Conferences, conventions, and meetings .				
20 Interest				
21 Payments to affiliates				
22 Depreciation, depletion, and amortization .				
23 Insurance				
24 Other expenses. Itemize expenses not covered above. (Expenses grouped together and labeled miscellaneous may not exceed 5% of total expenses shown on line 25 below.)				
a				
b				
c				
d				
e				
f All other expenses				
25 **Total functional expenses.** Add lines 1 through 24f				
26 **Joint Costs.** Check here ▶ ☐ if following SOP 98-2. Complete this line only if the organization reported in column (B) joint costs from a combined educational campaign and fundraising solicitation				

Form 990 (2008)   Page **11**

Part X — Balance Sheet

			(A) Beginning of year		(B) End of year
Assets	1	Cash—non-interest-bearing		1	
	2	Savings and temporary cash investments		2	
	3	Pledges and grants receivable, net		3	
	4	Accounts receivable, net		4	
	5	Receivables from current and former officers, directors, trustees, key employees, or other related parties. Complete Part II of Schedule L		5	
	6	Receivables from other disqualified persons (as defined under section 4958(f)(1)) and persons described in section 4958(c)(3)(B). Complete Part II of Schedule L		6	
	7	Notes and loans receivable, net		7	
	8	Inventories for sale or use		8	
	9	Prepaid expenses and deferred charges		9	
	10a	Land, buildings, and equipment: cost basis	10a		
	b	Less: accumulated depreciation. Complete Part VI of Schedule D	10b	10c	
	11	Investments—publicly traded securities		11	
	12	Investments—other securities. See Part IV, line 11		12	
	13	Investments—program-related. See Part IV, line 11		13	
	14	Intangible assets		14	
	15	Other assets. See Part IV, line 11		15	
	16	**Total assets.** Add lines 1 through 15 (must equal line 34)		16	
Liabilities	17	Accounts payable and accrued expenses		17	
	18	Grants payable		18	
	19	Deferred revenue		19	
	20	Tax-exempt bond liabilities		20	
	21	Escrow account liability. Complete Part IV of Schedule D		21	
	22	Payables to current and former officers, directors, trustees, key employees, highest compensated employees, and disqualified persons. Complete Part II of Schedule L		22	
	23	Secured mortgages and notes payable to unrelated third parties		23	
	24	Unsecured notes and loans payable		24	
	25	Other liabilities. Complete Part X of Schedule D		25	
	26	**Total liabilities.** Add lines 17 through 25		26	
Net Assets or Fund Balances		**Organizations that follow SFAS 117, check here ▶ ☐ and complete lines 27 through 29, and lines 33 and 34.**			
	27	Unrestricted net assets		27	
	28	Temporarily restricted net assets		28	
	29	Permanently restricted net assets		29	
		Organizations that do not follow SFAS 117, check here ▶ ☐ and complete lines 30 through 34.			
	30	Capital stock or trust principal, or current funds		30	
	31	Paid-in or capital surplus, or land, building, or equipment fund		31	
	32	Retained earnings, endowment, accumulated income, or other funds		32	
	33	Total net assets or fund balances		33	
	34	Total liabilities and net assets/fund balances		34	

Part XI — Financial Statements and Reporting

		Yes	No
1	Accounting method used to prepare the Form 990: ☐ Cash ☐ Accrual ☐ Other		
2a	Were the organization's financial statements compiled or reviewed by an independent accountant?	2a	
b	Were the organization's financial statements audited by an independent accountant?	2b	
c	If "Yes" to lines 2a or 2b, does the organization have a committee that assumes responsibility for oversight of the audit, review, or compilation of its financial statements and selection of an independent accountant?	2c	
3a	As a result of a federal award, was the organization required to undergo an audit or audits as set forth in the Single Audit Act and OMB Circular A-133?	3a	
b	If "Yes," did the organization undergo the required audit or audits?	3b	

Form **990** (2008)

SCHEDULE A (Form 990 or 990-EZ)	**Public Charity Status and Public Support** To be completed by all section 501(c)(3) organizations and section 4947(a)(1) nonexempt charitable trusts.	OMB No. 1545-0047 20**08**
Department of the Treasury Internal Revenue Service	▶ Attach to Form 990 or Form 990-EZ. ▶ See separate instructions.	**Open to Public Inspection**

Name of the organization	Employer Identification number

| **Part I** | **Reason for Public Charity Status** (All organizations must complete this part.) (see instructions) |

The organization is not a private foundation because it is: (Please check only **one** organization.)

1 ☐ A church, convention of churches, or association of churches described in **section 170(b)(1)(A)(i).**

2 ☐ A school described in **section 170(b)(1)(A)(ii).** (Attach Schedule E.)

3 ☐ A hospital or a cooperative hospital service organization described in **section 170(b)(1)(A)(iii).** (Attach Schedule H.)

4 ☐ A medical research organization operated in conjunction with a hospital described in **section 170(b)(1)(A)(iii).** Enter the hospital's name, city, and state: --

5 ☐ An organization operated for the benefit of a college or university owned or operated by a governmental unit described in **section 170(b)(1)(A)(iv).** (Complete Part II.)

6 ☐ A federal, state, or local government or governmental unit described in **section 170(b)(1)(A)(v).**

7 ☐ An organization that normally receives a substantial part of its support from a governmental unit or from the general public described in **section 170(b)(1)(A)(vi).** (Complete Part II.)

8 ☐ A community trust described in **section 170(b)(1)(A)(vi).** (Complete Part II.)

9 ☐ An organization that normally receives: (1) more than 33⅓ % of its support from contributions, membership fees, and gross receipts from activities related to its exempt functions—subject to certain exceptions, and (2) no more than 33⅓ % of its support from gross investment income and unrelated business taxable income (less section 511 tax) from businesses acquired by the organization after June 30, 1975. See **section 509(a)(2).** (Complete Part III.)

10 ☐ An organization organized and operated exclusively to test for public safety. See **section 509(a)(4).** (see instructions)

11 ☐ An organization organized and operated exclusively for the benefit of, to perform the functions of, or to carry out the purposes of one or more publicly supported organizations described in section 509(a)(1) or section 509(a)(2). See **section 509(a)(3).** Check the box that describes the type of supporting organization and complete lines 11e through 11h.

     a ☐ Type I   **b** ☐ Type II   **c** ☐ Type III–Functionally integrated   **d** ☐ Type III–Other

   e ☐ By checking this box, I certify that the organization is not controlled directly or indirectly by one or more disqualified persons other than foundation managers and other than one or more publicly supported organizations described in section 509(a)(1) or section 509(a)(2).

   f   If the organization received a written determination from the IRS that it is a Type I, Type II, or Type III supporting organization, check this box . . . . ☐

   g   Since August 17, 2006, has the organization accepted any gift or contribution from any of the following persons?

			Yes	No
	(i) A person who directly or indirectly controls, either alone or together with persons described in (ii) and (iii) below, the governing body of the supported organization?	11g(i)		
	(ii) A family member of a person described in (i) above?	11g(ii)		
	(iii) A 35% controlled entity of a person described in (i) or (ii) above?	11g(iii)		

   h   Provide the following information about the organizations the organization supports.

(i) Name of supported organization	(ii) EIN	(iii) Type of organization (described on lines 1–9 above or IRC section (see instructions))	(iv) Is the organization in col. (i) listed in your governing document?		(v) Did you notify the organization in col. (i) of your support?		(vi) Is the organization in col. (i) organized in the U.S.?		(vii) Amount of support
			Yes	No	Yes	No	Yes	No	
Total									

For Privacy Act and Paperwork Reduction Act Notice, see the Instructions for Form 990.   Cat. No. 11285F   Schedule A (Form 990 or 990-EZ) 2008

Part II | Support Schedule for Organizations Described in Sections 170(b)(1)(A)(iv) and 170(b)(1)(A)(vi)
(Complete only if you checked the box on line 5, 7, or 8 of Part I.)

Section A. Public Support

Calendar year (or fiscal year beginning in) ▶	(a) 2004	(b) 2005	(c) 2006	(d) 2007	(e) 2008	(f) Total
1 Gifts, grants, contributions, and membership fees received. (Do not include any "unusual grants.")						
2 Tax revenues levied for the organization's benefit and either paid to or expended on its behalf						
3 The value of services or facilities furnished by a governmental unit to the organization without charge						
4 **Total.** Add lines 1-3						
5 The portion of total contributions by each person (other than a governmental unit or publicly supported organization) included on line 1 that exceeds 2% of the amount shown on line 11, column (f)						
6 **Public support.** Subtract line 5 from line 4.						

Section B. Total Support

Calendar year (or fiscal year beginning in) ▶	(a) 2004	(b) 2005	(c) 2006	(d) 2007	(e) 2008	(f) Total
7 Amounts from line 4						
8 Gross income from interest, dividends, payments received on securities loans, rents, royalties and income from similar sources						
9 Net income from unrelated business activities, whether or not the business is regularly carried on						
10 Other income. Do not include gain or loss from the sale of capital assets (Explain in Part IV.)						
11 **Total support.** Add lines 7 through 10						

12 Gross receipts from related activities, etc. (see instructions) . . . . | **12** |

13 **First five years.** If the Form 990 is for the organization's first, second, third, fourth, or fifth tax year as a section 501(c)(3) organization, check this box and **stop here** . . . . ▶ ☐

Section C. Computation of Public Support Percentage

14 Public support percentage for 2008 (line 6, column (f) divided by line 11, column (f)) . . . . | **14** | %

15 Public support percentage from 2007 Schedule A, Part IV-A, line 26f . . . . | **15** | %

16a **33⅓ % support test—2008.** If the organization did not check the box on line 13, and line 14 is 33⅓ % or more, check this box and **stop here.** The organization qualifies as a publicly supported organization . . . . ▶ ☐

b **33⅓ % support test—2007.** If the organization did not check a box on line 13 or 16a, and line 15 is 33⅓ % or more, check this box and **stop here.** The organization qualifies as a publicly supported organization . . . . ▶ ☐

17a **10%-facts-and-circumstances test—2008.** If the organization did not check a box on line 13, 16a, or 16b, and line 14 is 10% or more, and if the organization meets the "facts-and-circumstances" test, check this box and **stop here.** Explain in Part IV how the organization meets the "facts-and-circumstances" test. The organization qualifies as a publicly supported organization . . . ▶ ☐

b **10%-facts-and-circumstances test—2007.** If the organization did not check a box on line 13, 16a, 16b, or 17a, and line 15 is 10% or more, and if the organization meets the "facts-and-circumstances" test, check this box and **stop here.** Explain in Part IV how the organization meets the "facts-and-circumstances" test. The organization qualifies as a publicly supported organization . . . . . ▶ ☐

18 **Private foundation.** If the organization did not check a box on line 13, 16a, 16b, 17a, or 17b, check this box and see instructions ▶ ☐

Schedule A (Form 990 or 990-EZ) 2008   Page **3**

Part III   **Support Schedule for Organizations Described in Section 509(a)(2)**
(Complete only if you checked the box on line 9 of Part I.)

Section A. Public Support

Calendar year (or fiscal year beginning in) ▶	(a) 2004	(b) 2005	(c) 2006	(d) 2007	(e) 2008	(f) Total
1 Gifts, grants, contributions, and membership fees received. (Do not include any "unusual grants.")						
2 Gross receipts from admissions, merchandise sold or services performed, or facilities furnished in any activity that is related to the organization's tax-exempt purpose . . .						
3 Gross receipts from activities that are not an unrelated trade or business under section 513						
4 Tax revenues levied for the organization's benefit and either paid to or expended on its behalf						
5 The value of services or facilities furnished by a governmental unit to the organization without charge . . .						
6 **Total.** Add lines 1-5						
7a Amounts included on lines 1, 2, and 3 received from disqualified persons .						
b Amounts included on lines 2 and 3 received from other than disqualified persons that exceed the greater of 1% of the total of lines 9, 10c, 11, and 12 for the year or $5,000						
c Add lines 7a and 7b						
8 **Public support** (Subtract line 7c from line 6.)						

Section B. Total Support

Calendar year (or fiscal year beginning in) ▶	(a) 2004	(b) 2005	(c) 2006	(d) 2007	(e) 2008	(f) Total
9 Amounts from line 6						
10a Gross income from interest, dividends, payments received on securities loans, rents, royalties and income from similar sources						
b Unrelated business taxable income (less section 511 taxes) from businesses acquired after June 30, 1975 . . .						
c Add lines 10a and 10b						
11 Net income from unrelated business activities not included in line 10b, whether or not the business is regularly carried on						
12 Other income. Do not include gain or loss from the sale of capital assets (Explain in Part IV.)						
13 **Total support.** (Add lines 9, 10c, 11, and 12.)						

14 **First five years.** If the Form 990 is for the organization's first, second, third, fourth, or fifth tax year as a section 501(c)(3) organization, check this box and **stop here** . . . . ▶ ☐

Section C. Computation of Public Support Percentage

15 Public support percentage for 2008 (line 8, column (f) divided by line 13, column (f)) . . .	**15**	%
16 Public support percentage from 2007 Schedule A, Part IV-A, line 27g	**16**	%

Section D. Computation of Investment Income Percentage

17 Investment income percentage for **2008** (line 10c, column (f) divided by line 13, column (f)) .	**17**	%
18 Investment income percentage from **2007** Schedule A, Part IV-A, line 27h	**18**	%

19a **33⅓ % support tests—2008.** If the organization did not check the box on line 14, and line 15 is more than 33⅓ %, and line 17 is not more than 33⅓ %, check this box and **stop here.** The organization qualifies as a publicly supported organization ▶ ☐

b **33⅓ % support tests—2007.** If the organization did not check a box on line 14 or line 19a, and line 16 is more than 33⅓ %, and line 18 is not more than 33⅓ %, check this box and **stop here.** The organization qualifies as a publicly supported organization ▶ ☐

20 **Private foundation.** If the organization did not check a box on line 14, 19a, or 19b, check this box and see instructions ▶ ☐

Schedule A (Form 990 or 990-EZ) 2008

Part IV **Supplemental Information.** Complete this part to provide the explanation required by Part II, line 10; Part II, line 17a or 17b; or Part III, line 12. Provide any other additional information. (see instructions)

Schedule B
(Form 990, 990-EZ,
or 990-PF)

Department of the Treasury
Internal Revenue Service

Schedule of Contributors

▶ Attach to Form 990, 990-EZ, and 990-PF.

OMB No. 1545-0047

2008

Name of the organization	Employer identification number

Organization type (check one):

Filers of: **Section:**

Form 990 or 990-EZ

☐ 501(c)(   ) (enter number) organization

☐ 4947(a)(1) nonexempt charitable trust **not** treated as a private foundation

☐ 527 political organization

Form 990-PF

☐ 501(c)(3) exempt private foundation

☐ 4947(a)(1) nonexempt charitable trust treated as a private foundation

☐ 501(c)(3) taxable private foundation

Check if your organization is covered by the **General Rule** or a **Special Rule**. (**Note.** Only a section 501(c)(7), (8), or (10) organization can check boxes for both the General Rule and a Special Rule. See instructions.)

General Rule

☐ For organizations filing Form 990, 990-EZ, or 990-PF that received, during the year, $5,000 or more (in money or property) from any one contributor. Complete Parts I and II.

Special Rules

☐ For a section 501(c)(3) organization filing Form 990, or Form 990-EZ, that met the 33⅓ % support test of the regulations under sections 509(a)(1)/170(b)(1)(A)(vi), and received from any one contributor, during the year, a contribution of the greater of **(1)** $5,000 or **(2)** 2% of the amount on Form 990, Part VIII, line 1h or 2% of the amount on Form 990-EZ, line 1. Complete Parts I and II.

☐ For a section 501(c)(7), (8), or (10) organization filing Form 990, or Form 990-EZ, that received from any one contributor, during the year, aggregate contributions or bequests of more than $1,000 for use *exclusively* for religious, charitable, scientific, literary, or educational purposes, or the prevention of cruelty to children or animals. Complete Parts I, II, and III.

☐ For a section 501(c)(7), (8), or (10) organization filing Form 990, or Form 990-EZ, that received from any one contributor, during the year, some contributions for use *exclusively* for religious, charitable, etc., purposes, but these contributions did not aggregate to more than $1,000. (If this box is checked, enter here the total contributions that were received during the year for an *exclusively* religious, charitable, etc., purpose. Do not complete any of the parts unless the **General Rule** applies to this organization because it received nonexclusively religious, charitable, etc., contributions of $5,000 or more during the year.) . . . . ▶ $ ....

Caution. Organizations that are not covered by the General Rule and/or the Special Rules do not file Schedule B (Form 990, 990-EZ, or 990-PF), but they **must** answer "No" on Part IV, line 2 of their Form 990, or check the box in the heading of their Form 990-EZ, or on line 2 of their Form 990-PF, to certify that they do not meet the filing requirements of Schedule B (Form 990, 990-EZ, or 990-PF).

For Privacy Act and Paperwork Reduction Act Notice, see the Instructions for Form 990. These instructions will be issued separately.   Cat. No. 30613X   Schedule B (Form 990, 990-EZ, or 990-PF) (2008)

Name of organization	Employer identification number

Part I Contributors (see instructions)

(a) No.	(b) Name, address, and ZIP + 4	(c) Aggregate contributions	(d) Type of contribution
......		$_____	Person ☐ Payroll ☐ Noncash ☐ (Complete Part II if there is a noncash contribution.)

(a) No.	(b) Name, address, and ZIP + 4	(c) Aggregate contributions	(d) Type of contribution
......		$_____	Person ☐ Payroll ☐ Noncash ☐ (Complete Part II if there is a noncash contribution.)

(a) No.	(b) Name, address, and ZIP + 4	(c) Aggregate contributions	(d) Type of contribution
......		$_____	Person ☐ Payroll ☐ Noncash ☐ (Complete Part II if there is a noncash contribution.)

(a) No.	(b) Name, address, and ZIP + 4	(c) Aggregate contributions	(d) Type of contribution
......		$_____	Person ☐ Payroll ☐ Noncash ☐ (Complete Part II if there is a noncash contribution.)

(a) No.	(b) Name, address, and ZIP + 4	(c) Aggregate contributions	(d) Type of contribution
......		$_____	Person ☐ Payroll ☐ Noncash ☐ (Complete Part II if there is a noncash contribution.)

(a) No.	(b) Name, address, and ZIP + 4	(c) Aggregate contributions	(d) Type of contribution
......		$_____	Person ☐ Payroll ☐ Noncash ☐ (Complete Part II if there is a noncash contribution.)

SCHEDULE C	**Political Campaign and Lobbying Activities**	OMB No. 1545-0047
(Form 990 or 990-EZ)	For Organizations Exempt From Income Tax Under section 501(c) and section 527	20**08**
Department of the Treasury Internal Revenue Service	▶ To be completed by organizations described below. ▶ Attach to Form 990 or Form 990-EZ.	**Open to Public Inspection**

If the organization answered "Yes," to Form 990, Part IV, line 3, or Form 990-EZ, Part VI, line 46 (Political Campaign Activities), then
- Section 501(c)(3) organizations: Complete Parts I-A and B. Do not complete Part I-C.
- Section 501(c) (other than section 501(c)(3)) organizations: Complete Parts I-A and C below. Do not complete Part I-B.
- Section 527 organizations: Complete Part I-A only.

If the organization answered "Yes," to Form 990, Part IV, line 4, or Form 990-EZ, Part VI, line 47 (Lobbying Activities), then
- Section 501(c)(3) organizations that have filed Form 5768 (election under section 501(h)): Complete Part II-A. Do not complete Part II-B.
- Section 501(c)(3) organizations that have NOT filed Form 5768 (election under section 501(h)): Complete Part II-B. Do not complete Part II-A.

If the organization answered "Yes," to Form 990, Part IV, line 5 (Proxy Tax), then
- Section 501(c)(4), (5), or (6) organizations: Complete Part III.

Name of organization	Employer identification number

Part I-A — To be completed by all organizations exempt under section 501(c) and section 527 organizations. See the instructions for Schedule C for details.

1 Provide a description of the organization's direct and indirect political campaign activities in Part IV.
2 Political expenditures . . . . ▶ $_____
3 Volunteer hours . . . . _____

Part I-B — To be completed by all organizations exempt under section 501(c)(3). See the instructions for Schedule C for details.

1 Enter the amount of any excise tax incurred by the organization under section 4955 . . . ▶ $_____
2 Enter the amount of any excise tax incurred by organization managers under section 4955 . ▶ $_____
3 If the organization incurred a section 4955 tax, did it file Form 4720 for this year? . . . . ☐ Yes ☐ No
4a Was a correction made? . . . . ☐ Yes ☐ No
b If "Yes," describe in Part IV.

Part I-C — To be completed by all organizations exempt under section 501(c), except section 501(c)(3). See the instructions for Schedule C for details.

1 Enter the amount directly expended by the filing organization for section 527 exempt function
   activities . . . . ▶ $_____
2 Enter the amount of the filing organization's funds contributed to other organizations for section
   527 exempt function activities . . . . ▶ $_____
3 Total of direct and indirect exempt function expenditures. Add lines 1 and 2 and enter here and
   on Form 1120-POL, line 17b . . . . ▶ $_____
4 Did the filing organization file **Form 1120-POL** for this year? . . . . ☐ Yes ☐ No
5 State the names, addresses and employer identification number (EIN) of all section 527 political organizations to which payments
   were made. Enter the amount paid and indicate if the amount was paid from the filing organization's funds or were political
   contributions received and promptly and directly delivered to a separate political organization, such as a separate segregated fund
   or a political action committee (PAC). If additional space is needed, provide information in Part IV.

(a) Name	(b) Address	(c) EIN	(d) Amount paid from filing organization's funds. If none, enter -0-.	(e) Amount of political contributions received and promptly and directly delivered to a separate political organization. If none, enter -0-.

For Privacy Act and Paperwork Reduction Act Notice, see the Instructions for Form 990.   Cat. No. 50084S   **Schedule C (Form 990 or 990-EZ) 2008**

Part II-A **To be completed by organizations exempt under section 501(c)(3) that filed Form 5768 (election under section 501(h)).** See the instructions for Schedule C for details.

A Check ▶ ☐ if the filing organization belongs to an affiliated group.

B Check ▶ ☐ if the filing organization checked box A and "limited control" provisions apply.

Limits on Lobbying Expenditures (The term "expenditures" means amounts paid or incurred.)	(a) Filing organization's totals	(b) Affiliated group totals
1a Total lobbying expenditures to influence public opinion (grass roots lobbying) . . .		
b Total lobbying expenditures to influence a legislative body (direct lobbying)		
c Total lobbying expenditures (add lines 1a and 1b)		
d Other exempt purpose expenditures		
e Total exempt purpose expenditures (add lines 1c and 1d)		
f Lobbying nontaxable amount. Enter the amount from the following table in both columns.		

If the amount on line 1e, column (a) or (b) is:	The lobbying nontaxable amount is:		
Not over $500,000	20% of the amount on line 1e.		
Over $500,000 but not over $1,000,000	$100,000 plus 15% of the excess over $500,000.		
Over $1,000,000 but not over $1,500,000	$175,000 plus 10% of the excess over $1,000,000.		
Over $1,500,000 but not over $17,000,000	$225,000 plus 5% of the excess over $1,500,000.		
Over $17,000,000	$1,000,000.		

	(a) Filing	(b) Affiliated
g Grassroots nontaxable amount (enter 25% of line 1f)		
h Subtract line 1g from line 1a. Enter -0- if line g is more than line a		
i Subtract line 1f from line 1c. Enter -0- if line f is more than line c		
j If there is an amount other than zero on either line 1h or line 1i, did the organization file Form 4720 reporting section 4911 tax for this year? . . . . ☐ Yes ☐ No		

4-Year Averaging Period Under Section 501(h)
(Some organizations that made a section 501(h) election do not have to complete all of the five columns below. See the instructions for lines 2a through 2f of the instructions.)

Lobbying Expenditures During 4-Year Averaging Period

Calendar year (or fiscal year beginning in)	(a) 2005	(b) 2006	(c) 2007	(d) 2008	(e) Total
2a Lobbying non-taxable amount					
b Lobbying ceiling amount (150% of line 2a, column(e))					
c Total lobbying expenditures					
d Grassroots non-taxable amount					
e Grassroots ceiling amount (150% of line 2d, column (e))					
f Grassroots lobbying expenditures					

Schedule C (Form 990 or 990-EZ) 2008   Page **3**

Part II-B **To be completed by organizations exempt under section 501(c)(3) that have NOT filed Form 5768 (election under section 501(h)).** See the instructions for Schedule C for details.

		(a)		(b)
		Yes	No	Amount
1	During the year, did the filing organization attempt to influence foreign, national, state or local legislation, including any attempt to influence public opinion on a legislative matter or referendum, through the use of:			
a	Volunteers?			
b	Paid staff or management (include compensation in expenses reported on lines 1c through 1i)?			
c	Media advertisements?			
d	Mailings to members, legislators, or the public?			
e	Publications, or published or broadcast statements?			
f	Grants to other organizations for lobbying purposes?			
g	Direct contact with legislators, their staffs, government officials, or a legislative body?			
h	Rallies, demonstrations, seminars, conventions, speeches, lectures, or any other means?			
i	Other activities? If "Yes," describe in Part IV			
j	Total lines 1c through 1i			
2a	Did the activities in line 1 cause the organization to be not described in section 501(c)(3)?			
b	If "Yes," enter the amount of any tax incurred under section 4912			
c	If "Yes," enter the amount of any tax incurred by organization managers under section 4912			
d	If the filing organization incurred a section 4912 tax, did it file Form 4720 for this year?			

Part III-A **To be completed by all organizations exempt under section 501(c)(4), section 501(c)(5), or section 501(c)(6).** See the instructions for Schedule C for details.

			Yes	No
1	Were substantially all (90% or more) dues received nondeductible by members?	1		
2	Did the organization make only in-house lobbying expenditures of $2,000 or less?	2		
3	Did the organization agree to carryover lobbying and political expenditures from the prior year?	3		

Part III-B **To be completed by all organizations exempt under section 501(c)(4), section 501(c)(5), or section 501(c)(6) if BOTH Part III-A, questions 1 and 2 are answered "No" OR if Part III-A, question 3 is answered "Yes."** See Schedule C instructions for details.

1	Dues, assessments and similar amounts from members	1	
2	Section 162(e) non-deductible lobbying and political expenditures **(do not include amounts of political expenses for which the section 527(f) tax was paid).**		
a	Current year	2a	
b	Carryover from last year	2b	
c	Total	2c	
3	Aggregate amount reported in section 6033(e)(1)(A) notices of nondeductible section 162(e) dues	3	
4	If notices were sent and the amount on line 2c exceeds the amount on line 3, what portion of the excess does the organization agree to carryover to the reasonable estimate of nondeductible lobbying and political expenditure next year?	4	
5	Taxable amount of lobbying and political expenditures (line 2c total minus 3 and 4)	5	

Part IV **Supplemental Information**

Complete this part to provide the descriptions required for Part I-A, line 1; Part I-B, line 4; Part I-C, line 5; and Part II-B, line 1i. Also, complete this part for any additional information.

....

....

....

....

....

....

Schedule C (Form 990 or 990-EZ) 2008

| Part IV | Supplemental Information *(continued)* |

| SCHEDULE D
(Form 990)

Department of the Treasury
Internal Revenue Service | **Supplemental Financial Statements**

▶ Attach to Form 990. To be completed by organizations that
answered "Yes," to Form 990, Part IV, line 6, 7, 8, 9, 10, 11, or 12. | OMB No. 1545-0047

2008

**Open to Public
Inspection** |

Name of the organization	Employer identification number

Part I   **Organizations Maintaining Donor Advised Funds or Other Similar Funds or Accounts.** Complete if the organization answered "Yes" to Form 990, Part IV, line 6.

	(a) Donor advised funds	(b) Funds and other accounts
1 Total number at end of year		
2 Aggregate contributions to (during year)		
3 Aggregate grants from (during year) .		
4 Aggregate value at end of year . . .		

5   Did the organization inform all donors and donor advisors in writing that the assets held in donor advised funds are the organization's property, subject to the organization's exclusive legal control? . . . . .   ☐ Yes   ☐ No

6   Did the organization inform all grantees, donors, and donor advisors in writing that grant funds may be used only for charitable purposes and not for the benefit of the donor or donor advisor or other impermissible private benefit? . . . .   ☐ Yes   ☐ No

---

Part II   **Conservation Easements.** Complete if the organization answered "Yes" to Form 990, Part IV, line 7.

1   Purpose(s) of conservation easements held by the organization (check all that apply).
    ☐ Preservation of land for public use (e.g., recreation or pleasure)   ☐ Preservation of an historically important land area
    ☐ Protection of natural habitat   ☐ Preservation of certified historic structure
    ☐ Preservation of open space

2   Complete lines 2a–2d if the organization held a qualified conservation contribution in the form of a conservation easement on the last day of the tax year.

		Held at the End of the Year
a Total number of conservation easements	2a	
b Total acreage restricted by conservation easements	2b	
c Number of conservation easements on a certified historic structure included in (a)	2c	
d Number of conservation easements included in (c) acquired after 8/17/06	2d	

3   Number of conservation easements modified, transferred, released, extinguished, or terminated by the organization during the taxable year ▶ ------------------

4   Number of states where property subject to conservation easement is located ▶ ------------------

5   Does the organization have a written policy regarding the periodic monitoring, inspection, violations, and enforcement of the conservation easements it holds? . . . .   ☐ Yes   ☐ No

6   Staff or volunteer hours devoted to monitoring, inspecting, and enforcing easements during the year ▶ ------------------

7   Amount of expenses incurred in monitoring, inspecting, and enforcing easements during the year ▶ $ ------------------

8   Does each conservation easement reported on line 2(d) above satisfy the requirements of section 170(h)(4)(B)(i) and section 170(h)(4)(B)(ii)? . . . .   ☐ Yes   ☐ No

9   In Part XIV, describe how the organization reports conservation easements in its revenue and expense statement, and balance sheet, and include, if applicable, the text of the footnote to the organization's financial statements that describes the organization's accounting for conservation easements.

Part III   **Organizations Maintaining Collections of Art, Historical Treasures, or Other Similar Assets.** Complete if the organization answered "Yes" to Form 990, Part IV, line 8.

1a   If the organization elected, as permitted under SFAS 116, not to report in its revenue statement and balance sheet works of art, historical treasures, or other similar assets held for public exhibition, education, or research in furtherance of public service, provide, in Part XIV, the text of the footnote to its financial statements that describes these items.

   b   If the organization elected, as permitted under SFAS 116, to report in its revenue statement and balance sheet works of art, historical treasures, or other similar assets held for public exhibition, education, or research in furtherance of public service, provide the following amounts relating to these items:
     (i)   Revenues included in Form 990, Part VIII, line 1 . . . . ▶ $ ------------------
     (ii)   Assets included in Form 990, Part X . . . . ▶ $ ------------------

2   If the organization received or held works of art, historical treasures, or other similar assets for financial gain, provide the following amounts required to be reported under SFAS 116 relating to these items:
   a   Revenues included in Form 990, Part VIII, line 1 . . . . ▶ $ ------------------
   b   Assets included in Form 990, Part X . . . . ▶ $ ------------------

---

For Privacy Act and Paperwork Reduction Act Notice, see the Instructions for Form 990.   Cat. No. 52283D   Schedule D (Form 990) 2008

Schedule D (Form 990) 2008   Page **2**

| **Part III** | Organizations Maintaining Collections of Art, Historical Treasures, or Other Similar Assets *(continued)* |

3 Using the organization's accession and other records, check any of the following that are a significant use of its collection items (check all that apply):

a ☐ Public exhibition   d ☐ Loan or exchange programs
b ☐ Scholarly research   e ☐ Other _____
c ☐ Preservation for future generations

4 Provide a description of the organization's collections and explain how they further the organization's exempt purpose in Part XIV.

5 During the year, did the organization solicit or receive donations of art, historical treasures, or other similar assets to be sold to raise funds rather than to be maintained as part of the organization's collection? . . . ☐ Yes ☐ No

| **Part IV** | **Trust, Escrow and Custodial Arrangements.** Complete if organization answered "Yes" to Form 990, Part IV, line 9, or reported an amount on Form 990, Part X, line 21. |

1a Is the organization an agent, trustee, custodian or other intermediary for contributions or other assets not included on Form 990, Part X? . . . . ☐ Yes ☐ No
b If "Yes," explain the arrangement in Part XIV and complete the following table:

		Amount
c	Beginning balance	1c
d	Additions during the year	1d
e	Distributions during the year	1e
f	Ending balance	1f

2a Did the organization include an amount on Form 990, Part X, line 21? . . . . ☐ Yes ☐ No
b If "Yes," explain the arrangement in Part XIV.

| **Part V** | **Endowment Funds.** Complete if organization answered "Yes" to Form 990, Part IV, line 10. |

		(a) Current year	(b) Prior year	(c) Two years back	(d) Three years back	(e) Four years back
1a	Beginning of year balance . . .					
b	Contributions					
c	Investment earnings or losses .					
d	Grants or scholarships					
e	Other expenditures for facilities and programs					
f	Administrative expenses . . .					
g	End of year balance					

2 Provide the estimated percentage of the year end balance held as:
a Board designated or quasi-endowment ▶ _____%
b Permanent endowment ▶ _____%
c Term endowment ▶ _____ %

3a Are there endowment funds not in the possession of the organization that are held and administered for the organization by:

		Yes	No
(i)	unrelated organizations	3a(i)	
(ii)	related organizations	3a(ii)	
b	If "Yes" to 3a(ii), are the related organizations listed as required on Schedule R?	3b	

4 Describe in Part XIV the intended uses of the organization's endowment funds.

| **Part VI** | **Investments—Land, Buildings, and Equipment.** See Form 990, Part X, line 10. |

Description of investment	(a) Cost or other basis (investment)	(b) Cost or other basis (other)	(c) Depreciation	(d) Book value
1a Land				
b Buildings				
c Leasehold improvements				
d Equipment				
e Other				

Total. Add lines 1a–1e. *(Column (d) should equal Form 990, Part X, column (B), line 10(c).)* . . . . ▶

Part VII   Investments—**Other Securities.** See Form 990, Part X, line 12.

(a) Description of security or category (including name of security)	(b) Book value	(c) Method of valuation: Cost or end-of-year market value
Financial derivatives and other financial products . .		
Closely-held equity interests		
Other		
--		
--		
--		
--		
--		
--		
--		
Total. *(Column (b) should equal Form 990, Part X, col. (B) line 12.)* ▶		

Part VIII   Investments—**Program Related.** See Form 990, Part X, line 13.

(a) Description of investment type	(b) Book value	(c) Method of valuation: Cost or end-of-year market value
Total. *(Column (b) should equal Form 990, Part X, col. (B) line 13.)* ▶		

Part IX   **Other Assets.** See Form 990, Part X, line 15.

(a) Description	(b) Book value
Total. *(Column (b) should equal Form 990, Part X, col. (B) line 15.)* . . . . ▶	

Part X   **Other Liabilities.** See Form 990, Part X, line 25.

(a) Description of liability	(b) Amount	
Federal income taxes		
Total. *(Column (b) should equal Form 990, Part X, col. (B) line 25.)* ▶		

In Part XIV, provide the text of the footnote to the organization's financial statements that reports the organization's liability for uncertain tax positions under FIN 48.

Part XI   Reconciliation of Change in Net Assets from Form 990 to Financial Statements

1	Total revenue (Form 990, Part VIII, column (A), line 12)	1
2	Total expenses (Form 990, Part IX, column (A), line 25)	2
3	Excess or (deficit) for the year. Subtract line 2 from line 1	3
4	Net unrealized gains (losses) on investments	4
5	Donated services and use of facilities	5
6	Investment expenses	6
7	Prior period adjustments	7
8	Other (Describe in Part XIV)	8
9	Total adjustments (net). Add lines 4–8	9
10	Excess or (deficit) for the year per financial statements. Combine lines 3 and 9	10

Part XII   Reconciliation of Revenue per Audited Financial Statements With Revenue per Return

1	Total revenue, gains, and other support per audited financial statements	1	
2	Amounts included on line 1 but not on Form 990, Part VIII, line 12:		
a	Net unrealized gains on investments	2a	
b	Donated services and use of facilities	2b	
c	Recoveries of prior year grants	2c	
d	Other (Describe in Part XIV)	2d	
e	Add lines 2a through 2d	2e	
3	Subtract line 2e from line 1	3	
4	Amounts included on Form 990, Part VIII, line 12, but not on line 1:		
a	Investment expenses not included on Form 990, Part VIII, line 7b .	4a	
b	Other (Describe in Part XIV)	4b	
c	Add lines 4a and 4b	4c	
5	Total revenue. Add lines 3 and 4c. (This should equal Form 990, Part I, line 12.)	5	

Part XIII   Reconciliation of Expenses per Audited Financial Statements With Expenses per Return

1	Total expenses and losses per audited financial statements	1	
2	Amounts included on line 1 but not on Form 990, Part IX, line 25:		
a	Donated services and use of facilities	2a	
b	Prior year adjustments	2b	
c	Losses reported on Form 990, Part IX, line 25	2c	
d	Other (Describe in Part XIV)	2d	
e	Add lines 2a through 2d	2e	
3	Subtract line 2e from line 1	3	
4	Amounts included on Form 990, Part IX, line 25, but not on line 1:		
a	Investment expenses not included on Form 990, Part VIII, line 7b .	4a	
b	Other (Describe in Part XIV)	4b	
c	Add lines 4a and 4b	4c	
5	Total expenses. Add lines 3 and 4c. (This should equal Form 990, Part I, line 18.)	5	

Part XIV   Supplemental Information

Complete this part to provide the descriptions required for Part II, lines 3, 5, and 9; Part III, lines 1a and 4; Part IV, lines 1b and 2b; Part V, line 4; Part X; Part XI, line 8; Part XII, lines 2d and 4b; and Part XIII, lines 2d and 4b.

SCHEDULE E	**Schools**	OMB No. 1545-0047

SCHEDULE E
(Form 990 or 990-EZ)

Department of the Treasury
Internal Revenue Service

Schools

► To be completed by organizations that
answer "Yes" to Form 990, Part IV, line 13, or Form 990-EZ, Part VI, line 48.

► Attach to Form 990 or Form 990-EZ.

OMB No. 1545-0047

20**08**

Open to Public
Inspection

Name of the organization	Employer Identification number

		YES	NO
1	Does the organization have a racially nondiscriminatory policy toward students by statement in its charter, bylaws, other governing instrument, or in a resolution of its governing body? **1**		
2	Does the organization include a statement of its racially nondiscriminatory policy toward students in all its brochures, catalogues, and other written communications with the public dealing with student admissions, programs, and scholarships? **2**		
3	Has the organization publicized its racially nondiscriminatory policy through newspaper or broadcast media during the period of solicitation for students, or during the registration period if it has no solicitation program, in a way that makes the policy known to all parts of the general community it serves? If "Yes," please describe. If "No," please explain **3**		

		YES	NO
4	Does the organization maintain the following?		
a	Records indicating the racial composition of the student body, faculty, and administrative staff? . . . **4a**		
b	Records documenting that scholarships and other financial assistance are awarded on a racially nondiscriminatory basis? **4b**		
c	Copies of all catalogues, brochures, announcements, and other written communications to the public dealing with student admissions, programs, and scholarships? **4c**		
d	Copies of all material used by the organization or on its behalf to solicit contributions? **4d**		
	If you answered "No" to any of the above, please explain. (If you need more space, attach a separate statement.)		

		YES	NO
5	Does the organization discriminate by race in any way with respect to:		
a	Students' rights or privileges? **5a**		
b	Admissions policies? **5b**		
c	Employment of faculty or administrative staff? **5c**		
d	Scholarships or other financial assistance? **5d**		
e	Educational policies? **5e**		
f	Use of facilities? **5f**		
g	Athletic programs? **5g**		
h	Other extracurricular activities? **5h**		
	If you answered "Yes" to any of the above, please explain. (If you need more space, attach a separate statement.)		

		YES	NO
6a	Does the organization receive any financial aid or assistance from a governmental agency? **6a**		
b	Has the organization's right to such aid ever been revoked or suspended? **6b**		
	If you answered "Yes" to either line 6a or line 6b, please explain using an attached statement.		
7	Does the organization certify that it has complied with the applicable requirements of sections 4.01 through 4.05 of Rev. Proc. 75-50, 1975-2 C.B. 587, covering racial nondiscrimination? If "No," attach an explanation. **7**		

For Privacy Act and Paperwork Reduction Act Notice, see the Instructions for Form 990.   Cat. No. 50085D   **Schedule E (Form 990 or 990-EZ) 2008**

Schedule F (Form 990)	**Statement of Activities Outside the United States**	OMB No. 1545-0047
		2008
Department of the Treasury Internal Revenue Service	▶ Attach to Form 990. Complete if the organization answered "Yes" to Form 990, Part IV, line 14b, line 15, or line 16.	**Open to Public Inspection**
Name of the organization		Employer identification number

| **Part I** | **General Information on Activities Outside the United States.** Complete if the organization answered "Yes" to Form 990, Part IV, line 14b. |

1 **For grantmakers.** Does the organization maintain records to substantiate the amount of the grants or assistance, the grantees' eligibility for the grants or assistance, and the selection criteria used to award the grants or assistance? . . . . ☐ **Yes** ☐ **No**

2 **For grantmakers.** Describe in Part IV the organization's procedures for monitoring the use of grant funds outside the United States.

3 Activities per Region. (Use Schedule F-1 (Form 990) if additional space is needed.)

(a) Region	(b) Number of offices in the region	(c) Number of employees or agents in region	(d) Activities conducted in region (by type) (i.e., fundraising, program services, grants to recipients located in the region)	(e) If activity listed in (d) is a program service, describe specific type of service(s) in region	(f) Total expenditures in region
Totals . . . . ▶					

For Privacy Act and Paperwork Reduction Act Notice, see the Instructions for Form 990.   Cat. No. 50082W   Schedule F (Form 990) 2008

Schedule F (Form 990) 2008

Page **2**

Part II **Grants and Other Assistance to Organizations or Entities Outside the United States.** Complete if the organization answered "Yes" to Form 990, Part IV, line 15, for any recipient who received more than $5,000. Check this box if no one recipient received more than $5,000 . . . . ▶ ☐
Use Schedule F-1 (Form 990) if additional space is needed.

1	(a) Name of organization	(b) IRS code section and EIN (if applicable)	(c) Region	(d) Purpose of grant	(e) Amount of cash grant	(f) Manner of cash disbursement	(g) Amount of non-cash assistance	(h) Description of non-cash assistance	(i) Method of valuation (book, FMV, appraisal, other)

2   Enter total number of organizations that are recognized as charities by the foreign country or for which the grantee or counsel has provided a section 501(c)(3) equivalency letter . . . . ▲ ▲

3   Enter total number of other organizations or entities . . . .

Schedule F (Form 990) 2008

Schedule F (Form 990) 2008

Page 3

Part III **Grants and Other Assistance to Individuals Outside the United States.** Complete if the organization answered "Yes" to Form 990, Part IV, line 16.
Use Schedule F-1 (Form 990) if additional space is needed.

(a) Type of grant or assistance	(b) Region	(c) Number of recipients	(d) Amount of cash grant	(e) Manner of cash disbursement	(f) Amount of non-cash assistance	(g) Description of non-cash assistance	(h) Method of valuation (book, FMV, appraisal, other)

SCHEDULE G	**Supplemental Information Regarding**	OMB No. 1545-0047
(Form 990 or 990-EZ)	**Fundraising or Gaming Activities**	2008
Department of the Treasury Internal Revenue Service	► Attach to Form 990 or Form 990-EZ. Must be completed by organizations that answer "Yes" to Form 990, Part IV, lines 17, 18, or 19, and by organizations that enter more than $15,000 on Form 990-EZ, line 6a.	**Open To Public Inspection**

Name of the organization	Employer identification number

Part I   **Fundraising Activities.** Complete if the organization answered "Yes" to Form 990, Part IV, line 17.

1   Indicate whether the organization raised funds through any of the following activities. Check all that apply.

a ☐ Mail solicitations   e ☐ Solicitation of non-government grants

b ☐ Email solicitations   f ☐ Solicitation of government grants

c ☐ Phone solicitations   g ☐ Special fundraising events

d ☐ In-person solicitations

2a   Did the organization have a written or oral agreement with any individual (including officers, directors, trustees or key employees listed in Form 990, Part VII) or entity in connection with professional fundraising services?   ☐ **Yes**   ☐ **No**

   b   If "Yes," list the ten highest paid individuals or entities (fundraisers) pursuant to agreements under which the fundraiser is to be compensated at least $5,000 by the organization. Form 990-EZ filers are not required to complete this table.

(i) Name of individual or entity (fundraiser)	(ii) Activity	(iii) Did fundraiser have custody or control of contributions?		(iv) Gross receipts from activity	(v) Amount paid to (or retained by) fundraiser listed in col. (i)	(vi) Amount paid to (or retained by) organization
		Yes	**No**			
Total . . . . ►						

3   List all states in which the organization is registered or licensed to solicit funds or has been notified it is exempt from registration or licensing.

For Privacy Act and Paperwork Reduction Act Notice, see the Instructions for Form 990.   Cat. No. 50083H   Schedule G (Form 990 or 990-EZ) 2008

Schedule G (Form 990 or 990-EZ) 2008   Page **2**

Part II   **Fundraising Events.** Complete if the organization answered "Yes" to Form 990, Part IV, line 18, or reported more than $15,000 on Form 990-EZ, line 6a. List events with gross receipts greater than $5,000.

		(a) Event #1 (event type)	(b) Event #2 (event type)	(c) Other Events (total number)	(d) Total Events (Add col. (a) through col. (c))
Revenue	1 Gross receipts				
	2 Less: Charitable contributions				
	3 Gross revenue (line 1 minus line 2)				
Direct Expenses	4 Cash prizes				
	5 Non-cash prizes				
	6 Rent/facility costs				
	7 Other direct expenses				

8   Direct expense summary. Add lines 4 through 7 in column (d) . . . . ▶   (   )

9   Net income summary. Combine lines 3 and 8 in column (d)   . . . . ▶

Part III   **Gaming.** Complete if the organization answered "Yes" to Form 990, Part IV, line 19, or reported more than $15,000 on Form 990-EZ, line 6a.

		(a) Bingo	(b) Pull tabs/Instant bingo/progressive bingo	(c) Other gaming	(d) Total gaming (Add col. (a) through col. (c))
Revenue	1 Gross revenue				
Direct Expenses	2 Cash prizes				
	3 Non-cash prizes				
	4 Rent/facility costs				
	5 Other direct expenses				
	6 Volunteer labor	☐ Yes _____% ☐ No	☐ Yes _____% ☐ No	☐ Yes _____% ☐ No	

7   Direct expense summary. Add lines 2 through 5 in column (d) . . . . ▶   (   )

8   Net gaming income summary. Combine lines 1 and 7 in column (d) . . . . . . ▶

		Yes	No
9 Enter the state(s) in which the organization operates gaming activities: ----------------------------			
a Is the organization licensed to operate gaming activities in each of these states?	**9a**		
b If "No," Explain:			
--			
10a Were any of the organization's gaming licenses revoked, suspended or terminated during the tax year?	**10a**		
b If "Yes," Explain:			
--			
11 Does the organization operate gaming activities with nonmembers?	**11**		
12 Is the organization a grantor, beneficiary or trustee of a trust or a member of a partnership or other entity formed to administer charitable gaming?	**12**		

Schedule G (Form 990 or 990-EZ) 2008

		Yes	No

13   Indicate the percentage of gaming activity operated in:

   a   The organization's facility . . . . **13a**   %

   b   An outside facility   . . . . **13b**   %

14   Provide the name and address of the person who prepares the organization's gaming/special events books and records:

     Name ▶ ....

     Address ▶ ....

15a   Does the organization have a contract with a third party from whom the organization receives gaming revenue? **15a**

   b   If "Yes," enter the amount of gaming revenue received by the organization ▶ $ .... and the amount of gaming revenue retained by the third party ▶ $ ....

   c   If "Yes," enter name and address:

     Name ▶ ....

     Address ▶ ....

16   Gaming manager information:

     Name ▶ ....

     Gaming manager compensation ▶ $ ....

     Description of services provided ▶ ....

     ☐ Director/officer   ☐ Employee   ☐ Independent contractor

17   Mandatory distributions:

   a   Is the organization required under state law to make charitable distributions from the gaming proceeds to retain the state gaming license? **17a**

   b   Enter the amount of distributions required under state law distributed to other exempt organizations or spent in the organization's own exempt activities during the tax year ▶ $

SCHEDULE H
(Form 990)

Department of the Treasury
Internal Revenue Service

Hospitals

▶ To be completed by organizations that answer "Yes" to Form 990,
Part IV, line 20.

▶ Attach to Form 990.

OMB No. 1545-0047

20**08**

Open to Public Inspection

Name of the organization

Employer identification number

Part I	Charity Care and Certain Other Community Benefits at Cost *(Optional for 2008)*

		Yes	No
1a	Does the organization have a charity care policy? If "No," skip to question 6a	**1a**		
b	If "Yes," is it a written policy?	**1b**		
2	If the organization has multiple hospitals, indicate which of the following best describes application of the charity care policy to the various hospitals.			
	☐ Applied uniformly to all hospitals ☐ Applied uniformly to most hospitals			
	☐ Generally tailored to individual hospitals			
3	Answer the following based on the charity care eligibility criteria that applies to the largest number of the organization's patients.			
a	Does the organization use Federal Poverty Guidelines (FPG) to determine eligibility for providing *free* care to low income individuals? If "Yes," indicate which of the following is the family income limit for eligibility for free care: . . . . ☐ 100% ☐ 150% ☐ 200% ☐ Other _____ %	**3a**		
b	Does the organization use FPG to determine eligibility for providing *discounted* care to low income individuals? If "Yes," indicate which of the following is the family income limit for eligibility for discounted care: . . . . ☐ 200% ☐ 250% ☐ 300% ☐ 350% ☐ 400% ☐ Other _____ %	**3b**		
c	If the organization does not use FPG to determine eligibility, describe in Part VI the income based criteria for determining eligibility for free or discounted care. Include in the description whether the organization uses an asset test or other threshold, regardless of income, to determine eligibility for free or discounted care.			
4	Does the organization's policy provide free or discounted care to the "medically indigent"?	**4**		
5a	Does the organization budget amounts for free or discounted care provided under its charity care policy?	**5a**		
b	If "Yes," did the organization's charity care expenses exceed the budgeted amount?	**5b**		
c	If "Yes" to line 5b, as a result of budget considerations, was the organization unable to provide free or discounted care to a patient who was eligible for free or discounted care?	**5c**		
6a	Does the organization prepare an annual community benefit report?	**6a**		
b	If "Yes," does the organization make it available to the public?	**6b**		
	Complete the following table using the worksheets provided in the Schedule H instructions. Do not submit these worksheets with the Schedule H.			

7   Charity Care and Certain Other Community Benefits at Cost

Charity Care and Means-Tested Government Programs	(a) Number of activities or programs (optional)	(b) Persons served (optional)	(c) Total community benefit expense	(d) Direct offsetting revenue	(e) Net community benefit expense	(f) Percent of total expense
a Charity care at cost (from *Worksheets 1 and 2*)						
b Unreimbursed Medicaid (from *Worksheet 3, column a*) . . .						
c Unreimbursed costs—other means-tested government programs (from *Worksheet 3, column b)*						
d Total Charity Care and Means-Tested Government Programs						
Other Benefits						
e Community health improvement services and community benefit operations (from Worksheet 4) .						
f Health professions education (from Worksheet 5)						
g Subsidized health services (from Worksheet 6)						
h Research (from Worksheet 7) . .						
i Cash and in-kind contributions to community groups (from Worksheet 8)						
j Total Other Benefits						
k Total (line 7d and 7j)						

For Privacy Act and Paperwork Reduction Act Notice, see the Instructions for Form 990.   Cat. No. 50192T   **Schedule H (Form 990) 2008**

Schedule H (Form 990) 2008   Page **2**

Part II   **Community Building Activities** Complete this table if the organization conducted any community building activities. *(Optional for 2008)*

		(a) Number of activities or programs (optional)	(b) Persons served (optional)	(c) Total community building expense	(d) Direct offsetting revenue	(e) Net community building expense	(f) Percent of total expense
1	Physical improvements and housing						
2	Economic development						
3	Community support						
4	Environmental improvements						
5	Leadership development and training for community members						
6	Coalition building						
7	Community health improvement advocacy						
8	Workforce development						
9	Other						
10	**Total**						

Part III   **Bad Debt, Medicare, & Collection Practices** *(Optional for 2008)*

Section A. Bad Debt Expense

		Yes	No
1	Does the organization report bad debt expense in accordance with Healthcare Financial Management Association Statement No. 15? **1**		
2	Enter the amount of the organization's bad debt expense (at cost) **2**		
3	Enter the estimated amount of the organization's bad debt expense (at cost) attributable to patients eligible under the organization's charity care policy. **3**		

4   Provide in Part VI the text of the footnote to the organization's financial statements that describes bad debt expense. In addition, describe the costing methodology used in determining the amounts reported on lines 2 and 3, or rationale for including other bad debt amounts in community benefit.

Section B. Medicare

5	Enter total revenue received from Medicare (including DSH and IME) **5**
6	Enter Medicare allowable costs of care relating to payments on line 5 . . . . . . **6**
7	Enter line 5 less line 6—surplus or (shortfall) **7**

8   Describe in Part VI the extent to which any shortfall reported in line 7 should be treated as community benefit and the costing methodology or source used to determine the amount reported on line 6, and indicate which of the following methods was used:

☐ Cost accounting system   ☐ Cost to charge ratio   ☐ Other

Section C. Collection Practices

9a Does the organization have a written debt collection policy? **9a**

 b If "Yes," does the organization's collection policy contain provisions on the collection practices to be followed for patients who are known to qualify for charity care or financial assistance? Describe in Part VI . . .   **9b**

Part IV   **Management Companies and Joint Ventures** *(Optional for 2008)*

	(a) Name of entity	(b) Description of primary activity of entity	(c) Organization's profit % or stock ownership %	(d) Officers, directors, trustees, or key employees' profit % or stock ownership %	(e) Physicians' profit % or stock ownership %
1					
2					
3					
4					
5					
6					
7					
8					
9					
10					
11					
12					
13					
14					

Schedule H (Form 990) 2008

Part V   **Facility Information** *(Required for 2008)*

Name and address	Licensed hospital	General medical & surgical	Children's hospital	Teaching hospital	Critical access hospital	Research facility	ER-24 hours	ER-other	Other (Describe)

Part VI	**Supplemental Information** *(Optional for 2008)*

Complete this part to provide the following information.

1   Provide the description required for Part I, line 3c; Part I, line 6a; Part I, line 7g; Part I, line 7, column (f); Part I, line 7; Part III, line 4; Part III, line 8; Part III, line 9b, and Part V. See Instructions.

2   **Needs assessment.** Describe how the organization assesses the health care needs of the communities it serves.

3   **Patient education of eligibility for assistance.** Describe how the organization informs and educates patients and persons who may be billed for patient care about their eligibility for assistance under federal, state, or local government programs or under the organization's charity care policy.

4   **Community information.** Describe the community the organization serves, taking into account the geographic area and demographic constituents it serves.

5   **Community building activities.** Describe how the organization's community building activities, as reported in Part II, promote the health of the communities the organization serves.

6   Provide any other information important to describing how the organization's hospitals or other health care facilities further its exempt purpose by promoting the health of the community (e.g., open medical staff, community board, use of surplus funds, etc.).

7   If the organization is part of an affiliated health care system, describe the respective roles of the organization and its affiliates in promoting the health of the communities served.

8   If applicable, identify all states with which the organization, or a related organization, files a community benefit report.

SCHEDULE I
(Form 990)

Department of the Treasury
Internal Revenue Service

Grants and Other Assistance to Organizations, Governments, and Individuals in the U.S.

▶ Complete if the organization answered "Yes," on Form 990, Part IV, lines 21 or 22.

▶ Attach to Form 990.

OMB No. 1545-0047

2008

Open to Public Inspection

Name of the organization

Employer identification number

Part I General Information on Grants and Assistance

1 Does the organization maintain records to substantiate the amount of the grants or assistance, the grantees' eligibility for the grants or assistance, and the selection criteria used to award the grants or assistance? . . . . □ Yes □ No

2 Describe in Part IV the organization's procedures for monitoring the use of grant funds in the United States.

Part II Grants and Other Assistance to Governments and Organizations in the United States. Complete if the organization answered "Yes" on Form 990, Part IV, line 21, for any recipient that received more than $5,000. Check this box if no one recipient received more than $5,000. Use Part IV and Schedule I-1 (Form 990) if additional space is needed ▶ □

1 (a) Name and address of organization or government	(b) EIN	(c) IRC section if applicable	(d) Amount of cash grant	(e) Amount of non-cash assistance	(f) Method of valuation (book, FMV, appraisal, other)	(g) Description of non-cash assistance	(h) Purpose of grant or assistance

2 Enter total number of section 501(c)(3) and government organizations . . . . ▲

3 Enter total number of other organizations . . . . ▲

For Privacy Act and Paperwork Reduction Act Notice, see the Instructions for Form 990. Cat. No. 50055P Schedule I (Form 990) 2008

Schedule I (Form 990) 2008

Part III **Grants and Other Assistance to Individuals in the United States.** Complete if the organization answered "Yes" on Form 990, Part IV, line 22.
Use Schedule I-1 (Form 990) if additional space is needed.

(a) Type of grant or assistance	(b) Number of recipients	(c) Amount of cash grant	(d) Amount of non-cash assistance	(e) Method of valuation (book, FMV, appraisal, other)	(f) Description of non-cash assistance

Part IV **Supplemental Information.** Complete this part to provide the information required in Part I, line 2, and any other additional information.

_____

_____

_____

_____

_____

_____

_____

_____

_____

_____

_____

_____

Schedule I (Form 990) 2008

Page 2

**SCHEDULE J
(Form 990)**

Department of the Treasury
Internal Revenue Service

Compensation Information

For certain Officers, Directors, Trustees, Key Employees, and Highest
Compensated Employees
▶ Attach to Form 990. To be completed by organizations
that answered "Yes" to Form 990, Part IV, line 23.

OMB No. 1545-0047

2008

**Open to Public
Inspection**

Name of the organization

Employer identification number

Part I	Questions Regarding Compensation

		Yes	No
1a	Check the appropriate box(es) if the organization provided any of the following to or for a person listed in Form 990, Part VII, Section A, line 1a. Complete Part III to provide any relevant information regarding these items.		

☐ First-class or charter travel   ☐ Housing allowance or residence for personal use
☐ Travel for companions   ☐ Payments for business use of personal residence
☐ Tax indemnification and gross-up payments   ☐ Health or social club dues or initiation fees
☐ Discretionary spending account   ☐ Personal services (e.g., maid, chauffeur, chef)

		Yes	No
b	If line 1a is checked, did the organization follow a written policy regarding payment or reimbursement or provision of all of the expenses described above? If "No," complete Part III to explain **1b**		
2	Did the organization require substantiation prior to reimbursing or allowing expenses incurred by all officers, directors, trustees, and the CEO/Executive Director, regarding the items checked in line 1a? . **2**		

3 Indicate which, if any, of the following the organization uses to establish the compensation of the organization's CEO/Executive Director. Check all that apply.

☐ Compensation committee   ☐ Written employment contract
☐ Independent compensation consultant   ☐ Compensation survey or study
☐ Form 990 of other organizations   ☐ Approval by the board or compensation committee

		Yes	No
4	During the year, did any person listed in Form 990, Part VII, Section A, line 1a:		
a	Receive a severance payment or change of control payment? **4a**		
b	Participate in, or receive payment from, a supplemental nonqualified retirement plan? **4b**		
c	Participate in, or receive payment from, an equity-based compensation arrangement? **4c**		

If "Yes" to any of lines 4a–c, list the persons and provide the applicable amounts for each item in Part III.

Only 501(c)(3) and 501(c)(4) organizations must complete lines 5–8.

		Yes	No
5	For persons listed in Form 990, Part VII, Section A, line 1a, did the organization pay or accrue any compensation contingent on the revenues of:		
a	The organization? **5a**		
b	Any related organization? **5b**		
	If "Yes" to line 5a or 5b, describe in Part III.		
6	For persons listed in Form 990, Part VII, Section A, line 1a, did the organization pay or accrue any compensation contingent on the net earnings of:		
a	The organization? **6a**		
b	Any related organization? **6b**		
	If "Yes" to line 6a or 6b, describe in Part III.		
7	For persons listed in Form 990, Part VII, Section A, line 1a, did the organization provide any non-fixed payments not described in lines 5 and 6? If "Yes," describe in Part III **7**		
8	Were any amounts reported in Form 990, Part VII, paid or accrued pursuant to a contract that was subject to the initial contract exception described in Regs. section 53.4958-4(a)(3)? If "Yes," describe in Part III **8**		

For Privacy Act and Paperwork Reduction Act Notice, see the Instructions for Form 990.   Cat. No. 50053T   **Schedule J (Form 990) 2008**

Schedule J (Form 990) 2008

Page **2**

Part II   **Officers, Directors, Trustees, Key Employees, and Highest Compensated Employees.** Use Schedule J-1 if additional space is needed.

For each individual whose compensation must be reported in Schedule J, report compensation from the organization on row (i) and from related organizations, described in the instructions, on row (ii). Do not list any individuals that are not listed on Form 990, Part VII.

Note. The sum of columns (B)(i)–(iii) must equal the applicable column (D) or column (E) amounts on Form 990, Part VII, line 1a.

(A) Name		(B) Breakdown of W-2 and/or 1099-MISC compensation			(C) Deferred compensation	(D) Nontaxable benefits	(E) Total of columns (B)(i)–(D)	(F) Compensation reported in prior Form 990 or Form 990-EZ
		(i) Base compensation	(ii) Bonus & incentive compensation	(iii) Other reportable compensation				
	(i)							
	(ii)							
	(i)							
	(ii)							
	(i)							
	(ii)							
	(i)							
	(ii)							
	(i)							
	(ii)							
	(i)							
	(ii)							
	(i)							
	(ii)							
	(i)							
	(ii)							
	(i)							
	(ii)							
	(i)							
	(ii)							
	(i)							
	(ii)							
	(i)							
	(ii)							
	(i)							
	(ii)							
	(i)							
	(ii)							
	(i)							
	(ii)							

Schedule J (Form 990) 2008

Part III   **Supplemental Information**

Complete this part to provide the information, explanation, or descriptions required for Part I, lines 1a, 1b, 4c, 5a, 5b, 6a, 6b, 7, and 8. Also complete this part for any additional information.

Page **3**

SCHEDULE K (Form 990)

Department of the Treasury
Internal Revenue Service

Supplemental Information on Tax-Exempt Bonds

▶ Attach to Form 990. To be completed by organizations that answered "Yes" to Form 990, Part IV, line 24a. Provide descriptions, explanations, and any additional information on Schedule O (Form 990).

OMB No. 1545-0047

2008

Open to Public Inspection

Name of the organization

Employer identification number

Part I   Bond Issues (Required for 2008)

(a) Issuer name	(b) Issuer EIN	(c) CUSIP #	(d) Date issued	(e) Issue price	(f) Description of purpose	(g) Defeased		(h) On behalf of issuer	
						Yes	No	Yes	No
A									
B									
C									
D									
E									

Part II   Proceeds (Optional for 2008)

	A		B		C		D		E	
1 Total proceeds of issue										
2 Gross proceeds in reserve funds										
3 Proceeds in refunding or defeasance escrows										
4 Other unspent proceeds										
5 Issuance costs from proceeds										
6 Working capital expenditures from proceeds										
7 Capital expenditures from proceeds										
8 Year of substantial completion										
	Yes	No	Yes	No	Yes	No	Yes	No	Yes	No
9 Were the bonds issued as part of a current refunding issue?										
10 Were the bonds issued as part of an advance refunding issue?										
11 Has the final allocation of proceeds been made?										
12 Does the organization maintain adequate books and records to support the final allocation of proceeds?										

Part III   Private Business Use (Optional for 2008)

	A		B		C		D		E	
	Yes	No	Yes	No	Yes	No	Yes	No	Yes	No
1 Was the organization a partner in a partnership, or a member of an LLC, which owned property financed by tax-exempt bonds?										
2 Are there any lease arrangements with respect to the financed property which may result in private business use?										

For Privacy Act and Paperwork Reduction Act Notice, see the Instructions for Form 990.   Cat. No. 50193E   Schedule K (Form 990) 2008

Schedule K (Form 990) 2008

Page **2**

Part III Private Business Use *(Continued)*

	A		B		C		D		E	
	Yes	No	Yes	No	Yes	No	Yes	No	Yes	No
3a Are there any management or service contracts with respect to the financed property which may result in private business use?										
b Are there any research agreements with respect to the financed property which may result in private business use?										
c Does the organization routinely engage bond counsel or other outside counsel to review any management or service contracts or research agreements relating to the financed property?										
4 Enter the percentage of financed property used in a private business use by entities other than a section 501(c)(3) organization or a state or local government ▶		%		%		%		%		%
5 Enter the percentage of financed property used in a private business use as a result of unrelated trade or business activity carried on by your organization, another section 501(c)(3) organization, or a state or local government ▶		%		%		%		%		%
6 Total of lines 4 and 5		%		%		%		%		%
7 Has the organization adopted management practices and procedures to ensure the post-issuance compliance of its tax-exempt bond liabilities?										

Part IV Arbitrage *(Optional for 2008)*

	A		B		C		D		E	
	Yes	No	Yes	No	Yes	No	Yes	No	Yes	No
1 Has a Form 8038-T, Arbitrage Rebate, Yield Reduction and Penalty in Lieu of Arbitrage Rebate, been filed with respect to the bond issue?										
2 Is the bond issue a variable rate issue?										
3a Has the organization or the governmental issuer identified a hedge with respect to the bond issue on its books and records?										
b Name of provider										
c Term of hedge										
4a Were gross proceeds invested in a GIC?										
b Name of provider										
c Term of GIC										
d Was the regulatory safe harbor for establishing the fair market value of the GIC satisfied?										
5 Were any gross proceeds invested beyond an available temporary period?										
6 Did the bond issue qualify for an exception to rebate?										

Schedule K (Form 990) 2008

SCHEDULE L
(Form 990 or 990-EZ)

Department of the Treasury
Internal Revenue Service

Transactions With Interested Persons
▶ Attach to Form 990 or Form 990-EZ.
▶ To be completed by organizations that answered
"Yes" on Form 990, Part IV, line 25a, 25b, 26, 27, 28a, 28b, or 28c,
or Form 990-EZ, Part V, line 38a or 40b.

OMB No. 1545-0047

2008

**Open To Public
Inspection**

Name of the organization

Employer identification number

Part I   **Excess Benefit Transactions** (section 501(c)(3) and section 501(c)(4) organizations only).
To be completed by organizations that answered "Yes" on Form 990, Part IV, line 25a or 25b, or Form 990-EZ, Part V, line 40b.

1	(a) Name of disqualified person	(b) Description of transaction	(c) Corrected?	
			Yes	No

2   Enter the amount of tax imposed on the organization managers or disqualified persons during the year
under section 4958 . . . . ▶ $ _____

3   Enter the amount of tax, if any, on line 2, above, reimbursed by the organization . . . . ▶ $ _____

Part II   **Loans to and/or From Interested Persons.**
To be completed by organizations that answered "Yes" on Form 990, Part IV, line 26, or Form 990-EZ, Part V, line 38a.

(a) Name of interested person and purpose	(b) Loan to or from the organization?		(c) Original principal amount	(d) Balance due	(e) In default?		(f) Approved by board or committee?		(g) Written agreement?	
	To	From			Yes	No	Yes	No	Yes	No

Total   . . . . ▶ $

Part III   **Grants or Assistance Benefitting Interested Persons.**
To be completed by organizations that answered "Yes" on Form 990, Part IV, line 27.

(a) Name of interested person	(b) Relationship between interested person and the organization	(c) Amount of grant or type of assistance

---

Part IV   **Business Transactions Involving Interested Persons.**
To be completed by organizations that answered "Yes" on Form 990, Part IV, line 28a, 28b, or 28c.

(a) Name of interested person	(b) Relationship between interested person and the organization	(c) Amount of transaction	(d) Description of transaction	(e) Sharing of organization's revenues?	
				Yes	No

For Privacy Act and Paperwork Reduction Act Notice, see the Instructions for Form 990.   Cat. No. 50056A   Schedule L (Form 990 or 990-EZ) 2008

SCHEDULE M
(Form 990)

Department of the Treasury
Internal Revenue Service

NonCash Contributions

► To be completed by organizations that answered "Yes"
on Form 990, Part IV, lines 29 or 30.
► Attach to Form 990.

OMB No. 1545-0047

2008

Open To Public Inspection

Name of the organization

Employer identification number

Part I   Types of Property

		(a) Check if applicable	(b) Number of contributions	(c) Revenues reported on Form 990, Part VIII, line 1g	(d) Method of determining revenues
1	Art—Works of art				
2	Art—Historical treasures				
3	Art—Fractional interests				
4	Books and publications				
5	Clothing and household goods				
6	Cars and other vehicles				
7	Boats and planes				
8	Intellectual property				
9	Securities—Publicly traded				
10	Securities—Closely held stock				
11	Securities—Partnership, LLC, or trust interests				
12	Securities—Miscellaneous				
13	Qualified conservation contribution (historic structures)				
14	Qualified conservation contribution (other)				
15	Real estate—Residential				
16	Real estate—Commercial				
17	Real estate—Other				
18	Collectibles				
19	Food inventory				
20	Drugs and medical supplies				
21	Taxidermy				
22	Historical artifacts				
23	Scientific specimens				
24	Archeological artifacts				
25	Other ► (......................)				
26	Other ► (......................)				
27	Other ► (......................)				
28	Other ► (......................)				

			Yes	No
29	Number of Forms 8283 received by the organization during the tax year for contributions for which the organization completed Form 8283, Part IV, Donee Acknowledgement	**29**		
30a	During the year, did the organization receive by contribution any property reported in Part I, lines 1–28 that it must hold for at least three years from the date of the initial contribution, and which is not required to be used for exempt purposes for the entire holding period?	**30a**		
b	If "Yes," describe the arrangement in Part II.			
31	Does the organization have a gift acceptance policy that requires the review of any non-standard contributions?	**31**		
32a	Does the organization hire or use third parties or related organizations to solicit, process, or sell noncash contributions?	**32a**		
b	If "Yes," describe in Part II.			
33	If the organization did not report revenues in column (c) for a type of property for which column (a) is checked, describe in Part II.			

For Privacy Act and Paperwork Reduction Act Notice, see the Instructions for Form 990.   Cat. No. 51227J   **Schedule M (Form 990) 2008**

SCHEDULE N
(Form 990 or 990-EZ)

Department of the Treasury
Internal Revenue Service

Liquidation, Termination, Dissolution, or Significant Disposition of Assets

To be completed by organizations that answer "Yes" to Form 990, Part IV, lines 31 or 32; or Form 990-EZ, line 36.

▶ Attach certified copies of any articles of dissolution, resolutions, or plans.

▶ Attach to Form 990 or 990-EZ.

OMB No. 1545-0047

2008

Open to Public Inspection

Name of the organization   **Employer identification number**

Part I   **Liquidation, Termination, or Dissolution.** Complete this part if the organization answered "Yes" to Form 990, Part IV, line 31, or Form 990-EZ, line 36. Use Schedule N-1 if additional space is needed.

1	(a) Description of asset(s) distributed or transaction expenses paid	(b) Date of distribution	(c) Fair market value of asset(s) distributed or amount of transaction expenses	(d) Method of determining FMV for asset(s) distributed or transaction expenses	(e) EIN of recipient	(f) Name and address of recipient	(g) IRC section of recipient(s) (if tax-exempt) or type of entity

		Yes	No
2	Did or will any officer, director, trustee, or key employee of the organization:		
a	Become a director or trustee of a successor or transferee organization?	2a	
b	Become an employee of, or independent contractor for, a successor or transferee organization?	2b	
c	Become a direct or indirect owner of a successor or transferee organization?	2c	
d	Receive, or become entitled to, compensation or other similar payments as a result of the organization's liquidation, termination, or dissolution?	2d	
e	If the organization answered "Yes" to any of the questions in this line, provide the name of the person involved and explain in Part III. ▶		

For Privacy Act and Paperwork Reduction Act Notice, see the Instructions for Form 990.   Cat. No. 50087Z   Schedule N (Form 990 or 990-EZ) 2008

Schedule N (Form 990 or 990-EZ) 2008   Page **2**

Part I   Liquidation, Termination, or Dissolution *(continued)*

		Yes	No
	Note. If the organization distributed all of its assets during the tax year, then Form 990, Part X, column (B) should equal -0-.		
3	Did the organization distribute its assets in accordance with its governing instrument(s)? If "No," describe in Part III	3	
4a	Did the organization request or receive a determination letter from EO Determinations that the organization's exempt status was terminated?	4a	
b	(If "Yes," provide the date of the letter ▶ _____)		
5a	Is the organization required to notify the attorney general or other appropriate state official of its intent to dissolve, liquidate, or terminate?	5a	
b	If "Yes," did the organization provide such notice?	5b	
6	Did the organization discharge or pay all liabilities in accordance with state laws?	6	
7a	Did the organization have any tax-exempt bonds outstanding during the year?	7a	
b	Did the organization discharge or defease tax-exempt bond liabilities in accordance with the Internal Revenue Code and state laws?	7b	
c	If "Yes," describe in Part III how the organization defeased or otherwise settled these liabilities. If "No," explain in Part III.		

Part II   Sale, Exchange, Disposition, or Other Transfer of More Than 25% of the Organization's Assets. Complete this part if the organization answered "Yes" to Form 990, Part IV, line 32, or Form 990-EZ, line 36. Use Schedule N-1 if additional space is needed.

1	**(a)** Description of asset(s) distributed or transaction expenses paid	**(b)** Date of distribution	**(c)** Fair market value of asset(s) distributed or amount of transaction expenses	**(d)** Method of determining FMV for asset(s) distributed or transaction expenses	**(e)** EIN of recipient	**(f)** Name and address of recipient	**(g)** IRC section(s) (if recipient is tax-exempt) or type of entity

2	Did or will any officer, director, trustee, or key employee of the organization:	Yes	No
a	Become a director or trustee of a successor or transferee organization?	2a	
b	Become an employee of, or independent contractor for, a successor or transferee organization?	2b	
c	Become a direct or indirect owner of a successor or transferee organization?	2c	
d	Receive, or become entitled to, compensation or other similar payments as a result of the organization's significant disposition of assets?	2d	
e	If the organization answered "Yes" to any of the questions in this line, provide the name of the person involved and explain in Part III.		

Schedule N (Form 990 or Form 990-EZ) 2008

SCHEDULE R (Form 990)

Related Organizations and Unrelated Partnerships

OMB No. 1545-0047

2008

Open to Public Inspection

Department of the Treasury
Internal Revenue Service

▶ Attach to Form 990. To be completed by organizations that answered "Yes" to Form 990, Part IV, line 33, 34, 35, 36, or 37.
▶ See separate instructions.

Name of the organization

Employer identification number

Part I   Identification of Disregarded Entities

(A) Name, address, and EIN of disregarded entity	(B) Primary activity	(C) Legal domicile (state or foreign country)	(D) Total income	(E) End-of-year assets	(F) Direct controlling entity

Part II   Identification of Related Tax-Exempt Organizations

(A) Name, address, and EIN of related organization	(B) Primary activity	(C) Legal domicile (state or foreign country)	(D) Exempt Code section	(E) Public charity status (if section 501(c)(3))	(F) Direct controlling entity

For Privacy Act and Paperwork Reduction Act Notice, see the Instructions for Form 990.   Cat. No. 50135Y   Schedule R (Form 990) 2008

Part III   Identification of Related Organizations Taxable as a Partnership

(A) Name, address, and EIN of related organization	(B) Primary activity	(C) Legal domicile (state or foreign country)	(D) Direct controlling entity	(E) Predominant income (related, investment, unrelated)	(F) Share of total income	(G) Share of end-of-year assets	(H) Disproportionate allocations?		(I) Code V—UBI amount in box 20 of Schedule K-1 (Form 1065)	(J) General or managing partner?	
							Yes	No		Yes	No

Part IV   Identification of Related Organizations Taxable as a Corporation or Trust

(A) Name, address, and EIN of related organization	(B) Primary activity	(C) Legal domicile (state or foreign country)	(D) Direct controlling entity	(E) Type of entity (C corp. S corp. or trust)	(F) Share of total income	(G) Share of end-of-year assets	(H) Percentage ownership

Schedule R (Form 990) 2008   Page **3**

Part V   Transactions With Related Organizations

Note. Complete line 1 if any entity is listed in Parts II, III, or IV.

		Yes	No
1 During the tax year, did the organization engage in any of the following transactions with one or more related organizations listed in Parts II–IV?			
a Receipt of **(i)** interest **(ii)** annuities **(iii)** royalties **(iv)** rent from a controlled entity	**1a**		
b Gift, grant, or capital contribution to other organization(s)	**1b**		
c Gift, grant, or capital contribution from other organization(s)	**1c**		
d Loans or loan guarantees to or for other organization(s)	**1d**		
e Loans or loan guarantees by other organization(s)	**1e**		
f Sale of assets to other organization(s)	**1f**		
g Purchase of assets from other organization(s)	**1g**		
h Exchange of assets	**1h**		
i Lease of facilities, equipment, or other assets to other organization(s)	**1i**		
j Lease of facilities, equipment, or other assets from other organization(s)	**1j**		
k Performance of services or membership or fundraising solicitations for other organization(s)	**1k**		
l Performance of services or membership or fundraising solicitations by other organization(s)	**1l**		
m Sharing of facilities, equipment, mailing lists, or other assets	**1m**		
n Sharing of paid employees	**1n**		
o Reimbursement paid to other organization for expenses	**1o**		
p Reimbursement paid by other organization for expenses	**1p**		
q Other transfer of cash or property to other organization(s)	**1q**		
r Other transfer of cash or property from other organization(s)	**1r**		

2 If the answer to any of the above is "Yes," see the instructions for information on who must complete this line, including covered relationships and transaction thresholds.

(A) Name of other organization(s)	(B) Transaction type (a–r)	(C) Amount involved
(1)		
(2)		
(3)		
(4)		
(5)		
(6)		

Schedule R (Form 990) 2008

Schedule R (Form 990) 2008

Page **4**

Part VI Unrelated Organizations Taxable as a Partnership

Provide the following information for each entity taxed as a partnership through which the organization conducted more than five percent of its activities (measured by total assets or gross revenue) that was not a related organization. See instructions regarding exclusion for certain investment partnerships.

(A) Name, address, and EIN of entity	(B) Primary activity	(C) Legal domicile (state or foreign country)	(D) Are all partners section 501(c)(3) organizations?		(E) Share of end-of-year assets	(F) Disproportionate allocations?		(G) Code V—UBI amount in box 20 of Schedule K-1 (Form 1065)	(H) General or managing partner?	
			Yes	No		Yes	No		Yes	No

Schedule R (Form 990) 2008